Social
Conservatism
and the
Middle Classes
in Germany,
1914-1933

Social Conservatism and the Middle Classes in Germany, 1914-1933

by
Herman
Lebovics

PRINCETON

UNIVERSITY PRESS

Princeton, New Jersey

1969

*Printed in
the United States of America
by Princeton University Press
Princeton, New Jersey*

*This book
has been composed
in 10 point Linotype
Baskerville
with display in
Melior*

For Victoria

Preface

CONTRARY to inherited wisdom, taking the middle course is all too often the worst path out of a crisis. This is a study of the efforts of a number of German thinkers to effect first an intellectual, then a social, and finally a political *modus vivendi* between the values of the feudalized capitalism and the Marxian socialism of the years between World War I and the triumph of National Socialism. Their purpose was nothing less than the fabrication—in the worlds both of thought and of institutions—of a socialism for the German middle classes.

The accelerating pace of economic development, the loss of the war, and the consequent revolution disabused all but the most irreconcilable conservatives of their faith in the utility of the socioeconomic arrangements of the late Empire. In the days of the Republic artisans, shopkeepers, peasants, professional men, and white-collar employees came to feel with ever greater intensity that the trends of the age were funnelling them between the grinding wheels of organized capital and organized labor. Imperial governments had offered them some encouragement and minimal protection; but now the governments of the Republic proved themselves much more tightfisted in the disbursement of both. By the mid-twenties many members of the middle classes realized that neither order suited their special socioeconomic, and therefore political, needs. Haltingly, but in growing numbers, they turned their backs on the antiquated values of the Empire: monarchy, aristocracy, and privilege. And in growing numbers, too, they rejected the Republican values of democracy, liberalism, and capitalism.

Acknowledging the world of industrial capitalism, and acknowledging the validity of some of the criticisms of this world by its socialist opponents, but still gripped by nos-

talgia for the happier aspects of the lost world of Bismarck's Reich, a group of conservative scholars, intellectuals, and publicists set out in the years of the Republic to
supply a new interpretation for the new situation. For the
destruction of the middle classes, they agreed, would demol-
ish society's most valuable bridge back to the past—and
paradoxically—ahead to the better future. In the 1920s
and early 1930s these theorists worked out for themselves,
and for the middle classes, an explanation of their misfortunes, a vindication of their demands, and the outlines of
a program for action. Their efforts resulted in an ideology
which, they believed, updated the viable socioeconomic values of the Imperial era and yet transcended those of both
contemporary capitalism and socialism.

The ideology bore various labels, depending on what
themes an author chose to emphasize. Early in his career
Werner Sombart referred to such ideas simply as "German
Anti-Capitalism." Later, during the depression, he wrote of
a "German Socialism," which he contrasted with Marxian
"Proletarian Socialism." Edgar Salin sought to institution-
alize the "beautiful life" in a new Reich along the hazy
guidelines set down by the poet Stefan George. The Viennese
economist Othmar Spann expounded a philosophy of "Universalism," systematically contrasting it with a set of doctrines he termed "Individualism." For Oswald Spengler, the
path to a new social order lay through "Prussian Socialism";
at the same time, the socialist Ernst Niekisch tried to organize support for a "National Bolshevism." Finally, in the
depths of the depression, Ferdinand Fried and the circle
which put out the periodical *Die Tat* advocated the creation
of a "Third Front" to carry out the "revolution of the intelligentsia." Such ideas appeared in vulgarized form in the
politics of the street as the program and aspirations of the
National Socialist German Workers' Party.

For the purposes of this study I have grouped this complex of ideas under the general label "social conservatism."
My term has, as yet, no strong emotional overtones. Moreover, late nineteenth-century social reformers—Heinrich
Herkner, for example, in *Die Arbeiterfrage* (1st edn., Ber-

lin, 1905) —employed it to describe a similar approach to the "social question" of their day. As I use it, the term grasps the two basic emphases of the twentieth-century intellectual movement: the rejection of many of the features of the twentieth-century industrial market economy, and the desire to modernize many of the social and economic values of the pre-industrial era. The major goals of this study of some aspects of the economic and social thought of Germany's "conservative revolutionaries" are to search for something approximating a pattern in the literature of social conservatism, to assess the internal cohesion of these ideas, and to understand their relation to social and economic realities. The men I have chosen as subjects knew each other's work and, to a significant degree, shared common values and analyses. My prime concern here, however, is the pattern of ideas and its social significance; the idiosyncratic outlook of this or that writer is secondary.

I have largely ignored the question of whether ideas or circumstances are primary. Keynes's "madmen in authority, who hear voices in the air" but who in reality "are distilling their frenzy from some academic scribblers of a few years back," hear through a social filter. Moreover, as the poet Gregory Corso reminds us, "even paranoids have enemies." Admittedly, it would be foolish to expect an isomorphic relation between ideology and empirical reality. The vagaries of thinkers who project ideological schemes, and the function of ideology as a kind of public relations effort, prohibit such a pattern. But, in spite of these limitations, it does seem that social conservative ideas and Germany's unhappy social and economic realities were closely and functionally linked. The ideas discussed in this study might be understood most properly as sets of proposals, put forth by intelligent men speaking to a literate audience, for wrong solutions to real problems and reasonable solutions to misconceived problems. Thus, in Chapter I, and wherever appropriate, I have tried to specify the socioeconomic situations to which social conservative ideas were a response and which social conservative thinkers were trying to reshape.

A word about organization is necessary. I have ordered

this study according to several complementary principles. To begin with, the treatment is roughly chronological. The first two writers discussed, Werner Sombart and Edgar Salin (as a Georgian), were intellectually active before 1914. The subsequent chapters concentrate on the 1920s and early 1930s. The Conclusion takes the story up to 1933. There is, secondly, a development from the level of high abstraction to that of concrete proposals. In other words, the professors of economics give way, in the end, to the economic "experts" of the NSDAP. Finally, the study progresses from theorists speaking to the ˙condition of peasants, artisans, shopkeepers, and the old white-collar middle class (Sombart, Salin, and Spann) to thinkers more concerned with the new white-collar middle class of industrial society (Niekisch, Spengler, and Fried). Here, too, the National Socialists united the major tendencies.

But just because it was, in the end, the National Socialists who capitalized most effectively on the corpus of social conservative ideology, and on the social discontent which prompted it, does not mean that the two were identical. Representative social conservative thinkers, unlike most Nazis, were not racists. Moreover, as Chapters II through VI show, most social conservatives did not become adherents of National Socialism. Had the brothers Strasser prevailed against Hitler, or General Schleicher against the NSDAP, the intellectual and institutional issues of social conservatism in Germany—at least up to 1933—would, as the Conclusion suggests, have been approximately the same. Social conservatives were not crypto-Nazis; rather, the Nazis were vulgar social conservatives. What connected them was their common middle class orientation. Their audience understood some kinds of language better than others, so both spoke in mutually intelligible dialects. Some words our social conservatives tried to avoid—like "race" and "bloodletting." Some things these intellectuals would not do—like march, canvass door-to-door, and fight in the streets. In 1933-1934 the success of the political deed made the subtle discrimination of words and ideas pointless, and social conservatism expired with the victory of its most powerfully armed adherents.

It is hoped that this study will illuminate a vital aspect of recent German social thought and perhaps suggest some hypotheses for the study of German society itself in the future. Its findings may have relevance for the understanding of contemporary problems, not just in Germany, but perhaps in our part of the Western world.

H. L.

June 1968
Stony Brook, N. Y.

Acknowledgments

THE STUDY of so murky a body of literature about a very muddy set of aspirations can only benefit from the control which the advice of teachers, colleagues, and friends exercises. Although none of the people I wish to thank should be blamed for the final product, each, in one way or another, helped curb the author's apparently innate drive for obscurity, imprecision, and inaccuracy.

I wish first to express my appreciation to Hajo Holborn, of Yale University, who served as my adviser both during the dissertation-writing stage of this study and when I was revising it for publication. Leonard Krieger, now of the University of Chicago, read and criticized some of the first sections of the dissertation. Ivo J. Lederer read and criticized it. The encouragement and advice of Henry A. Turner were very helpful.

Walter Struve, of the College of the City of New York, whose own work on German conservatism served me as a model for excellence, was liberal with his counsel and criticism. The good sense and knowledge of my Stony Brook colleagues Werner T. Angress, Bernard Semmel, and David Trask aided my work, as did the kind interest of Val Lorwin, of the University of Oregon.

I can only list some of the other people who aided me in various ways in completing this work: Jesse Clarkson, Sabine Jessner, Gary Spackey, Sonia Sbarge, Holger Herwig, and Mrs. Shirley Lerman.

The study was supported by fellowships from the Graduate School of Yale University, the Deutscher Akademischer Austauschdienst, and the Research Foundation of the State University of New York.

Finally, I wish to express my appreciation to Sanford G. Thatcher, of Princeton University Press, for the care and good judgment he displayed in his editorial work with the manuscript.

Contents

Social
Conservatism
and the
Middle Classes
in Germany,
1914-1933

An Introduction
to the Mittelstand

IN THE COURSE of the nineteenth century Germany passed from the ranks of the relatively underdeveloped regions of Central Europe to become, by the end of the century, the most advanced industrial society in Europe. Starting after both Britain and France, Germany by the beginning of the twentieth century had surpassed her two Western neighbors in the production of pig iron, chemicals, and electrical power.[1] In his book *Imperial Germany and the Industrial Revolution* Thorstein Veblen argued that the relative lateness of the advent of German industrialization permitted her to avoid "the penalty of taking the lead." The Germans, he pointed out, could borrow on a massive scale from the accumulated knowledge and technology of already industrialized societies. Although this judgment is doubtless correct on the purely technological level, it is not true that German society made the transition from the basically agrarian-commercial society of the mid-nineteenth century to the predominantly industrial society of the twentieth century without penalties.[2] In recent years specialists on the developing nations have directed our attention to the dislocation, hardships, and complexities which the processes of industrialization, urbanization, and modernization are introducing into traditional

[1] John H. Clapham, *Economic Development of France and Germany, 1815-1914* (4th edn., Cambridge, Eng., 1955), pp. 283, 303-9.

[2] Thorstein Veblen, *Imperial Germany and the Industrial Revolution* (New York, 1915), pp. 17-41. Veblen, more than most contemporary social scientists, was of course aware that there were social penalties. However, he predicted the payment of the penalties for a later, more advanced period. He did not detect Germany's grave social malaise in the years before the war.

societies. In our scholarly concern with the problems of development in the non-Western world we have, until quite recently, tended to forget that large segments of the populations of European societies, too, had to be "dragged kicking and screaming into the twentieth century," to use Adlai Stevenson's telling phrase.[3]

Many socially conservative intellectuals, gripped by the same anxieties, came forward with proposals for an ideology for those threatened by the progress of democracy and of industrial capitalism. In Germany the greatest portion of this threatened population was to be found in the middle strata of the society.

In Germany and Austria in the course of the nineteenth century and into the twentieth, students of society regularly referred to individuals engaged in such disparate activities as small-scale farming, keeping shop, artisan industry, teaching, the professions, and clerical work as being all members of a "Mittelstand." The use of so vague a term, meaning literally "middle estate," to describe social groups with such divergent specific economic interests, so different in their styles of living and in their life expectations, and so lacking in the kind of political unity displayed by great landowners, big businessmen, and workers was more an expression of wishful thinking on the part of those in Central Europe who searched for consensus in an ever more conflict-ridden society than of commitment to objective

---

[3] See, e.g., Daniel Lerner, *The Passing of Traditional Society: Modernizing the Middle East* (Glencoe, Ill., 1958) and Amitai and Eva Etzioni, eds., *Social Change* (New York, 1964), esp. the essay by Reinhard Bendix, "Industrialization, Ideologies, and Social Structure," pp. 300-309. See also the provocative application of the model of social crisis amidst social change of the school of Talcott Parsons in Neil Smelser's *Social Change in the Industrial Revolution: An Application of Theory to the British Cotton Industry* (Chicago, 1959). That this recognition has come in United States history is evidenced in the excellent interpretative essay by Samuel P. Hays, *The Response to Industrialism, 1885-1914* (Chicago, 1957). An elaborate bibliographical essay on various aspects of the problem of "modernization" may be found in C. E. Black's *The Dynamics of Modernization: A Study in Comparative History* (New York, 1966), pp. 175-99.

analysis.[4] But, even if the concept of a middle estate with its implications of a pre-industrial society organized in *Stände*, or corporate bodies, could represent no economic or social reality after the middle of the nineteenth century,[5] it could, and did, represent a unity of aspiration and of fear for the future.

In the second half of the nineteenth century, as Germany experienced with increasing intensity and tempo the consequences of capitalistic industrialization, common fears worked to enforce the beginnings of unity on the middle strata of the society. This was not the unity of the self-conscious entrepreneurs of the heavy industry sector, nor that of the growing social democratic movement. It was rather a unity in the negative sense. Fears of economic irrelevance, loss of livelihood, and above all loss of status stalked the middle classes. In the late nineteenth century and the early part of the twentieth the terrible abstractions of "capital" and "labor" came to loom over the middle classes,

[4] Efforts to define these groups in terms of income, status, or economic function have been numerous and generally of little value. See, e.g., J. Wernicke, *Kapitalismus und Mittelstandspolitik* (Jena, 1922), pp. 13ff.; A. Leimgruber, *Christliche Wirtschaftsordnung und Mittelstand* (Lucerne, 1923), *passim*; Rudolf Küstenmeier, *Die Mittelschichten und ihr politischer Weg* (Potsdam, 1933), *passim*; Fritz Marbach, *Theorie des Mittelstandes* (Bern, 1942), pp. 102ff.; Emil Grünberg, *Der Mittelstand in der kapitalistischen Gesellschaft: Eine ökonomische und soziologische Untersuchung* (Leipzig, 1932), pp. 72ff.; and a critique of such an approach in L. D. Pesl, "Mittelstandsfragen: Der gewerbliche und kaufmännische Mittelstand," *Grundriss der Sozialökonomik* (Tübingen, 1926), IX, Part 1, 72ff. A more recent reevaluation of this problem of definition appears in Fritz Croner, *Soziologie der Angestellten* (Cologne, 1962), pp. 41ff. For modern discussions of the problem of delineating the middle class, see further E. A. Johns, *The Social Structure of Modern Britain* (Oxford, 1965), pp. 65-75, and C. Wright Mills, *White Collar: The American Middle Classes* (New York, 1951).

[5] For excellent examinations of the role of the German middle classes in the Revolution of 1848 in Germany, see Theodore S. Hamerow, *Restoration, Revolution, Reaction: Economics and Politics in Germany, 1815-1871* (Princeton, 1958), and Paul Noyes, *Organization and Revolution: Working Class Associations in the German Revolutions of 1848-49* (Princeton, 1966).

beckoning to them yet at the same time threatening to destroy them. Under conditions of great common hardship, as in the terrible twentieth-century depression, artisans, small shopkeepers, peasant proprietors, and white-collar workers could find little guidance or comfort in the ideological blandishments of either big business or big labor. Their economic problems, as they understood them, were different from those of both capital and labor.

Analysis of the most general economic worries of the members of the Mittelstand around 1900 permits us to differentiate three large areas of uneasiness within contemporary commercial and industrial society; these areas of concern coincide with the three major socioeconomic divisions within the Mittelstand.

The most numerous part of the middle strata, in the period of this study, was the old Mittelstand, composed of peasant proprietors, artisans, and small businessmen working at what might broadly be called "pre-industrial" occupations. This group could be expected to take the most reactionary stance in the face of commercial and industrial advance. Four features of modern economic life impinged especially heavily upon their activities. First, as members of an economic sector constantly in need of capital, who often had to mortgage their farms or shops to obtain credit, they resented the prevailing credit and banking systems of Imperial and Weimar Germany. Second, like their larger competitors, they suffered from the fluctuations of the market economy; but, unlike the larger business enterprises, they were rarely able to get favorable legislation or to create monopolies to limit such fluctuations. Third, they could not compete, nor deal effectively with, the larger firms which could buy and sell in bulk. Finally, they were unable, and often unwilling, to match the massive production and distribution systems of estate agriculture, efficient factories, and large commercial enterprises.[6]

---

[6] Arthur Schweitzer, *Big Business in the Third Reich* (Bloomington, Ind., 1964), p. 76. Chapter II of this work is the latest and best concise introduction to the economic problems of the "pre-industrial" middle classes.

The second segment of the Mittelstand comprised the members of the so-called new middle class. These clerical workers, lower management employees, and technicians, holding jobs created for the most part by industrialization, depended on the continued prosperity of Germany's capitalist society for their economic welfare. Those employed in these occupations wished above all to maintain a status clearly distinct from, and superior to, that of manual workers. Although their definition of what their status should be was based largely on pre-industrial values, their employment in a modern economy had to supply the means by which they could live according to their station. Whereas the concerns of the old middle class tended to dominate the theories of social conservatives in the decades before World War I, the interests of the new middle class loomed large in social conservative thought in the Weimar era.[7]

Constituting the final segment of the Mittelstand were those who had taken up pursuits that had been held in great esteem in the days before industry transformed German national life. State officials, university students, lawyers, doctors, and school teachers were involved in activities only indirectly related to the capitalist economy of Germany. Thus they tended to view economic prosperity as a guarantee of their social position, while having to fear only the indirect effects of serious economic downswings. Nevertheless, intellectually aware members of such occupational groups could not fail to realize to what degree their own status and eco-

[7] The classic work on the origins and composition of the "new middle class" remains Emil Lederer's *Die Privatangestellten in der modernen Wirtschaftsordnung* (Tübingen, 1912); also valuable is his work (written in collaboration with Jacob Marschak), "Der neue Mittelstand," in *Grundriss der Sozialökonomik*, Vol. IX, Part 1. Of the more impressionistic literature, the best are still Siegfried Kracauer's *Die Angestellten* (3rd unaltered edn., Bonn, 1959) and the novel by Hans Fallada (pseud. for Rudolf Ditzen), *Kleiner Mann, Was Nun?* (Berlin, 1932), about the pitiable distress of a salesman working in a department store during the depression. A useful introduction to the problems of the new middle classes during the Weimar period is available in Walter Struve, "Hans Zehrer as a Neoconservative Elite Theorist," *American Historical Review*, LXX (1965), 1035-57.

nomic position depended upon the continuation of the social structure in which, before 1914, they had found a com-
fortable place.[8] Consequently, many of the members of this
section of the Mittelstand, as well as of the other two, were
inclined to identify themselves with the status quo under the
Empire and with the social conservative conceit of a stable,
harmonious, and justly stratified society in the years of the
Weimar Republic.

However much a peasant or white-collar employee might
wish to identify his interests with those of the great landowners or high corporate management, an unfavorable economic reality all too often posed a barrier. At the same
time, despite attempts first by Socialists and, after 1919, by
Communists to convince the peasant and the white-collar
worker to join their ranks, this group on the whole stubbornly rejected "proletarianization." Even in the depths of
the great depression of the early 1930s, when middling peasants continued to follow the lead of the Junkers or pushed
their Center party to the right, or, worse, voted National
Socialist, when white-collar employees continued to spurn
membership in Socialist white-collar unions, the sophisticated Socialist writer Emil Grünberg could not grasp the
futility of applying the Marxian concept of "false consciousness" to explain the behavior of the Mittelstand. He could
still write in 1932 that just because "white-collar workers
and bureaucrats see themselves as members of the Mittelstand and not as proletarians alters nothing of the objective
fact of their proletarian situation, their proletarian destiny,
and their proletarian interests vis-à-vis capital."[9] What-

[8] The specific literature on these groups will be cited at appropriate
points in the discussion.

[9] Emil Grünberg, *Der Mittelstand in der kapitalistischen Gesellschaft*,
p. 169. There existed within the Social Democratic Party another
point of view which contended that the dependent middle classes had
special problems and that the party would have to modify its ideology
and thereby reorient itself to the needs of white-collar workers if it
were to win them over. The leading spokesman for this position was
Emil Lederer. See his *Die Privatangestellten*, Chs. II-III, and his "Die
Umschichtung des Proletariats," *Die neue Rundschau*, Aug. 1929.
Ambivalence on the question of the Mittelstand plagued the Socialist
movement (see Chs. I and V below).

ever merit this mode of analysis may have, it tells us little about the positive aspirations of members of the middle classes.

Income level or relationship to the means of production was, in fact, to them secondary to the question, as one scholar put it, of "who sits with whom at the *Stammtisch*."[10] But even at the *Stammtisch* of a small town *Ratskeller* the primary school teacher did not generally sit with the housepainter, nor the peasant with the office worker.[11] Nevertheless, each was inclined to see himself as a part of society's middle stratum. For the very concept of Mittelstand bespoke real sources of comfort for Germany's "little men." It was an affirmation of the continued vitality of elements of the population which, according to the implications of classical economic theory and the expectations of Marxist doctrine, were destined to disappear with continued economic progress. It signified a social status somewhat above that of the manual workers but blessedly below that of the corrupt world of business and finance. Moreover, it denied the Marxist category of "class" and therefore belied class conflict. To many members of the middle classes the concept, shared by both workers and their employers, that society was nothing more than aggregates of economic power in conflict was abhorrent. Reality permitting, they preferred to view society as an organism in equilibrium. And, of course, they liked to conceive of themselves as the heart or, better, the soul of the social body.

But in the late nineteenth century the cruel reality of economic development and governments more receptive to the demands of powerful economic pressure groups than to the needs of smaller enterpreneurs threatened this dream. In response, addressing members of the Evangelisch-sozialer

[10] Karl Dietrich Bracher, *Die Auflösung der Weimarer Republik* (3rd edn., Villingen-Schwarzwald, 1960), p. 163. A *Stammtisch* is a table regularly reserved by a circle of friends at their habitual café or neighborhood bar.

[11] See, e.g., the scenes set in the *Ratskeller* of a small town in the fine novel—and insightful document of social history—by Heinrich Mann, *Der Untertan*.

Kongress in 1897, Gustav Schmoller, Germany's leading expert on the problems of the agricultural and industrial Mittelstand, assured his auditors of the continued economic and social vigor of the middle strata of society. He offered his audience of distinguished social scientists, religious leaders, and officials concerned with social questions an analysis of the German social structure which concluded that the Mittelstand still comprised more than half the population. Further, he saw "tendencies for the reconstruction of the Mittelstand," which would insure its future importance.[12] Imperial governments did manifest a degree of sensitivity to the plight of the Mittelstand.[13] The measures of protection put forward, however, were at best holding actions and usually mere palliatives. Still, conservative intellectuals and occasionally the Imperial authorities did show their concern about the survival of this social group, wedded neither to the perpetuation of capitalism nor to the growth of socialism. And it did survive.

Although between the census years 1895 and 1907 the agricultural population had declined, in 1907 it still constituted 28.6 percent of the nation's total population. Moreover, the number of middling farms (five to twenty hectares) had increased by 9.4 percent. The great industrial

[12] Die Verhandlungen des 8. Evangelisch-sozialen Kongresses, abgehalten zu Leipzig am 10. und 11. Juni 1897. Nach den stenographischen Protokollen (Göttingen, 1897), pp. 159-60.

[13] Beginning in the Bismarck era a modest program of peasant resettlement was carried on in northeastern Germany; in 1889 rural cooperatives were permitted; various states set up land banks to supply the rural Mittelstand with credit; in 1895 various business practices, travelling sales activities, and "excessive" advertising—deemed harmful by the Mittelstand—were prohibited; in 1897 the activities of urban cooperatives and the rights of their members to resell goods were curbed; in 1897, also, artisan gilds were strengthened in various ways (without giving artisans monopoly control of that branch of production); and, finally, in 1903 the Reichstag passed a new set of high protective restrictions on the import of grains (which aided large growers much more than the peasantry). See my article " 'Agrarians' versus 'Industrializers': Social Conservative Resistance to Industrialism and Capitalism in Late Nineteenth-Century Germany," International Review of Social History, XII (1967), Part 1, 56-61.

firms and large-scale commerce, it is true, continued to thin
the ranks of the small artisan and commercial enterprises;
the increase of enterprises employing between one and six
workers lagged behind that of large enterprises and, indeed,
behind the general growth of population. Nevertheless,
while the artisan population was declining in numbers and
economic importance, the forces undermining it were creating a new Mittelstand to augment the ranks of the old. Employees in trade and commerce were the most rapidly growing segment of the labor force, up from 5,966,846 in 1895 to
8,278,239 in 1907 (counting their families).[14] As Germany
approached industrial maturity, Schmoller's hoped-for renewal of the Mittelstand was taking place in the form of the
growth of a new white-collar employee stratum.

Large numbers of economically inefficient artisans and
peasants continued to ply their crafts up to the outbreak of
World War I. The Imperial and state bureaucracies continued to grow. White-collar workers, in private employ,
continued to increase in numbers. The nationalistic Mittelstand greeted the outbreak of war with enthusiasm. But by
1918 patriotic fervor had given way to anger and despair.
In the war years industry benefited more than agriculture,
and large firms, of necessity, were favored by governmental
policies over their smaller industrial and commercial competitors.[15] White-collar workers were uprooted from the

[14] *Ibid.*, pp. 61-62; Statistisches Reichsamt, *Deutsche Wirtschaftskunde*
(Berlin, 1930), pp. 1, 8-9; A. Sartorius von Waltershausen, *Deutsche
Wirtschaftsgeschichte, 1815-1914* (2nd expanded edn., Jena, 1923),
pp. 449-503; August Skalweit, *Agrarpolitik* (Berlin, 1924), p. 203;
Joseph Schumpeter, *Business Cycles: A Theoretical, Historical, and
Statistical Analysis of the Capitalist Process* (2 vols.; New York,
1939), I, 439-44; Heinz Spitz, "Das Organisationswesen im Handwerk,"
in Bernhard Harms, ed., *Strukturwandlungen der deutschen Volkswirtschaft* (2 vols.; 2nd edn., Berlin, 1929), II, 42ff.; M. Biermer,
article "Mittelstandsbewegung," in *Handwörterbuch der Staatswissen-
schaften* (3rd edn., Jena, 1910), VI, 740-41; René König, "Zur Soziologie
der Zwanziger Jahre," in Leonard Reinisch, ed., *Die Zeit ohne Eigen-
schaften: Eine Bilanz der zwanziger Jahre* (Stuttgart, 1961), p. 85.

[15] Heinrich Bechtel, *Wirtschaftsgeschichte Deutschlands* (3 vols.;
Munich, 1956), III, 363-79; W. F. Bruck, *Social and Economic History
of Germany from William II to Hitler* (New York, 1962), pp. 134-43;

humdrum of their daily activities and in the trenches were transformed into heroes and ruffians—men, as the Weimar years would show, not easily reintegrated into the nine-to-five world. The military adventure of Imperial Germany served only to erode further the social basis of that society. When the last German Emperor, William II, crossed the border into Holland, the passing of this symbol of the failure of the Empire to adequately protect the Mittelstand evoked relatively little regret among Germany's middle strata.[16]

The German Revolution of 1918 was the penultimate calamity of the Mittelstand. The Revolution destroyed the political order of Imperial Germany without, however, furthering the destruction of the inherited economic and social order. From the point of view of the Mittelstand, the Revolution placed its archenemies at the head of a new Republican state which followed—or, more often, threatened to follow—policies which would lead to its social and economic extinction. If some members of the Mittelstand, especially those who voted initially for the parties of the Weimar coalition, could see the first days of the Republic as an opportunity for a new consolidation of their social position, most looked to the future with trepidation.

Gustav Stolper, *German Economy, 1870-1940* (New York, 1940), pp. 108-20; and esp. Gerald D. Feldman, *Army, Industry, and Labor in Germany, 1914-1918* (Princeton, 1966), pp. 116-17, 166-67, 459-73.

16 Walter H. Kaufmann, *Monarchism in the Weimar Republic* (New York, 1953), *passim*.

I. Organize or Perish
THE MITTELSTAND
IN WEIMAR GERMANY

ARTICLE 164 of the Weimar Consti-
tution stipulated that "the independent agricultural, industrial, commercial Mittelstand shall be fostered by legislation
and administration, and shall be protected against oppression and exploitation." The next article brought salaried
employees, grouping them with wage-earners, under the protection of the new state.[1] How most of the governments of
the Republic understood the provisions was perhaps most accurately expressed by Wolfgang Reichardt of the Ministry
of Economics in a survey of the problems of the middle
classes written on the eve of the depression. He denied that
the state was obligated to give special preference to the interests of the middle classes. The state had only to insure
their "*free* participation in the economic process." Their
needs were to be recognized by the authorities only to a degree "commensurate with their numbers as well as with
their vitality."[2] That was to say, in effect, that the state
would protect those interests which could make their weight
felt in politics, while guaranteeing to weak and strong alike
the right to compete at the marketplace. But big business,
big agriculture, and big labor all achieved positions of economic and political power in Republican Germany which

[1] An English text may be found in the Appendix to René Brunet,
The New German Constitution, tr. Joseph Gollomb (New York, 1928),
pp. 297-339.
[2] Italics mine. "Probleme der Handwerkerspolitik," in Harms, ed.,
Strukturwandlungen der deutschen Volkswirtschaft, II, 80: ". . . wie
es sowohl seinem äusseren Bestande wie seiner inneren Lebenskraft
entspricht." This collection of essays will hereafter be cited as
Strukturwandlungen.

the middle classes never attained. It was precisely *special* state protection which the various segments of the middle classes needed to survive socially and economically. Why was this special state protection not forthcoming? Why did the leadership of the Republic generally prove either unable or unwilling to aid the Mittelstand? Why could the Mittelstand not force concessions from the Republic and yet marshal enough political unity and power to help bring down the Republic? The answers to these questions may be found in the history of the socioeconomic disasters of the Weimar era.

The social history of the Republic may be understood in terms of the consequences of structural and cyclical distress —exacerbated by unwise and, all too often, inconclusive policy decisions—for the various segments of German society. If the fate of the Weimar Republic teaches any lesson about the relationship of economics to politics, it is that liberal democracy and prosperity are functionally related. In the Weimar period prosperity meant in practice, as Alexander Gerschenkron has argued, high and steady employment, rising incomes, and improving welfare.[3] No large segment of German society, it is true, enjoyed great prosperity throughout the 1920s and early 1930s. Members of the middle classes had to endure repeated economic and social setbacks, as of course did other members of the society. Even so, given the constitution of that society, the final defection of these middle strata in 1933 proved decisive in bringing about the death of German democracy. The economic constituents of ruin, we can see in retrospect, were already taking shape in the very first days of the new Republic.

DEFEAT, REVOLUTION, AND FISCAL COLLAPSE

It was the sad paradox of the first years of the Republic that defeat produced more revolutionary consequences than did the Revolution. The Revolution completed the demolition of the political order of the Empire; it spurred on the members of the Mittelstand in their search for a new polit-

[3] Alexander Gerschenkron, *Bread and Democracy in Germany* (Berkeley, 1943), p. 9.

ical shelter. But it was the implications of a lost war, especially in the area of the economy, that turned them in the direction of the radical right.

In 1920 Germany's population was 13 percent below the level it had reached in 1913. Since the soldiers for the most part were Germany's physically and intellectually most vigorous males, the statistics cannot express the loss of talent that Germany suffered. The military shot off munitions to the value of 157 billion measured in stable gold marks. The figure does not include the cost of replacing worn-out equipment and of conversion to peacetime production.[4] Moreover, the inflationary method of war financing robbed all consumers of a percentage of their incomes. The burden weighed most heavily on the rentier class and those on fixed incomes. But all paid equally for the consequent ruin of the nation's credit abroad. The authors of the peace treaty took the unprecedented step of expropriating the private assets of nationals of the enemy state.[5] The lost war cost Germany 14.3 percent of her arable land and 15 percent of her productive capacity. It forced her into the position of a debtor nation. Before the war Germany had exported capital; after the war she had to import it at high interest charges.[6] Devastating as these initial losses were, the armistice signed on 11 November 1918, which—along with the expected provisions about German surrender of arms, airplanes, and warships—demanded the handing over of trucks, locomotives, rolling stock, and coal and railroad yards, warned the Germans that the Entente powers would make economic

[4] Ferdinand Friedensburg, *Die Weimarer Republik* (Berlin, 1946), p. 15; James W. Angell, *The Recovery of Germany* (New Haven, 1929), pp. 15, 363. The 13% includes population losses accruing from the cession of territory.

[5] M. J. Bonn, *Das Schicksal des deutschen Kapitalismus* (Berlin, 1931), pp. 11-12. The German government compensated the owners of confiscated goods and the managements of firms first, rendering restitutions to the stockholders only partially, if at all.

[6] Angell, *The Recovery of Germany*, pp. 10, 363; Gerschenkron, *Bread and Democracy*, p. 97, n. 13; Albert Hesse, *Die Wirkungen des Friedens von Versailles auf die Wirtschaft des deutschen Ostens* (Jena, 1930), p. 26.

demands going beyond mere reparations for neutral Belgium.[7]

The Treaty of Versailles stipulated Germany's obligation to make restitution for war damages, but it did not include the total sum of Germany's liability. By the time the Reparations Commission set the sum (1 May 1921), the British had effected the inclusion of war pensions in the financial demands. The final bill of 132 billion gold marks was termed excessive by the Germans and fair by the Entente powers.[8] But the sum was not what hurt Germany; it was never paid. It was rather the ambiguity of the intentions of the Western powers, especially France, and the method hit upon to keep payments flowing from Germany that did the harm.

Germany was given the option to pay in cash or commodities. In either case her capacity to pay depended on her productivity and on her ability to sell abroad. These in turn were conditioned by the heights of prosperity the nations participating in the world economy could achieve.[9] The extent and rapidity of German recovery was not predictable immediately after the war and certainly not in the midst of the serious postwar depression. When Germany was again in a position to sell abroad, the Western nations proved unwilling to buy German exports.[10] They—in particular, France—envisioned the use of reparations income as a means of reducing their own war debts, not as a means of stimulating the recovery of the German economy. Yet, if Germany were to pay any significant amount, she had to be strong enough economically to do so. Economic recovery was also a necessary condition for great power status in the

[7] The text of the armistice may be found in Appendix G, pp. 426-32, of Harry Rudin, *Armistice, 1918* (New Haven, 1944).

[8] This was equivalent to 31.5 billion dollars. For a useful discussion of the origins and early history of reparations, see Philip Mason Burnett, *Reparations at the Paris Peace Conference* (2 vols.; New York, 1940), esp. Vol. I.

[9] Harold Moulton and Leo Pasvolsky, *War Debts and World Prosperity* (New York, 1932), pp. 416-22.

[10] Charles P. Kindleberger, *International Economics* (Homewood, Ill., 1958), p. 363.

twentieth century.[11] The disastrous French invasion of the
Ruhr resulted from the French effort to follow simultaneously policies of national security, collection of reparations,
and the inhibition of German economic recovery. Up to
1923 Germany paid reparations from her own assets.[12] The
final destruction of the currency and the immobilization of
the economy in that year altered the nature of the reparations problem as part of the initiation of yet another
fundamental transformation of the German economy.

There is no need to rehearse at any length the opportunities missed in the course of the German Revolution. By
mediating a political revolution, but not a radical social or
economic transformation, the champions of social revolution, the Social Democratic Party (in alliance, to be sure,
with the not so revolutionary Catholic Center and Democratic Parties), missed an opportunity to give the new Republic an enduring social base.[13]

Because of the unique economic heritage of Germany, the
intensification of prewar trends during the war, the economic dislocations of the peace, and the incomplete social
revolution, the economy of the Republican era was no
longer a fully capitalist one. Nor could it be properly labelled socialist. It was rather an economy being reformed
from above, following no plan, without the wherewithal to
cover both business needs and reform expenditures. It was,
as Joseph Schumpeter aptly put it, "a deadening laborism
[which] threatened everybody and satisfied nobody."[14] To

[11] Angell, *The Recovery of Germany*, p. 29.

[12] Friedrich Lütge, "An Explanation of the Economic Conditions
which Contributed to the Victory of National Socialism," in the
UNESCO-sponsored volume, Maurice Baumont et al., eds., *The Third
Reich* (New York, 1955), pp. 419-21. Germany claimed to have paid
51.7 billion marks up to 1924; the Reparations Commission credited
her with having paid only 8 billion.

[13] Arthur Rosenberg, *Imperial Germany: The Birth of the German
Republic, 1871-1918*, tr. Ian F. W. Morrow (Boston: Beacon Press
paperback, 1964), pp. 233-74; *idem, A History of the Weimar Republic*
(London, 1936); Bonn, *Schicksal*, pp. 9-11.

[14] Schumpeter, *Business Cycles*, II, 715.

its inherited powers of operating the national railroads and
the postal system with the connected telephone, telegraph,
radio, and postal savings facilities, to its inherited functions
of determining tariff levels and granting subsidies to various
branches of the economy, the state added new powers of
direct involvement in the production process. The state and
communities financed the construction of housing. They
built and ran gas and electrical generating works. The weak
credit market necessitated such intervention, for only in this
way could these vital, but low short-term return, needs be
filled.[15] Moreover, for the first time since the foundation
of the Second Empire the national government gained direct access to income and property taxes.[16]

Perhaps new state expenditures on reparations, compen-
sations to citizens and firms for war losses, pensions, and
social welfare obligations were necessary, even exemplary;
still, they were economically unproductive. The government, having assumed so decisive a role in many major areas
of the economy while failing really to control it, had to endure the denunciations of the critical without being in
either an ideological or a practical position to administer
effective remedies. A case in point was the fiscal collapse of
1923.

The conclusion of hostilities did not relieve the regime
of its fiscal burdens. The printing presses had to be kept
running to finance the demobilization. Returning soldiers
unable to find work had to be supported. The government
also assumed the responsibility of easing industrial demobilization and reconversion by extending credit to firms
short on capital. Fulfillment of these obligations was complicated by the inevitable postwar decline in patriotic
fervor. No one wished to save; peace, to most Germans,
meant consumption. The German states encountered gen-

15 Johannes Popitz, "Die Probleme der Finanzpolitik des Reiches,"
Strukturwandlungen, II, 426, 430ff.; Gustav Stolper, "Oeffentliche und
private Wirtschaft," *Der deutsche Volkswirt*, 14 Oct. 1927, pp. 43-44.
16 Before the war the power of taxation resided primarily within
the competence of the states of the Empire. W. Gerloff, "Reichs-,
Landes-, und Gemeindefinanzen," *Strukturwandlungen*, II, 417.

eral indifference on the part of the public when they placed long-term bonds on the market.[17] In 1914 one dollar bought 4.2 marks. By 1919 the mark had lost half its value, falling to 8.9 to the dollar. In the spring of 1922 the exchange rate of dollars to marks was 1 for 290, and by early November it had plummeted to 1 for 9,150.[18]

When France and Belgium invaded the Ruhr in January 1923, the serious inflation was converted into a runaway inflation. The value of the mark collapsed on the international market as fearful traders unloaded their holdings in German currency. German governmental revenue sank when the French confiscated tax and customs revenues and blocked financial transfer out of the occupied zone. German workers and officials stopped work as part of a massive passive resistance campaign in the Ruhr, and the German government took on the obligation of paying the salaries and wages of the strikers when their employers could not or would not.

So astronomical was the outstanding bank-note circulation, and so much greater the need, that near the height of the inflation the presses of the Reichsbank and 150 printing firms, supplied with bank-note paper by 300 paper mills, could not keep abreast of the demand. On 20 November 1923 the value of the mark hit bottom with a quotation of 4.2 trillion marks to one dollar.[19]

The inflation was brought to a halt by means as classical as those which had caused it. The Reichsbank stopped issuing currency. The president of the bank, Hjalmar Schacht, took the next step in a bit of fiscal hocus-pocus which earned him the appellation, "the wizard." A new bank, the Rentenbank, was created and empowered to issue a new currency, the Rentenmark. The new currency was an expression of the psychological willingness of the public and the business community to end the inflation by any means short

[17] Rudolf Stucken, *Deutsche Geld- und Kreditpolitik* (Hamburg, 1937), pp. 44-45.
[18] Stolper, *German Economy*, p. 151; Lütge, *The Third Reich*, p. 423.
[19] Stolper, p. 154.

of a fundamental fiscal reform. Its value was backed by the value of German land and industrial property. A person owning a bill issued by the Rentenbank could not, however, cash it in for a few hectares of agricultural land or a lathe from Krupp. Nor did such a bill have any value on the international market. Nevertheless, the public showed sufficient confidence to turn in their essentially worthless old marks for the new currency.[20]

The inflation and the stabilization etched deep scars in the German economy and society. Different elements of the society paid the price of economic disaster in different ways. Hardest hit were individuals occupying creditor positions. Debtors benefited in the short run but in the long run lost out, too. Savings accounts were wiped out. Small investors and individuals on fixed incomes suffered most.[21] Members of the upper middle classes paid a high price for their patriotism when the war bonds they had bought with such enthusiasm lost their value. The cushion against hardship which such bonds and savings represented was gone, leaving behind a hatred for what they thought was the incompetence or the viciousness of the Republic. Moreover, doctors, lawyers, and other members of the free professions, as well as retired officials living on what had once been good pensions, could often no longer pay for the university education of their sons. Many students had to leave the universities to earn a living at jobs below their social expectations.

The holders of real property, and the entrepreneurial class in general, held their own and even benefited from the inflation. The value of real property rose with the decline in currency. Businessmen could pay off debts contracted in good money with inflated currency. Anyone with sufficient capital bought real estate and industrial properties. But such investments were made with an eye to hedging

20 Stucken, *Deutsche Geld- und Kreditpolitik*, pp. 64ff.; cf. Schacht's description of the miracle in his book *Die Stabilisierung der Mark* (Stuttgart, 1927).

21 Franz Eulenberg, "Die sozialen Wirkungen der Währungsverhältnisse," in *Schriften des Vereins für Sozialpolitik* (Munich, 1925), CLXX, 87-108; Bonn, *Schicksal*, pp. 17-18.

against inflation or making a quick profit rather than on the basis of sound long-term return calculations. After stabilization owners and big investors discovered the economic costs of such unwise and indiscriminate capital investments. They had borrowed heavily to make their investments, often at extremely high interest rates. After 1924 these high cost investments burdened German industry with heavy interest and amortization obligations, requiring in turn rapid and tremendous increases in productivity merely to break even.[22]

Not all of the strata of the middle classes were hurt by the inflation. Peasants, like the upper class Junker cultivators, could pay off their debts in cheap money. An estimated total agricultural debt of 17.5 billion gold marks in 1913 had been reduced to only 2.7 billion gold marks by the end of 1923. The inflation had the secondary effect of subsidizing agricultural (as well as industrial) exports. For a short time German grain exporters could undersell their hard-money competitors abroad. At home they could not be undersold. However, the short-run benefits were soon outweighed by rapidly mounting debts,[23] a serious shortage of capital in the countryside, and an unfortunate abatement of the pressures for greater efficiency and crop diversification.

STABILITY IN THE SHORT RUN: 1924-1929

With the inflation brought to a halt, Germany was left with no foreign exchange, a serious shortage of capital, and the requirement to resume reparations payments. The restoration of political confidence, a necessary first step for recovery, was accomplished by the formation of a moderate

[22] Bonn, *ibid.*; Stucken, *Deutsche Geld- und Kreditpolitik*, pp. 59. Hugo Stinnes was one such inflation profiteer; after the currency was normalized, his economically senseless empire of steel, coal mines, banks, newspapers, hotels, and sundry other firms in various unrelated industries went bankrupt. See the unsigned article "Stinnes Liquidation," *Der deutsche Volkswirt*, 15 Oct. 1926, pp. 75-77, for an evaluation of the number and value of the Stinnes holdings.

[23] Schumpeter, *Business Cycles*, II, 740; Gerschenkron, *Bread and Democracy*, p. 108; Max Sering, *Deutsche Agrarpolitik auf geschichtlicher und landeskundlicher Grundlage* (Leipzig, 1934), p. 26.

government under the premiership of the Centrist Wilhelm Marx and by the efforts of the foreign minister, Gustav Stresemann, who negotiated the withdrawal of the armies of occupation from the Ruhr and, in October 1925, the Locarno Pacts. Simultaneously, the United States proposed the Dawes Plan and the Dawes loans in the hope of regularizing Germany's international finances and the payment of reparations.

The committee of representatives of the major Western powers, under the chairmanship of the American banker General Charles Dawes, formulated a schedule of reparations payments combined with the concession of American loans to ease the strains of the first payments. The Germans undertook to deliver the requisite sum in their new Reichsmarks. It was up to Parker Gilbert, the Dawes Plan commissioner, to convert the suspect Reichsmarks into pounds and francs for payment in the recipient's currency.

The Dawes Plan aroused great animosity in Germany. Foreigners, indeed former enemies, held a "mortgage" on the Reichsbahn. The central note-issuing bank had to defer to the vetoes of its foreign directors. An American gained the right to dispose of a billion marks a year on the international money market. Any ill-will on his part or on the part of his government, or even a miscalculation, could once again reduce Germany to fiscal ruin. German nationalists, not unjustifiably, felt their country was being treated like a bankrupt "banana republic" or Middle Eastern sheikdom. In the words of Joseph Schumpeter, the "Dawes tribute was *morally* unacceptable to Germany and *economically* unacceptable to the recipient countries."[24]

Germany's creditors, refusing to permit German exports to compete with their own production, largely barred payment by the transfer of German goods. As a result, Germany met her reparations obligations largely out of the 25 billion Reichsmarks in public and private loans received from abroad—nearly 40 percent of the sum from the United States—in the years between 1924 and late 1931. Sometimes

[24] Schumpeter, II, 704, n. 1 (italics in the original).

called reparations, sometimes repayment of inter-Allied war debts, and sometimes U. S. loans to Germany, this circular flow of credits guaranteed the success of the Dawes Plan and, after 1929, the Young Plan—by not testing the German capacity to pay.[25]

The issue of reparations in the democratic Republic was a constant irritant to a sensitized national pride. But reparations did not impoverish Germany. The debilitating consequences of the payment of reparations on the economy were primarily indirect, albeit important. The payments intensified the chronic capital shortage from which the economy suffered. They increased Germany's foreign indebtedness without directly enhancing her productive capacity. Germany's foreign debts, in turn, exposed her economy to the cyclical movements of the economies of her creditors, in a way that rendered ineffectual the usual defenses of economic nationalism—tariffs, currency controls, monopoly pricing, and import-export regulation. Reparations did not cause the German depression; but, together with the loans made for other purposes, they laid the lines which carried the full shock of the American depression to Central Europe.

Only about 20 percent of German foreign borrowing went directly to the national, state, and local governments. Industry, primarily heavy industry, received most of the remainder.[26] The bulk of this capital was employed in financing the rationalization movement of industry and commerce.

"The escape into tangible assets" (*Flucht in die Sachwerte*) of the inflationary period left German industry greatly overcapitalized and too big for the existing markets. Amortization and interest obligations were extremely high. Industrialists responded immediately by reducing their in-

---

[25] Friedensburg, *Die Weimarer Republik*, p. 286; Lütge, *The Third Reich*, p. 426; Carl Bergmann, "Das Problem der deutschen Reparationsleistungen," *Strukturwandlungen*, II, 451-60. The two classical assessments of German capacity to pay reparations—in retrospect, an irrelevant issue—are John Maynard Keynes, *The Economic Consequences of the Peace* (New York, 1920), arguing that Germany could not have paid, and Étienne Mantoux, *The Carthaginian Peace* (New York, 1952), arguing that she could have paid.

[26] Friedensburg, p. 286.

ventories and by converting their short-term debts into long-
term loans.[27] Their long-range policies aimed at limiting
the repercussions of an unpredictable market, while at the
same time increasing profit margins. The inflation had stimulated the organization of vertical combinations in industry
and commerce. Under such conditions control of the productive process from raw materials to sales reduced uncertainties by giving firms control of costs. Currency stabilization exposed such vertical combinations to new competitive
pressures, in the face of which their often hastily established
and uneconomic organizations proved unresilient. Their
wholesale demise led to a new wave of cartel-building and,
beyond that, to the creation of vast trusts.[28]

The directors of industrial and commercial firms tried to
solve the problems which were brought to the fore by stabilization by means of business rationalization. The first step
involved the intensification of horizontal integration in industry and commerce as a way of improving their position
in the domestic and foreign markets. In 1925 combination
in the chemical industry took final form in the creation of
the chemical trust, I. G. Farben. In May 1926 the largest
steel-producing firms—Thyssen, Rhein-Elbe Union, Phoenix
and Rheinstahl—created the steel trust. The Krupp firm remained outside the organization because of its strong
interest in preserving family control, but it worked closely
with the trust. Most branches of heavy industry discovered
the economic advantage of trustification in the following

   [27] Gustav Stolper, "Investions- oder Konsumkonjunktur?" *Der deutsche Volkswirt*, 7 Oct. 1927, pp. 11-13.

   [28] Rudolf K. Michels, *Cartels, Combines, and Trusts in Post-War
Germany* (New York, 1928), p. 82; Schumpeter, *Business Cycles*, II,
763; Walter Meakin, *The New Industrial Revolution* (London, 1928),
pp. 101-2. A German cartel was usually the product of an *ad hoc*
agreement among the major independent firms in an industry regu-
lating some or all aspects of the production and marketing process. A
trust, on the other hand, was an amalgamation of firms. The directors
of the participating companies (not the stockholders) elected the
board of directors of the trust, or holding company, which then
dominated the industry as a single firm.

half decade and organized themselves accordingly. Commercial firms followed the same path, although by no means as extensively or as intensively. After the war large restaurant chains, like Kempinski and Aschinger, spread rapidly in the big cities of Germany. Large department stores and chain stores also proliferated. In 1925 the Karstadt chain owned thirty-two retail outlets. In 1928 the firm of Leonard Tietz operated seventeen outlets.[29]

Business reorganization led to administered prices. Trade union pressures made it difficult for managers to make savings by wage reductions. Sticky price and wage levels permitted increases in the profit margins only by reduction of fixed and operating costs. Thus the second step of business rationalization involved the systematic application of science to business activities. Cartels and trusts closed down unprofitable and over-aged operations. Careful cost-accounting procedures were introduced. Labor-saving and other more productive machinery, installed and linked in continuous flow systems, was made as automatic in its operation as possible. The use of chemical processes and electrical power, wherever feasible, was increased. The techniques of scientific management were linked to methods of mass production to streamline important sectors of the economy.[30]

The short-range goals of the sponsors of rationalization were generally achieved: costs were trimmed and profits rose. The textile industries, both woolen and cotton, were modernized. Machine tool production was rationalized, along with gas and electrical generation and transmission. Commercial enterprises of many sorts achieved important economies in this way. So efficient did the German coal mines become that between early 1925 and the end of 1926

[29] Meakin, pp. 101-4, 125ff. In 1927 the steel trust produced nearly as much raw iron as the whole of British output. In 1931 the Karlstadt chain, founded in 1920, did an annual business of 310.6 million Reichsmark. Robert Brady, *The Rationalization Movement in German Industry* (Berkeley, 1933), p. 283.

[30] Brady, pp. 3-4, 295; Meakin, pp. 40ff.; Friedrich Mayenberg, "Rationalisierung der technischen Betriebsorganisation," *Strukturwandlungen*, I, 225-47.

the average output per man per shift increased by 21.8 percent.[31]

Viewed from a broad perspective, the rationalization movement appears as the attempt of the leaders of the German economy to catch up with the other major industrial countries of the world and, indeed, to forge ahead of them. In the narrow business sense the ventures were largely successful. Their very success, however, posed fundamental questions about the structure of the economy which received no clear or unified answers from the leaders of the society. The rationalization movement was part of the general trend of the German economy away from the classical capitalist economy with its competitive markets and minimum of regulation. A return to that order would have been extremely difficult, even had any large or important segment of the society desired a return. Robert Brady stated the problem well when, in the midst of the depression, he observed that the Germans "seem to lack the social philosophy, the singleness of purpose and the will to take the next step. Every development in the rationalization movement has called for more comprehensive and far-sighted social and economic planning; yet every year appears to have passed with a deepening confusion as to objective and methods." By tampering with the classical economic structure and insulating large segments of it as much as possible from its ever more sluggish cyclical fluctuations, the movers of the economy reduced the effectiveness of the old self-equilibrating mechanisms. Yet they could present nothing in their stead.[32] The intensity of the depression in Germany was the price of this business indifference and of governmental failure to find the solution.

Very few voices were raised in protest against the impairment of the self-regulating mechanisms of the market economy. The first years of prosperity since the war were not years in which the nay-sayers could expect to receive much

[31] Meakin, pp. 63, 137-45ff. (cf. also p. 36); Wilhelm Kalveram, "Rationalisierung der kaufmännischen Betriebsorganisation," *Struktur-wandlungen*, I, 248-86.

[32] Brady, *The Rationalization Movement*, pp. 321-22.

attention from their fellow Germans. Political stability, a sounder currency, and a steady stream of foreign credits permitted business to progress at a better than usual rate. Unemployment was relatively low. Exports were rising. By 1927 the index of production had surpassed the levels of 1913. By 1929 most industries were producing at levels 10 to 20 percent above prewar output.[33]

THE MIDDLE CLASSES UNDER THE REPUBLIC

The quality of German life had changed radically in a generation's time. Mass production, increased organization, and urban culture all stimulated the emergence of a mass culture in the 1920s. Factories and even artisan shops employed machinery of a greater complexity to a greater degree. Typewriters, dictating machines, intercom systems, telephones, and efficiency experts with their stopwatches became the norm in the offices of progressive business firms. The *Hausfrau* was learning increasingly how to operate a textile machine or a piece of office equipment as readily as she had handled her potato peeler. And, as a result, she began to demand the introduction of labor-saving devices, such as vacuum cleaners and her husband, into the work of the household. If she and her family lived outside one of the great cities, they could see the world growing before their very eyes. Especially disturbing to the small-town middle classes was the rapid transformation of their little communities of a few thousand into genuine urban centers.[34] The increasing penetration of industrial and commercial society into all aspects of life seemed to many middle class Germans, especially those who suffered from it directly, to be "removing the magic from the world" (*Entzauberung der Welt*).[35]

---

[33] Friedensburg, *Die Weimarer Republik*, p. 297.

[34] Between 1925 and 1933 the number of towns with between 5,000 and 20,000 inhabitants increased by 7.9%. Statistisches Reichsamt, *Wirtschaft und Statistik*, Sonderheft 12 (1934), pp. 13-15.

[35] Werner Sombart used the phrase, taken from Schiller, in his *Die Rationalisierung in der Wirtschaft* (Düsseldorf, 1927), p. 11. Perhaps the most graphic artistic interpretations of the impact of the

Three important aspects of the socioeconomic history of Weimar Germany must be understood if the position, the attitudes, and the fate of the Mittelstand are to be properly appreciated. First, a socially and politically significant segment of these middling strata continued to exist in the twenties and early thirties. Second, many of these people lived under conditions of constant economic crisis. Finally, not being as well organized as the numerically larger labor movement and the financially powerful business community, the middle classes were always at a competitive disadvantage in the frequently savage interest politics of Republican Germany.

Despite the fundamental transformations in the social climate and in the structure of business enterprise since the advent of industrialism, changes in the structure of occupations proceeded more slowly. The Republic had a labor force (counting dependents) of 57 million in the mid-1920s. Of these, official statistics listed 21 percent as independent, 10 percent as employed in family enterprises, 19 percent as clerical and bureaucratic, and 50 percent as workers. If these data are compared with the results of the occupational census of 1907, almost no alteration in the relative size of the blue-collar working population is evident. Only a slight increase (2 percent) of those working at their family business or farm had occurred; "independents," meaning primarily rentiers, as well as self-employed shopkeepers, artisans, and farmers, had declined by 6 percent; while the clerical and bureaucratic labor force had expanded by 5 percent.[36] As the old Mittelstand continued to shrink, the new Mittelstand grew to replace the victims of modernity.

---

machine and of the organization of life around the machine were the films *Metropolis* (1927) by Fritz Lang and, after the onset of the depression, *Modern Times* (1936) by Charlie Chaplin.

[36] If this same labor force is broken down according to branches of activity, the 1925 census reveals the following distribution of employment: 23.0% in agriculture and forestry, 41.3% in industry and artisan trades, 16.9% in transport and commerce, 5.1% in administration and free professions, 3.1% in household service and the like, and 9.1% in no job (or none given). *Deutsche Wirtschaftskunde*, p. 47; Croner, *Soziologie der Angestellten*, p. 197.

The old middle classes, however, had by no means departed from the scene.

In the mid-twenties peasant proprietors remained dominant in the countryside almost everywhere but in the regions of the great Junker estates east of the Elbe. The most successful of these small landowners—that is, the most successfully market-oriented—were usually the cultivators of from five to one hundred hectares of land.[37] Progressive though they were, these peasant cultivators were nevertheless in economic difficulty throughout most of the Republican era. Despite some tariff protection, they had difficulty maintaining themselves in the face of foreign competition. They suffered from a chronic shortage of credit, which they needed to finance necessary improvements, and, when they did get it, had to pay exorbitant rates of interest, as even industrialists and Junkers were compelled to do. Compared with the Junkers, however, who had better tariff protection, with the industrialists, who could keep administered prices high regardless of economic conditions, and with the industrial workers, who were protected by powerful unions, the peasants were relatively unshielded from the adverse effects of free-market forces.[38] It has been estimated that by the mid-1920s perhaps 52 percent of all farms were operating at a loss. In late June 1926 the agricultural debt stood at 3.7 billion marks. By late March 1930 it had risen to 7.66 billion. In that same year 2,554 farms went under the hammer. In 1929, moreover, 3,173 farms, big and small, had failed.[39] The period of relative prosperity for industry

[37] In 1925 farms of this size constituted 22.6% of the total number and accounted for the cultivation of 62.6% of the farm land. *Deutsche Wirtschaftskunde*, p. 67. It must be emphasized that the goal of these peasant farmers was not profit for its own sake but rather the security of their family and above all the maintenance of the family patrimony. Gerhardt Albrecht, "Das deutsche Bauerntum im Zeitalter des Kapitalismus," *Grundriss der Sozialökonomik*, IX, Part 1, 61ff.

[38] Fritz Beckmann, "Die weltwirtschaftlichen Beziehungen der deutschen Landwirtschaft," *Strukturwandlungen*, I, 143-46. Cf. also Fritz Baade, "Die Stabilisierung der Schweinepreise," *Der deutsche Volkswirt*, 9 Sept. 1927, pp. 1574-78.

[39] Brady, *The Rationalization Movement*, p. 273; Schumpeter, *Busi-*

and labor between 1924 and 1929 was one of hardship for
all of agriculture. Naturally, the peasantry—with limited
working capital, poor access to new capital, foreign competition, and weakened political leverage in Republican Germany—suffered most intensely.

The post-stabilization business prosperity brought few
benefits for artisans and small shopkeepers. Although the
size of this sector in the mid-twenties is difficult to estimate,
one informed guess put its size at 11.2 percent of the total
labor force, or 2.88 million. The vast majority of artisan enterprises were small shops operated by the owner with the
aid of a few clerks or helpers.[40] Their number and size depended both on general economic conditions and on the
economic status of the specific industry. For the most part,
though, their numbers waxed and waned inversely with the
rate of industrial employment. The number of small businesses had increased immediately after the war when many
returning veterans could not return to their old jobs and
decided to start in business for themselves. During the 1923
inflation small businesses laid off employees, reverting often
to one-man operations. In the depression years many unemployed workers and salaried employees tried their hand at
earning a living by setting up little shops.[41] Thus, in times of

---

ness Cycles, II, 740. Cf. the somewhat higher estimates of indebted-
ness in John Bradshaw Holt, *German Agricultural Policy, 1918-1934:
The Development of a National Philosophy toward Agriculture in
Postwar Germany* (Chapel Hill, 1936), pp. 134-37; Gerschenkron,
Bread and Democracy, p. 125.

[40] Grünberg, *Der Mittelstand in der kapitalistischen Gesellschaft*, p.
78. A census of very doubtful reliability conducted by artisan organizations in 1926 indicated that about 60% of the small businesses were
operated by one man working alone, that another 20% employed two
men, and that over 10% had three workers. Certain branches of industry and commerce, such as food services, construction, and wood-
working, continued to be heavily dominated by artisan labor. J.
Dethloff, "Das Handwerk in der kapitalistischen Wirtschaft," *Strukturwandlungen*, II, 12, 16.

[41] Dethloff, p. 13; Statistisches Reichsamt, *Volks-, Berufs-, und Be-
triebszählung vom 16 Juni 1933: Statistik des deutschen Reiches*,
CCCCLIII, Heft 2, 17-18.

economic adversity, not only was the Mittelstand hardest hit, but also more Germans shared its distress.[42]

Unlike the old middle classes, the new white-collar middle classes grew in size and importance as a consequence of economic progress. The German economy, having achieved industrial maturity, followed the familiar pattern of extension of distribution and service activities. This extension in itself required the hiring of more nonproduction employees, like clerks and record keepers. Similarly, greater emphasis on production planning, control, and administration called forth expansion of the business bureaucracy. Increased governmental activity, too, necessitated a commensurate increase in the staffs of public bodies. Even members of the so-called free professions found themselves joining the dependent middle classes in significant numbers. Thus engineers, chemists, architects, and lawyers accepted employment with large firms, while many medical doctors, nominally independent, received much of their income—at fixed rates—from the public health insurance program.

By 1925 every tenth gainfully employed person was a salaried employee. For every four manual workers there was one white-collar worker. Of a total of 5.27 million private and public salaried employees, 63 percent worked in administration in industry, commerce, or government. Another 30 percent were individuals with special training or technicians. The rest were mainly supervisory personnel.[43]

The primary goal of the white-collar worker was advancement within the white-collar hierarchy. The function of his salary, therefore, was to permit a style of living appropriate to his rank and to indicate the degree of this advancement. Unlike the worker in the production departments, he saw his employment as a *Beruf*, a vocation. Very often his con-

---

[42] Schweitzer, *Big Business in the Third Reich*, pp. 65ff., offers a good general survey of the economic problems of the old middle classes in the Weimar period. These problems were largely the same as those at the turn of the century but were more intense and more intensely felt.

[43] Hans Speier, "The Salaried Employee in Modern Society," *Social Research*, I (1934), 115-16; *Deutsche Wirtschaftskunde*, pp. 54-55.

ception of his vocation led him to identify his own interests
with those of the management, rather than with those of the
manual worker. An impressive title was almost as important to him as a high salary. Although he was, in large measure, as dependent as the manual worker, he stubbornly refused to acknowledge any equality of status with this "proletarian." Despite his high self-evaluation, however, his pro-
motions, his salary, and his very job were all subject to the
play of the same labor market as that which affected manual workers. And, whereas manual workers had powerful
trade unions to speak for them, the salaried worker had to
depend, to a much greater degree, on the good will of his
employer. Efficient managers tended to view the clerical pay-
roll as an unproductive, if necessary, expense; accordingly,
their good will fluctuated with the phases of the business
cycle. The Mittelstand experienced little which might have
improved its economic position during the years of prosperity. A 10 percent rate of unemployment and growing
foreign indebtedness attest to the fact that in the years of
relative prosperity between 1924 and 1929 neither labor nor
capital found fundamental long-range solutions to their own
economic problems. The Junkers, business, and labor
nevertheless were sufficiently organized to exert political leverage to protect and advance their interests. This, within
the framework of Republican institutions, the Mittelstand could not achieve.

Owing to the failure of the social revolutionary impulse,
the Junker lands and most industrial holdings remained in
the possession of their old owners. The Republic gave half-
hearted encouragement to a program of peasant resettlement, and coal mining, potash mining, and steel industries
were organized into "autonomous authorities." But Junkers
and industrialists alike still endeavored, as they had before
the war, to stave off both socialism and the "nightmare of
free competition."

Moreover, the Junkers continued to speak in behalf of
the "landed interest." In 1921 a union of the two largest
agricultural pressure groups formed the Reichslandbund
(National Agrarian League) and brought a membership of

more than 5.5 million cultivators under Junker control. Members of the Reichslandbund owned or operated a total of 1.7 million farms or estates.[44]

The new organization of the leading industrial firms was the Reichsverband der Deutschen Industrie (National Association of German Industry). For questions affecting the relationship of management and labor there arose the Vereinigung Deutscher Arbeitgeberverbände (Confederation of German Employers' Associations).[45]

In the field of parliamentary politics the party which most closely represented the interests of the big industrialists, especially those in exporting industries, was the Deutsche Volkspartei (German People's Party). Industrialists less in sympathy with the basically nineteenth-century liberal economic orientation of the DVP joined the eastern landowners in the ranks of the Deutschnationale Volkspartei (German National People's Party). At their maximum combined strength in 1924 the two parties managed to win just under one-third of the Reichstag seats.[46]

Neither party worked comfortably in the parliamentary politics of Republican Germany. As long as Stresemann led the DVP (until his death in 1929), it did not openly repudiate the Constitution, and it tolerated German participation in the League of Nations. Most of the members of the DNVP, on the other hand, opposed the Republic. The restoration of the monarchy ceased to appeal to most members of the DNVP early in the 1920s. Although implicated in the reactionary Kapp Putsch of 1920, the DNVP did not become a decisive instrument in the overthrow of the Republic until 1928, on the eve of the depression, when Alfred

[44] Gerschenkron, Bread and Democracy, pp. 75-76, 105.

[45] On the activities of these and lesser industrialists' pressure groups, see Robert Brady, "Policies of National Manufacturing Spitzenverbände," Political Science Quarterly, LVI (1941), 199ff., 379ff., 515ff.

[46] Sigmund Neumann, Die deutschen Parteien: Wesen und Wandel nach dem Kriege (Berlin, 1932), pp. 53ff., 60ff., 120. This total consisted of 111 seats for the DNVP and 51 for the DVP out of the 493 contested in the election of December 1924, immediately after Stresemann had effected the withdrawal of the French troops occupying the Ruhr.

Hugenberg became its leader. After that date the party engaged actively in the search for a dictator to replace the
lost Kaiser.

There is little doubt that restorative yearnings were present in the hearts of most big businessmen and Junkers. Perhaps Abraham Frowein expressed best the hope common to
big industrialists and large landowners when he opened the
meeting of the main committee of the Reichsverband on
12 February 1926 with the fervent wish "that we recover
in [the new] Germany what we had before the war."[47]

The class of industrial workers was the most populous
social group in the Republican era. Industrial workers and
their families comprised perhaps one-half of the total population. Their occupational interests were well represented by
their trade unions. The free trade unions, associated with
the Social Democratic Party, were the outstanding spokesmen for unionized labor. In labor relations the Catholic
trade unions worked closely with the Socialist organization.
Mirroring the employers' organizations, the unions were
consolidated in the Allgemeiner Deutscher Gewerkschaftsbund (General Confederation of German Labor).[48]

A half-century of socialist education, propaganda, and
activity had given most members of this group a sense of
class solidarity and a common vision of a better socialist
future. The new era would dawn, the proletariat was
taught, when socialist activity and industrial development
under capitalism came to a decisive juncture. Within the
ranks of labor strong disagreements existed on the questions
of the nearness of that day, the means of bringing about
the revolution, and the role of the nonsocialist political

[47] *Veröffentlichungen des Reichsverbandes der deutschen Industrie,*
XXX (April 1926), 6—cited by Bracher, *Die Auflösung der Weimarer
Republik,* p. 206.

[48] Richard Woldt, "Die deutschen Gewerkschaften in der Nachkriegszeit," *Strukturwandlungen,* I, 503ff. This estimate of the size
of the industrial proletariat must be considered at best a thoughtful
guess. It is based on the conclusions of the best available study of the
social structure: Theodore Geiger, *Die soziale Schichtung des deutschen
Volkes* (Stuttgart, 1932), pp. 73-74. Cf. also the statistics in *Deutsche
Wirtschaftskunde,* p. 103.

forces in the process. In the politics of Weimar Germany the differing views on these questions crystallized about the two poles of the moderate Social Democratic Party (SPD) and the radical Communist Party (KPD).

The SPD committed itself fully to the principles of parliamentary democracy. Rejecting revolution, its leaders worked to construct a welfare state in Germany which, with the gradual expiration of free-market capitalism, would slowly and démocratically assume the shape of a socialist commonwealth. They worked willingly with the "democratic bourgeois" forces in German society. At its numerical height, in 1930, the SPD counted just over a million members. It had won a little less than 40 percent of the mandates to the Constituent Assembly in 1919, but the vote it received never broke the "one-third barrier" between 1920 and 1933. Support for the SPD at the polls rose and fell in direct proportion to the economic fortunes of the state with which it was so intimately identified.[49]

The Communist Party was formed by dissident Socialists in 1919. It espoused in theory at least, if not (after 1920) in practice, revolutionary seizure of power by the proletariat led by a party vanguard. It claimed a membership of only 200,000, but each member was expected to view himself as an active, full-time revolutionary. Like the SPD, it recruited its membership primarily from the class of manual workers, most successfully from among unskilled workmen, rural laborers, and the lower levels of the unemployed. Unlike the SPD, however, which as part of the new Establishment tended to lose votes when the Republic experienced misfortune, the Communist Party increased its voter support fairly steadily throughout the 1920s and the early 1930s. During the depression it gained many voters at the expense of the SPD, although the SPD, with its close links to the unions, kept the loyalty of the employed workers. Receiving only 4 seats in the Reichstag elections of 1920, the KPD by No-

---

[49] Neumann, *Die deutschen Parteien*, pp. 28-29, 120, and 123, n. 8. For a history of the party during the Republican era, see Richard Hunt, *German Social Democracy, 1918-1933* (New Haven, 1964), esp. pp. 111-30 on the SPD vote.

vember 1932 had garnered 17.1 percent of the mandates, or
100 seats, making it the third strongest German party after
the National Socialists (196 seats) and the SPD (121
seats).[50]

The middle classes, too, formed occupational and political organizations to represent them. But, in contrast to
those of capital and labor, these organizations, representing the narrow interests of various occupational groups
(for they could not work out unified action programs
among themselves), proved too weak. Peasants joined organizations like the Reichslandbund, the Deutscher Land-
wirtschaftsrat (German Agricultural Council), and the
Vereinigung Christlicher Deutscher Bauernvereine (Federation of Christian German Peasants' Unions). The intensity of the agricultural depression prompted these bodies to
merge in a broad agrarian Green Front in March 1929. The
conclusion of such an alliance revealed the despair of the
peasantry, for their leaders surely realized that the Junkers
would dominate it just as they had dominated the Reichslandbund. Purely peasant parties in the Reichstag never attained a strength of more than 5 percent of the mandates.
After 1930 the peasant vote went increasingly to the
DNVP and the National Socialists.[51]

The organizations of tradesmen and shopkeepers were
even weaker. The Association of German Artisans, comprising in 1925 the craft organizations of sixty-three different skills, represented 910,388 artisans belonging to 17,543
gilds. Under the provisions of the still valid Imperial legislation, 83 percent of these gilds were mandatory by 1929;

[50] Neumann, pp. 88ff. On the history of the KPD, see Ossip K.
Flechtheim, *Die Kommunistische Partei Deutschlands in der Weimarer
Republik* (Offenbach-am-Main, 1948).

[51] The Württemberger Land League, the German Peasants Party,
and the Christian Peasants Party together won 4.2% of the seats in
1928 and only 4.85% in the depression year of 1930. Cf. the table in
Holt, *German Agricultural Policy*, p. 97. Rudolf Heberle, *Landbevölkerung und Nationalsozialismus: Eine soziologische Untersuchung der
politischen Willensbildung in Schleswig-Holstein, 1918-1932* (Stuttgart,
1963), pp. 29, 118-33; Bracher, *Die Auflösung der Weimarer Republik*,
p. 207.

that is, they were empowered to regulate membership, training, and the employment of journeymen. The small retailers were united in forty-five trade organizations, which together could speak for only approximately half of all retailers. The two distinctly artisans' and shopkeepers' parties, the Wirtschaftspartei (Economy Party) and the Christlich-Sozialer Volksdienst (Christian-Social Peoples Service), must be numbered among the insignificant minority parties. Here, too, when members of this stratum voted at all, they tended to support the DNVP or Nazi candidates.[52]

Since white-collar workers could join organizations allied with the major power blocs, their potential for political influence was great. However, active recruitment by the SPD-oriented Allgemeiner Freier Angestelltenbund (General Confederation of Free Salaried Employees) had resulted, by the coming of the depression, in the enrollment of only about 12 percent of the total number. They preferred to join "professional" organizations, like the moderate Gewerkschaftsbund der Angestellten (Trade Union of Salaried Employees), or the oldest and biggest white-collar association, the Deutschnationaler Handlungsgehilfen-Verband (German National Commercial Employees Society). The DHV was closely connected with the DNVP. Like the peasants and farmers, the white-collar workers could not marshal their political power effectively in their own parties; but, because they were so vocal and so well-connected, they could, unlike the old middle classes, keep their interests on the agendas of the major parties.[53]

On the eve of the depression important segments of the society had insulated themselves, more or less securely, against economic misfortune. The heavy industries operated behind high tariff barriers with administered prices.

[52] Schweitzer, *Big Business in the Third Reich*, pp. 66-67; Neumann, *Die deutschen Parteien*, pp. 66-72.

[53] Speier, *Social Research*, I (1934), 125; Emil Lederer and Jakob Marschak, "Der neue Mittelstand," *Grundriss der Sozialökonomik*, IX, Part 1, 134ff.; Fritz Croner, "Die Angestelltenbewegung nach der Währungsstabilisierung," *Archiv für Sozialwissenschaften und Sozialpolitik*, XX (1928), 103-46.

Large landowners suffered little from foreign competitors because of the high grain tariffs maintained by the Republican government. When indebtedness threatened the loss of their estates, they could turn to the government, as they did during the depression, for special subsidies. Industrial workers benefited from the large body of social legislation, receiving the additional cushion of unemployment insurance in 1927. Their representatives in the Reichstag effectively looked after their interests. Such safeguards did not prove sufficiently effective under the unprecedented stress of the depression, but they were more effective than any the middle classes had.

For the Mittelstand, more than any other element of the society, lived and worked in the only significant corners of the economy still controlled by a free market. Small businessmen, artisans, and peasants, when they could get credit, borrowed at high free-market interest rates; they sold their products under relatively free-market conditions; and they had to compete with larger and more efficient competitors at home and often, too, with foreign competitors whose exports German tariffs did not completely drive off the market. Poorly organized white-collar workers participated in a much freer labor market than their industrial counterparts. Even state employees and members of the free professions suffered from the fluctuations of the business cycle to an unprecedented degree. Gripped by a mood of economic and social crisis, members of the middle classes realized, however dimly, that neither capitalism nor socialism would fit their needs. The depression intensified their search for an alternative ideology, for alternative state policies, and— lacking a state sufficiently interested in their problems—for a new German state.

DEPRESSION

Signs of a deflationary downturn were already evident in Germany at the beginning of 1929. In January 1928 the level of unemployment had stood at 1.8 million. By the end of February of the following year 3.1 million were unemployed. In the depth of the depression (spring 1932) 8 million workers would be without jobs.[54] The German depression was not primarily an import from the United States, as some economists have suggested.[55] It struck all the nations deeply enmeshed in the world economy, which more or less by default was led by the United States. There is ample evidence that internal German structural and cyclical factors precipitated the crisis, which American developments then exacerbated.[56] The number of explanations for the depression are legion, but no single one has found general acceptance among economists.[57] A cyclical downswing was, of course, expected after the years of prosperity during the 1920s. New investigations into the business cycle had uncovered sufficient periodicity to permit the Harvard Economic Society to predict such a downturn for 1929.[58] Yet no one predicted the enormity or the duration of the great depression.[59] If the German economy had been a "normal" one in 1929, the crisis would doubtless have been both healed and "healing," as cyclical downturns of the nineteenth century had been.[60] But the "healing" mechanisms no longer functioned; in large measure they were not

[54] Gustav Stolper, "Wirtschaftskrise," *Der deutsche Volkswirt*, 8 Dec. 1929, pp. 591-92; Wilhelm Grotkopp, *Die Grosse Krise: Lehren aus der Überwindung der Wirtschaftskrise, 1929-1933* (Düsseldorf, 1954), p. 14.

[55] Most recently, John K. Galbraith, *The Great Crash* (Boston: Riverside Press paperback, 1961), pp. 93ff., 173ff.

[56] Gerhard Kroll, *Von Weltwirtschaftskrise zur Staatskonjunktur* (Berlin, 1958), pp. 83ff.

[57] Galbraith, *The Great Crash*, pp. 173-74; see the survey of the theories in Paul Einzig, *The World Economic Crisis, 1929-1931* (London, 1932), pp. 23-28ff.

[58] Galbraith, p. 76. Schumpeter's retrospective prediction also pointed to the same conclusion. See his *Business Cycles*, II, 906ff.

[59] Except perhaps Joseph Stalin, who had been doing so since 1924. Cf. David J. Dallin, "Politics and the World-Economy in the Great Depression of 1929-1934," *Review of Politics*, VII (1945), 15ff.

[60] Theories based largely on the assumptions of a classical model, or ones very much like it, made up the core of economic orthodoxy in Germany during this period. Cf. Grotkopp, *Die Grosse Krise*, pp. 21-22, esp. p. 21, n. 1; and also Schumpeter, *History of Economic Analysis*, ed. from the manuscript by Elizabeth Boody Schumpeter (New York, 1954), pp. 1126-35.

permitted to function. Hence the orthodox anti-depression policies of the Brüning government enjoyed neither the economic nor the social—nor the temporal—prerequisites for success.

The German economy of the late 1920s cannot fairly be described as self-regulating.[61] Heavy state intervention, together with controlled prices and wages, had seriously limited the operation of the free-market machinery. Prices did not fall rapidly in all sectors; nor did there develop a sufficient gap between declining raw material prices and those of finished goods. Thus, while the world prices for mineral raw materials from January 1929 to January 1932 fell by an amount between 30 and 50 percent, in Germany the drop was only 22 percent. And over the same period the decline in German monopolistic heavy industry prices was just 19 percent, even though in the less well-organized branches of raw material production the reduction at times reached 50 percent. Price cuts in steel, coal, and chemicals were not commensurate with the fall in world prices, either. The downward trend of agricultural food prices, finally, did not exceed 15 percent despite a world free-market plunge of from 40 to 70 percent.[62]

In addition, not all marginally inefficient producers were forced out of business. Relatively unimportant small producers, it is true, very often were obliged to close down, but economic giants were better cushioned. Thus, although farm mortgage foreclosures increased from 3,173 in 1929 to 6,121 in 1932, most of the farms struck were under peasant proprietorship. Again, while tariffs on the importation of wheat and rye, the specialties of the Junker agriculturalists,

[61] Perceptive observers like Gustav Stolper, even before the coming of the depression, had predicted that ominous consequences would ensue from the ongoing restriction of the play of the free market in large sectors of the economy if business activity were to take a downswing. "Der gefesselte Kapitalismus," *Der deutsche Volkswirt*, 18 May 1928, pp. 1115-17.

[62] Adolf Sturmthal, *Die Grosse Krise* (Zurich, 1937), pp. 148-50. These estimates are based on the drop in posted prices. In practice many firms violated cartel agreements by selling below their posted prices.

remained high, resulting in stable prices for these grains throughout the depression (rye prices even rose between 1931 and the beginning of 1933), tariff protection for beef, butter, and pork products, the primary output of peasant farms, was slight. Moreover, as a consequence of Junker demands, tariff barriers were erected against foreign animal fodder, thus forcing peasants to pay the higher domestic prices for Junker-grown animal feeds.[63]

But even high tariffs did not offer sufficient protection to large growers. The domestic market could absorb only so much of the agrarian overproduction, and large, as well as small, cultivators still faced the fundamental problem posed by the shortage of credit. The lot of the Junkers differed markedly from that of the peasants, however. In the spring of 1931 the Reichstag passed the Ost-Hilfe (Aid to the East), which made a billion and a half marks available to East Elbian cultivators for debt conversion. In addition, local taxes and freight rates in the East were lowered. In 1932 nearly half of the Ost-Hilfe funds went to farms of one hundred hectares or more, that is to Junker farms.[64]

In industry, likewise, inefficient large producers with monopoly control were not driven from the market. Their position of power and the effect of governmental policies, especially increased tariff protection, repealed the law of economic survival of the fittest. Many small firms collapsed, but the total number increased as the unemployed tried to

[63] Holt, *German Agricultural Policy*, p. 139; see the statistics in *Der deutsche Volkswirt*, 27 Jan. 1933, p. 542; Gerschenkron, *Bread and Democracy*, pp. 134-38. In light of the evidence, Fritz Baade's argument that there existed no real conflict of interest between big and peasant cultivators is misleading. "Roggenpolitik und bäuerliche Veredelungswirtschaft," *Der deutsche Volkswirt*, 14 Nov. 1930, pp. 211-16.

[64] Cf. the article by M. K., "Das Getreideprogramm der Reichsregierung," *Der deutsche Volkswirt*, 6 Dec. 1929, pp. 302-4; Gerschenkron, *Bread and Democracy*, pp. 150-51. Cf. also an earlier, more blatantly self-serving aid plan proposed by the Green Front in the fall of 1929, which would have given agriculture governmental grants-in-aid financed by increased duties on feed grains. Rye and wheat growers were thus to be subsidized at the expense of peasant pig breeders of the Northwest and Southwest. M. K., "Ein neues Hilfsprogramm für die Landwirtschaft," *Der deutsche Volkswirt*, 1 Nov. 1929, pp. 142-45.

eke out a living by setting up small businesses. In Berlin alone in 1932 an estimated 60,000 men subsisted by working as canvassers and door-to-door salesmen.[65] The effect of this development, however, was simply to intensify further the competitive pressures weighing upon the established small businessmen.

At the heart of the abnormality of the German depression lay the intolerable structure of credit. By the late 1920s foreign investment and big business profits had become sufficiently great to permit large enterprises to finance their operations without recourse to private bankers. Often, like I. G. Farben, these businesses created their own banks. Private banks, some owned by Jewish families, meanwhile specialized in financing firms of medium size and smaller.[66]

The shortage of credit began at the level of banking. German banks had borrowed abroad in the 1920s to cover their credit needs. By September 1930 total German foreign indebtedness lay between 16.3 and 17.3 billion marks. After 1928 these loans had frequently been contracted for the short term, so that short-term loans comprised nearly half of the total borrowing. To further expand credit, bankers had followed the dangerous policy of lending funds of their depositors in excessive amounts. Before the war the average ratio of banking capital to deposited funds had been about three or four to one; by the time of the depression it had grown to almost fifteen or twenty to one. In the context of such banking practices, which the Reichsbank had no legal power to curb, there existed a constant risk that a liquidity crisis might be triggered by only a minor rush on the banks, a rush which could be initiated at any moment by the large number of foreign creditors the high interest rates had attracted.[67]

[65] Carl Dreyfuss, *Occupation and Ideology of the Salaried Employee* (2 vols.; New York, WPA Translation Project, 1938), I, 183—a translation of the German original, *Beruf und Ideologie der Angestellten* (Munich, 1933), citing the newspaper *Welt am Abend*, XXXII (1932), No. 42.

[66] Gustav Stolper, "Renaissance des Privaten Bankiers," *Der deutsche Volkswirt*, 20 April 1928, pp. 967-68.

[67] Gustav Stolper, "Banksorgen," *Der deutsche Volkswirt*, 13 April

The American crash of October 1929 produced that rush. American investors caught short on the stock exchange called in their short-term loans to meet rising margin requirements. Parallel with the bursting of the American speculative bubble was the collapse of the stock exchanges in London, Paris, Amsterdam, and Germany. German investors started a run on their banks, but all too often they placed second in the race with the Americans. In May 1931 the Austrian Kreditanstalt, perhaps the greatest of the Austrian banks, collapsed. In July the German Darmstädter- und National Bank (Danat Bank) followed suit. The Brüning government was forced to declare a bank holiday. The banks struggled to meet their obligations by recalling outstanding short-term loans to industry and agriculture, which for want of other alternatives had been invested for long-term purposes. The debtors could not sell buildings, equipment, and livestock rapidly enough. The financial crisis had provoked an industrial depression and worsened the existing agricultural depression.[68] Nevertheless, interest rates in Germany did not plummet as expected.

Firms tried to reduce costs by reorganizing and lowering wages. But, with the annual contracts of powerful trade unions hindering a policy of heavy wage cuts, the result instead was an increase in unemployment. Paring expenses where possible, businessmen laid off as many of their white-collar personnel as they could spare. The salaried employees, being the most expendable in cost-accounting terms, fared worse than the manual workers. In 1931, for example, the Brandenburg Labor Bureau received requests to fill 369 openings in salaried commercial positions. It received applications from 31,780 unemployed workers belonging to this category. But even these figures do not express fully the extent of white-collar joblessness, since out of considerations

1928, pp. 927-30; Georg Katona, "Die Auslandsverschuldung Deutschlands," *Der deutsche Volkswirt*, 5 Dec. 1930, p. 311; Lütge, "An Explanation of the Economic Conditions which Contributed to the Victory of National Socialism," *The Third Reich*, p. 432.

[68] Gustav Stolper, "Börsenkrise," *Der deutsche Volkswirt*, 25 Oct. 1929, p. 107; Lütge, *The Third Reich*, p. 432.

of status many such individuals refused to avail themselves
of public employment agencies. Many instead wrote literally hundreds of letters of inquiry—only to receive either a
negative response or no response at all.[69] Their despera-
tion knew no limits. In 1929, only the first year of the depression, a study conducted by the Deutschnationaler
Handlungsgehilfen-Verband concluded that, of the members who had died in that year, 16.28 percent of them had
taken their own lives. The suicide rate for the general population was 3.54 of every 100 deaths.[70]

Those salaried employees who were allowed to keep their
positions had to accept reductions in salary. In times of prosperity most had earned just a little more than skilled workmen.[71] As the depression continued, the income gap, to the
dismay of the salaried employees, closed.

Not only were large numbers of the existing class of white-
collar workers unemployed, but the future generation also
could not find work. Throughout the 1920s the number of
students graduated increasingly exceeded the number of positions open for them.[72] Perhaps a third of a million jobs
required academic training. The annual number of vacan-
cies in these positions approximated 11,000 or 12,000. Be-

[69] Dreyfuss, *Occupation and Ideology*, II, 65; Speier, *Social Research*, I, 119.

[70] Dreyfuss, II, 65-66. Such estimates must, of course, be viewed with
extreme suspicion; yet the despair of white-collar workers and of
their spokesmen is surely reflected in the use of suicide statistics as
an index of unemployment.

[71] *Deutsche Wirtschaftskunde*, pp. 279, 281.

[72] In 1925 the enrollment of students in institutions of higher learning had been 89,481. By 1930 this figure had jumped to 132,090. Over
half of this student population came from families of small landowners, artisans, shopkeepers, white-collar workers, the professions,
and the middle ranks of officialdom. Nearly a third more were from
upper middle and upper class families. Only 5.8% came from rural or
industrial working class backgrounds. Walter M. Kotschnig, *Unemployment in the Learned Professions* (London, 1937), pp. 13, 57. See
further the statistics on the growth of middle class enrollment at the
universities from 1835 to 1925 in the study of the Bayerisches Statistisches Landesamt, *Sozialer Auf- und Abstieg im deutschen Volk*
(Munich, 1930), Heft 117, p. 32.

tween 1929 and 1933, on the average, 25,000 students finished their schooling each year. Thus, even if only 80 percent of them had degrees in hand, there would still have
been at least two applicants for every job under normal
economic conditions.

Unemployment was highest among law graduates, secondary school teachers, engineers, and doctors.[73] A system
which could not offer such university graduates a means of
livelihood, in a society which viewed education as the primary means of social mobility within the middle classes, was
sure to incur their hatred. It was no cause for surprise, then,
that university students and recent graduates, like the rest
of the middle classes, were growing increasingly receptive
to ideologies of the middle class which promised to better
their lot.

The economic reality of the last days of the Republic
did not reflect the model of economic behavior which most
of its policymakers had learned at the university. Prices
were not falling sufficiently, nor were industrial wages. The
inefficient firms were not collapsing, only the unprotected
ones. Interest rates remained relatively high. Firms could
not sell off their overstock. Most important, no signs of the
restoration of business confidence, such as businessmen
undertaking fresh investments, were evident. Capitalism, at
least the textbook variety, seemed to be coming to an
end.[74]

If recovery were to be achieved, governmental action
would have to fill the economic void. But what policies
should the leaders of Germany follow? Germany's best economic minds could not agree. Some warned against any governmental activity. Many wanting governmental intervention could not agree on the form it should take.[75] Brüning,

[73] Kotschnig, pp. 57, 118-21.

[74] See the succinct differentiation between the depression economy
and the classical liberal economy in Lionel Robbins, *The Great Depression* (New York, 1936), pp. 1-11.

[75] See the conclusions of such important economists as Lautenbach,
Emil Lederer, and Ernst Wagemann, head of the government's
Institut für Konjunkturforschung (Institute for Business Cycle Re-

the last chancellor dedicated to preserving the Republic, chose to follow a compromise course of "classical liberal intervention." In the midst of the depression he initiated a deflationary policy with the prime purpose of stimulating business investment by making capital once more available. He reduced governmental expenditures by cutting civil service salaries in several steps between July and December 1930 by 12.5 to 16 percent. He decreased the amount and period of unemployment compensation in July 1931 and again in the summer of 1932. He replaced the defunct market mechanisms by governmental fiat. On 8 December 1931 he had a presidential order issued under the extra-parliamentary Article 48 of the Constitution which cut wages to the level of 1 January 1927, limited interest rates on bonds to 6 percent, cut rents by 10 percent, and pressured producers to lower their prices by 10 percent. In the international arena he hoped that price reductions would increase German sales abroad, which in turn would supply German producers with profits with which they could pay off their debts and make new capital investments. He also sought to increase the marketing area friendly to Germany with a plan for a customs union with Austria in 1931, but French political fears frustrated this project.[76]

Perhaps in the long run Brüning's policies might have achieved the goal of sparking a revival. In the late spring of 1932 the economy seemed to be responding with a slight decline in the rate of unemployment.[77] But there was no long run for the Republic. The German economy was, after all, integrated into a real society, and, even though Brün-

---

search) , that the automatic mechanisms could not be expected to function sufficiently well to bring recovery. Grotkopp, *Die Grosse Krise*, pp. 22, 30-31.

[76] Louis R. Franck, "An Economic and Social Diagnosis of National-Socialism," *The Third Reich*, pp. 550-51; Lütge, *The Third Reich*, pp. 432-33. Although exports were not increased, imports declined sufficiently to yield a positive balance of international trade in the years between 1930 and 1932. Grotkopp, p. 220. A succinct treatment of the Austrian customs union debacle may be found in Bracher, *Die Auflösung der Weimarer Republik*, pp. 398ff.

[77] Grotkopp, p. 14.

ing's deflationary policy may have been a sound textbook solution, it was not equipped to cope with conflicts that engendered strong political pressures and counterpressures. Moreover, Brüning had neither apparently nor dramatically reduced unemployment. In fact, during his two years in office, between 1930 and 1932, it had increased rapidly until the spring of 1932, at which time it had dropped by only a little more than 100,000. Business, big and small, had not reacted favorably to cuts in prices. The political prestige Brüning had gained from his negotiations with the Allies concerning an increase in the size of the German army and the effective, if not the legal, end of reparations with the Lausanne Agreement of June 1932 was lost when the customs union with Austria was blocked.[78] When Brüning tried to stop the irregularities in the administration of the Ost-Hilfe and made an effort to divide up some of the big Junker estates, President von Hindenburg, a Junker himself, asked for his resignation.[79] The premierships of Franz von Papen and his "cabinet of barons" and of General von Schleicher, with no party affiliation, followed. Finally, on 30 January, Hitler was asked by the President to head a new government. And it was this new regime which, at least initially, earned the gratitude of many members of the Mittelstand for pursuing an active and sympathetic economic policy aimed at overcoming the depression.[80]

In achieving a working definition of the Mittelstand, we have thus come to see something of its plight. The collapse of the Empire had blown away the sheltering, if leaky, umbrella protecting the middle classes. The governments of the Republic did little to help them, and, in the face of both long-term and short-term economic disasters, made no move to prevent many members of these middle strata

[78] Stolper, *German Economy*, pp. 221, 231.

[79] In the words of Gustav Stolper, "The German crisis of state is upon us." "Staatskrise," *Der deutsche Volkswirt*, 3 June 1932, p. 1179.

[80] On the measures devised by von Papen and Schleicher to fight the depression and their adoption by Hitler's first coalition government for the purpose of rearmament, see the excellent discussion by Dieter Petzina, "Hauptprobleme der deutschen Wirtschaftspolitik, 1932-33," *Vierteljahrshefte für Zeitgeschichte*, XV (1967), 18-55.

from being hurt. Organized labor and organized capital, by implication (and often in fact), virtually taunted the middle classes to organize themselves into a powerful, unified pressure group if they wished to remain a force in German public life.

It was in this context that a number of conservative thinkers attempted to devise a theory of society, economics, and political action designed to meet the needs and aspirations of the Mittelstand. Their language was often obscure or intemperate, but they did not theorize in a world of fantasy. Above all, they sought to supply orientation and a program to a middle class bewildered and hurt by the forces of capitalist industrial society. The chapters that follow deal with these attempts—largely uncoordinated, it is true, differing in sophistication and in nuance, but arising from the same impulses and pointing in the same direction for solutions—to formulate a social conservative ideology for the Mittelstand.

The most important thinker engaged in this task was the distinguished economist Werner Sombart, whose intellectual career spanned the whole first third of the twentieth century. During this time he marked the path that social conservative thought was to take throughout the years of the Republic. The twentieth-century movement was initiated by his search for a suitable ideology for the especially and obviously hard-pressed members of the old middle classes.

II. Werner Sombart

THE AGE OF
LATE CAPITALISM

IT WAS Werner Sombart who formu-
lated the basic principles of that complex of ideas and
values which, for the years of the Weimar Republic, we
have termed social conservatism. Major theorists, such as
Edgar Salin and Othmar Spann, important publicists, such
as Oswald Spengler and Ferdinand Fried, and, to some extent, even the National Socialists all assumed his basic
diagnosis of the ailments of the contemporary economic and
social order and, in essentials, his outline for the desirable
society of the future.

Sombart served the cause of social conservatism in several
major ways. Not only did he forge most of the arguments
against Marxism in the social conservative arsenal, but,
more important, he extracted and classified those precepts
of the Marxist canon which conservatives could employ
against liberal capitalism. Indeed, he offered other social
conservatives theories by means of which both capitalism
and socialism might be swept off the field of intellectual
contention. Most important of all, he pointed the way to
the transcendence of the more reactionary impulses of
nineteenth-century varieties of conservatism—the primitivist
hostility to industrialism and machinery, the extremes of
hierarchical thinking, the religious obscurantism, and the
disregard for the common man. Success in this intellectual
enterprise, he and other social conservatives hoped, would
mean the intellectual—and then institutional—triumph of
an ideology beyond both capitalism and socialism. Sombart
labelled his version of the ideal "German Socialism."

Like anarchism, the anti-industrialism of the left, social

conservatism was strongly influenced in its development by
the personalities of its leading thinkers. Many social conservatives, among them Sombart, had the special gift of being
able to feel and articulate the aspirations, the frustrations,
and the material needs of elements of the population less
able to give coherent expression to their grievances. Sombart, like many of the others who shared his outlook,
had an almost aesthetic perception of the world in which he
lived. A strong moral sense informed even his most prosaic
condemnations of modern industrial society and moved him
to an early concern with the social question. Very early in
his intellectual career he evinced a special interest in the lot
of all the social groups threatened and made miserable by
the progress of industrial capitalism. He looked first to the
Socialist movement in Germany as the best hope of the
downtrodden. But, when he realized that Marxian socialism
was at once too radical (it sought to overthrow a great deal
of the inheritance of the past which he wished to save) and
too conservative (it did not oppose the spread of industry
and the values of industrial society), he began to fight
against it. The repudiation of Marx and of any sympathy
he might have had for Marxism made his search for an ideology for the disadvantaged of industrial society all the
more difficult. With the formulation of German Socialism
he believed he had at last found a coherent ideology for the
old middle classes. But this metamorphosis required several
decades to work itself out.

In his *Socialism and the Social Movement in the Nineteenth Century*, first published in 1896, Sombart elaborated
the two guiding principles which were to assume the central
place in the works of all social conservative thinkers. Above
the issues of class or of class struggle, he argued, were the
two forces which shape all history, the *social* and the *national*, each conceived in its broadest sense.[1] Sombart's intellectual biography is the story of his changing interpretation

---

[1] *Sozialismus und die soziale Bewegung im 19. Jahrhundert* (Jena,
1896). The English translation by Anson P. Attenburg, *Socialism and
the Social Movement* (New York, 1898), pp. 2-3, is the text that will
hereafter be cited as *Social Movement*.

of these concepts. His final systematization laid the theoretical basis for social conservative economic thought in the Weimar period.

Sombart was born in Emersleben-am-Harz in 1863, the son of the wealthy landowner and industrialist Anton Ludwig Sombart.[2] The elder Sombart, originally a land surveyor, had through hard work become a man of means and had been elected to the Prussian Diet. A liberal and something of a reformer, he had divided his large manorial farm into small holdings for peasant settlers in 1885. The wealth of his father enabled the young Sombart to travel and even to study abroad. It also guaranteed him a good education. After attending gymnasium in Berlin and Schlessingen, Werner enrolled in 1882 at the University of Berlin. There he studied economics under Adolf Wagner and Gustav Schmoller, the latter of whom considered Sombart one of his outstanding students. While doing graduate work at the University of Pisa, Sombart prepared his doctoral dissertation on the Roman Campagna. His sympathy with the misery of the Italian poor was spontaneous and warm. Italy's industrial workers lived on a level below that of workers in the rest of Europe, but the agrarian popula-

[2] For biographical data on Sombart, I have drawn on M. Epstein, "Obituary, Werner Sombart (1863 - 13 May 1941)," *Economic Journal,* LI (1941), 523-26; Gustav Schmoller, review of Sombart's *Der moderne Kapitalismus,* in *Schmollers Jahrbuch,* XXVII (1903), 291; Leopold von Wiese, "Werner Sombart zum 70. Geburtstag," *Kölner Vierteljahrshefte für Soziologie,* XI (1932/33); Emil Ludwig, *The Nation,* 26 Oct. 1932, p. 391; article "Werner Sombart," in *Biographisches Jahrbuch und Deutscher Nekrolog,* III (1898), 253; Werner Krause, *Werner Sombarts Weg von Kathedersozialismus zum Faschismus* ([East] Berlin, 1962), p. 13; and esp. M. J. Plotnik, *Werner Sombart and his Type of Economics* (New York, 1937), pp. 24-43. In addition, there is the correspondence between the young Sombart and the Swiss Socialist Otto Lang which Arthur Mitzman used for his paper "Tönnies, Sombart, and the German Tradition," given at the Toronto meeting of the American Historical Association (30 Dec. 1967). These letters came to my attention too late to be used for this study. For a more detailed examination of the psychological makeup of the young Sombart, see Mr. Mitzman's forthcoming study of late Imperial German sociological thought.

tion was even more impoverished. Sombart feared that Italian culture could not long continue thriving when so many of her people were bereft of the essentials of a decent existence. He was especially distressed by the absence of a "storm-fast peasantry"; he observed a predominance only of "unsteady, uncertain, rootless, small holders and sharecroppers."[3]

After completing his studies in 1888, Sombart took the post of secretary of the Bremen Chamber of Commerce. In 1890 he was named to a professorship of economics at the University of Breslau. In this relatively unsophisticated Silesian town Sombart's behavior aroused general interest and much unfriendly criticism. Emil Ludwig, a former student, has given us the following description of his teacher:

> Werner Sombart was a revolutionary in his late thirties. His reputation as a Don Juan made him an object of curiosity to his students, of distressful emotions to the faculty, and of holy terror to the citizenry. He had a splendid delivery and was, or appeared to be, a socialist, which made him doubly fascinating, since these views were anathema in Prussian institutions of higher learning. I saw in him a new type of the combination of the man of the world and artist, for undoubtedly he was both; and though not supposed to be a poet, he went driving in Byronic fashion with the handsomest opera singer. At concerts he lolled in his seat, often passing his delicate hands through his long lustrous black hair. And this was the man whose definitions had a classical lucidity, who could always, without wearying his audience, bring home the most complicated economic statistics both to mind and imagination.[4]

Because of his radical political views, the gifted and popular teacher was forced to remain in "exile" for fifteen years, until

[3] *Archiv für soziale Gesetzgebung und Statistik*, II (1889), 280.

[4] *Gifts of Life: A Retrospect*, ed. Ethel C. Mayne, tr. M. I. Robertson (Boston, 1931), p. 89. I have altered the wording of this passage slightly to bring it into conformity with the usages of the English language.

1905, when he received an appointment at the Handels-
hochschule (School of Commerce) in Berlin. Only in 1917,
after his reputation as a scholar had long been established
and he had published attacks on Marxist socialists in his
extremely nationalistic *Händler und Helden* (*Merchants
and Heroes*), did he become professor of economics at the
University of Berlin. Only in democratic Germany did
Sombart receive the recognition he deserved. He became a
member of both the Prussian and Bavarian Academies, serv-
ing also as president of the Verein für Sozialpolitik from
1932 to 1935. On his seventieth birthday, on 19 January
1933, socialist organs remembered and hailed the old leftist
Sombart, while the right-radical press praised the new Sombart, the social conservative economist.[5]

In later life Sombart once reminisced on the dilemma of
being both a radical and a professor of economics in Imperial
Germany: "I was then [in his thirties] a convinced Marxist
and at the same time a Royal Prussian University Professor." He felt he could resolve the contradiction with the insight that "value judgments had no place in science. [He]
could therefore conduct scientific inquiry quite independ-
ently from [his] value preferences."[6] Such a distinction was
quite important for a man of his passionate nature, since
the object of his study, to which he devoted a lifetime of
thought, was modern capitalism.

Before we investigate the results of his analyses of capitalism, we must first consider briefly Sombart's method, for
aspects of it were to become important in social conservative thought. Sombart represented a third generation of
the German historical school of economics.[7] Thus he started
with an anti-classical bias, a repudiation of universal laws
of economics, and an emphasis on the relativity of economic

[5] Plotnik, *Werner Sombart*, p. 41.

[6] Von Wiese, *Kölner Vierteljahrshefte für Soziologie*, XI, 254. See
also his statement in support of Max Weber when the latter proposed
the elimination of ethical values from scientific investigation at the
stormy meeting of the Verein für Sozialpolitik in Vienna in 1909.
Schriften, CXXXII, 572.

[7] Schumpeter links him with the two gifted social scientists, Max
Weber and Arthur Spiethoff, in this grouping; see his *History of
Economic Analysis*, pp. 815ff.

eras and systems.[8] From Marx he took the concept of an *economic system* as a mode of production in a specific era.

In the history of economic thought Sombart found three types (he termed them "epochs") of methodology, which we may, for our purposes, designate as the pre-classical, the classical, and the type Sombart championed, the method of *Verstehen* (sympathetic understanding) .[9] Proponents of the method of *Verstehen* had always opposed the classical approach to economics on national and ethical grounds. But Sombart went farther in his attack, for he maintained that followers of classical economics were wrong to base their model on the natural sciences.[10] He drew a distinction between natural sciences and human sciences, holding them to be basically different in kind and method—a distinction commonly made in the German historicist tradition. Most sophisticated social conservatives, such as Othmar Spann an Edgar Salin, also skillfully employed this dichotomy for their own purposes.[11] By means of the disciplined empathy of *Verstehen*, Sombart "felt himself into" the object of his inquiry; he believed that by employing such an approach he could capture the essence, the spirit, of a historical economic system. Sombart devoted a lifetime to the study of the origins, the spirit, and the development of capitalism. The detailed results of his inquiries—contained in at least nine full volumes, many related studies, and innumerable articles—need not detain us here, but his general conclusions about the nature and tendencies of modern capitalism

[8] Talcott Parsons, " 'Capitalism' in Recent German Literature: Sombart and Weber," *Journal of Political Economy*, XXXVI (1928), 648. Parsons offers the best available guide to Sombart's analysis of capitalism; I have followed the outlines of his argument in my discussion.

[9] *Die drei Nationalökonomien* (Munich, 1930), Ch. I. Sombart elaborated on his methodology only after he had completed his major works.

[10] *Ibid.*, pp. 140-51.

[11] For a well-reasoned negative critique of themes divorcing the natural from the human sciences and of "The Operation Called *Verstehen*," see the article of that title by Theodore Abel in Feigl and Brodbeck, eds., *Readings in the Philosophy of Science* (New York, 1953) , pp. 319-53.

bear directly on the story of social conservatism in Germany.

Sombart differentiated three components undergirding every economic system: a unique spirit animating it, its own form and plan of organization, and its body of technology.[12] Applying his analysis to capitalism, Sombart arrived at a description of a system consisting of the following elements: first of all, a spirit of acquisition and competition, along with economic rationality; then, formally, a scheme based on exchange and private enterprise; and, finally, a modern technology upon which all else rested and which in turn depended upon scientific discovery.[13]

Under mercantilism (early capitalism) state officials who implemented the policies of their princes directed the economy. In the era of high capitalism during the nineteenth century control passed into the hands of the entrepreneurs.[14] Of the ingredients of the spirit of capitalism—acquisitiveness, enterprise, and rationality—acquisitiveness was clearly the oldest. The desire for gain was a constant of all economic behavior; its existence was quite independent of the dominant system. Evidence of the spirit of enterprise, however, Sombart found first about the time of the Renaissance embodied in the spirit of adventure, of seeking, and of inquiry. The spirit of enterprise was not unique to capitalism either, but business activity proved eminently suitable to satisfying the urge for conquest and domination. The tendency toward acquisition and enterprise, strengthened by competition, led to the destruction of the system of medieval handicraft economy, reinforced the insatiable desire for gain, and, as a consequence, fostered the beginnings of the business mentality.

The spirit of capitalism did not emerge fully, however, until the bourgeois spirit had become integrated into it. It

[12] Sombart, "Economic Theory and Economic History," *Economic History Review*, II (1929), 14.

[13] Sombart, "Die prinzipielle Eigenart des modernen Kapitalismus," *Grundriss der Sozialökonomik* (Tübingen, 1925), IV, 1-26.

[14] Sombart, "Entfaltung des modernen Kapitalismus," in Bernard Harms, ed., *Kapital und Kapitalismus* (2 vols.; Berlin, 1931), I, 86—hereafter cited as "Entfaltung."

was this spirit that supplied the final element of rationality. Sombart wrote, much as Marx had written, of the achievements of the bourgeois class in moving history forward and, therefore, closer to the era of socialism: "How gladly would I speak of the great historic mission which this class has fulfilled!" He waxed lyrical about "the wonderful development which this class has given to the material forces of production."[15] Some segments of the bourgeoisie had stimulated the growth of the bourgeois spirit more than others. Breaking down the ingredients of the bourgeois spirit, Sombart sought for explanations in the psychological peculiarities of various peoples. The Jews, especially, had contributed greatly to the evolution of the modern spirit of capitalism in general and to the spirit of rationality in particular. Their religious beliefs, their intellectualism, and their long history as wanderers had implanted within them character traits which permitted them to develop the "idea" of capitalism to its highest level.[16]

Under the influence of the bourgeois spirit, the spirit of enterprise was structured and molded into institutions. In what Sombart called the "objectification" of the capitalist spirit, the bourgeois spirit and that of enterprise were transferred to the firm. The firm became an enterprising, rational entity, quite independent now from the personal qualities of its owners. It gained a life of its own—its own will, its

[15] *Social Movement*, p. 8.

[16] *The Jews and Modern Capitalism* (London, 1913), pp. 21ff.— tr. M. Epstein from the original *Die Juden und das Wirtschaftsleben* (Leipzig, 1911). Sombart apparently intended nothing invidious in singling out the Jews in this way. Before World War I he evinced a great admiration for the Jews and their "unique" characteristics. He even wrote a pamphlet on the Jewish question in which he showed great sympathy for the persecuted Jews of Eastern Europe and advocated Zionism (the return to Palestine) as a solution to their plight. For Western Jews, especially those of Germany, he recommended a policy of cultural pluralism, i.e., continuation of their own culture and toleration of them by the rest of the society. He counselled the Jews to accept their exclusion from university posts and the officer corps. Although they ought to enjoy civic equality, they should, he urged, be temperate in the exercise of their rights. See his *Die Zukunft der Juden* (Leipzig, 1912).

own mode of understanding, and its own special character.[17] Indeed, it made increasingly greater demands on men's time and efforts, forcing them into its service through its voracious ingestion of economic power.

Sombart, like most new conservatives, viewed economic history as being cyclical.[18] Each epoch of economic democracy is necessarily followed by an epoch of economic aristocracy, which in turn must give way to an era of economic democracy. In Europe the cycles had been: democracy of the most primitive order, the society of nomadic herders (aristocratic), the village community (democratic), manorialism (aristocratic), the handicraft system (democratic), and, finally, aristocratically organized capitalism. Sombart believed it reasonable to predict that the downfall of capitalism would usher in an era of economic democracy under socialism.[19]

The study of modern capitalism by Sombart "the dispassionate scientist" led to its indictment by Sombart "the reformer." Already in Breslau his friends were fond of referring to him as the "salon demagogue," while his enemies spoke of him as "the Red Professor." But Sombart's radicalism in the 1890s was even then somewhat peculiar. In her memoirs the Socialist leader Lily Braun tells of conversations about German foreign policy she and her husband (an SPD revisionist and publisher of some of Sombart's early pieces) had with the young academic socialist sympathizer. In these conversations Sombart pressed the view that the major international question confronting Germany was that of white or nonwhite domination of the world. Sombart's later virulent nationalism was foreshadowed in his support of Germany's construction of a large fleet and her acquisition of colonies.[20]

[17] "Entfaltung," pp. 89-90.
[18] Armin Mohler, *Die Konservative Revolution in Deutschland, 1918-1932: Grundriss ihrer Weltanschauung* (Stuttgart, 1950), pp. 106-46.
[19] Sombart, *Economic History Review*, II, 15-16.
[20] Lily Braun, *Memoiren einer Sozialistin* (2 vols.; Munich, 1911), II, 391-92. Heinrich Braun edited the socially liberal-oriented *Archiv*

Yet, despite his advocacy of imperialism, a heresy which had also cropped up in the ranks of the SPD,[21] Sombart must be considered one of the most important bourgeois interpreters of Marxist thought in late nineteenth-century Germany. The aged Engels himself praised Sombart's article on the third volume of *Capital* for displaying a basically correct understanding of Marx.[22] It has even been claimed that the influence of his book *Socialism and the Social Movement* in winning friends for Marxism all over the world was greater than that achieved by any writings of members of the movement itself.[23] He first delivered the contents of this slim red volume in a series of lectures he gave in Switzerland in 1896. When he published it in the same year, it met with immediate acclaim on the left and assured the continuation of his exile in Breslau.

This work was a pithy description of the origins, nature, and prospects of socialism in Western Europe. Hailing Marx's conception of history as the history of the class struggle as "one of the greatest truths that fill our century," Som-

---

für soziale Gesetzgebung und Statistik. In 1904 Sombart, Edgar Jaffé, and Max Weber took this journal over, renaming it the *Archiv für Sozialwissenschaft und Sozialpolitik.*

[21] Abraham Ascher, "National Solidarity and Imperial Power: The Sources and Early Development of Social Imperialist Thought in Germany, 1871-1914" (Ph.D. diss., Columbia University, 1957; also available in microfilm edition from University Microfilms, Ann Arbor, 1958), pp. 203 ff.

[22] Sombart's piece, entitled "Zur Kritik des ökonomischen Systems von Karl Marx," appeared in the *Archiv für Gesetzgebung und Statistik,* VII (1894), 555-94; Engels's praise in *Neue Zeit,* XIV (1895/96), 9.

[23] Von Wiese, *Kölner Vierteljahrshefte für Soziologie,* XI, 254. See also Friedrich Hayek's statement in his *Road to Serfdom* (Chicago: Phoenix Books paperback, 1944), pp. 168-69, asserting the great influence of Sombart the Marxist. So intent is Professor Hayek on proving that the triumph of Hitler was a victory of "socialism" that he distorts the meaning of the term as it was then used in Germany and as it is commonly used today. As a result, he neglects completely the great change that Sombart's thinking underwent. In the years of the Republic Sombart opposed Marx, Marxism, the SPD, and the KPD. Hayek seems to have fallen sufficiently under the spell of social conservative rhetoric to be misled into identifying a very special brand of "anti-capitalism" with socialist ideology and policy.

bart showed how the uncertainty and exposure of the workers under capitalism had provoked resentments which had then flowered into the social movement. Writing with the nostalgia which has come to be the hallmark of social conservative thinkers, he characterized the era of free competition as having "stamped itself upon all spheres of life. Every man strives with others, no one feels himself sure, no one is content with his condition. The beauty and peace of repose are gone."[24]

The German working class, he argued, could take one of three possible paths out of the capitalist bog. It could emulate the revolutionary workers' movement in France. Or it could continue the trend toward revisionism, which was then the cause of so much dispute within the SPD. The third way, that of English non-political trade unionism, was the way Sombart believed most desirable.[25] For he was distressed by the lack of sympathy for religion and for the national interest characteristic of socialism in Germany. He understood the workers' mistrust of "official Christianity," which had resulted from the use of religion by the ruling class as a prop to support capitalism and the monarchy. He had hopes, however, that the Christian-Social movement of Adolf Stöcker, the favorite preacher of Wilhelm II, would be effective in lessening the mistrust of the workers and in opening up the possibility of Christianizing the proletariat. Of the internationalism of the German working class movement, he predicted that "an artificial sympathy with the most downtrodden people would prove too weak to restrain a sound national self-interest." If workers were better treated, he contended, they could accept, and would follow, the leaders of the nation. When the workers were integrated as full members of the society, they too would become good nationally minded Germans. Yet he advised Socialists to avoid any compromise with middle class elements, some of whom had already found their way into the movement. The thrust of Sombart's first important statement on the social question, then, was in the direction of advocacy of a legal class strug-

[24] *Social Movement*, pp. 1, 12-13, 16.
[25] *Ibid.*, pp. 53-54.

gle. "So long as the battle rages legally and honorably," he concluded, "we need not worry about the future of our civilization."[26]

As early as 1896, as we have seen, the outlines of the doctrines which Sombart would call German Socialism in the years of the Republic were beginning to take shape. His opposition to capitalism on aesthetic and moral grounds was unequivocal. His advocacy of workers' action no more radical than militant trade unionism was also clear. His nationalism and his linking of social reform with nationalism, which were to assume a dominant place in his subsequent thought, were already developing. But what stands out above all in this picture of the young Sombart is the stress he laid on social harmony.

Many German intellectuals, social scientists in particular, believed this harmony to be in imminent danger around the turn of the century. Social peace and rapid change rarely go hand in hand. Young, tinged with radicalism, and more sophisticated than many other German academicians, Sombart realized the futility of attempting to hold fast to the status quo. Nothing could be gained by opposing social and economic trends so deep and so powerful. Sombart carefully followed the statistical war over the number and viability of the old Mittelstand, which the publication of the census of 1895 had stimulated.[27] At the height of the debate, in 1896, he seemed to take his stand against the old Mittelstand and with the forces of modernity. In *Socialism and the Social Movement* he counselled the advancing Social Democratic movement to beware of alliance with "the notoriously declining classes" of artisans and other such petty bourgeois groups.[28] A few years later at a meeting of the Verein für Sozialpolitik he warned against policies which

[26] *Ibid.*, pp. 162-63, 165, 167, 172-77.

[27] Hans Rosenberg, *Grosse Depression und Bismarckzeit: Wirtschaftsablauf, Gesellschaft, und Politik in Mitteleuropa* (Berlin, 1967), pp. 58-61; Lebovics, "'Agrarians' versus 'Industrializers,'" *International Review of Social History*, XII, 43-53; Sombart, "Zur neueren Literatur über das Handwerk," *Archiv für Gesetzgebung und Statistik*, IX (1896), 624-39.

[28] *Social Movement*, p. 197.

might give small shopkeepers special protection in their competition with modern commercial enterprises.[29] And his 1904 *Gewerbewesen*, a small primer on manufacture, was almost a syllabus of the errors in the arguments advanced in behalf of artisan industry. "Artisan industry," he wrote, "will prove itself capable of holding on . . . only insofar as it takes on the specific features of capitalistic organization."[30] To do this, as Sombart well knew, artisans would have to give up being self-conscious about their status and instead become little capitalists. Sombart had schooled himself too well in the dialectical view of history to offer his readers a simplistic doctrine of return to a golden age in the past. The creation of a German community would have to be a post-capitalist phenomenon. But he did not consider the Socialist movement fit for the task.

Social Democracy, instead of having intensified its hostility to capitalism in the years before the war, had, in Sombart's view, accepted it. In 1903 he noted that, in an era when the conflict between pre-capitalist classes and the capitalists had become more acute than that between labor and capital, the Marxian Socialist movement was changing from a revolutionary party, led by a band of heroes, to a mass reform party. It had become "boring." Lured by the prospects of limited reforms, Socialists had betrayed their principles. Sombart, looking beyond the issue of orthodoxy versus revisionism, concluded that "the old sect of utopians, revolutionaries, and men of principle [*Prinzipienreiter*] [had] become the great party of opportunists and accommodationists."[31] The war crystallized his disenchantment with the movement.

In reaction to Entente propaganda, which often tarred

[29] *Schriften des Vereins für Sozialpolitik*, LXXXVIII (1899), 137-57.

[30] *Gewerbewesen*, Sammlung Göschen (2 vols.; Leipzig, 1904), II, 30-31; see further 59-97.

[31] Sombart, *Die deutsche Volkswirtschaft im neunzehnten Jahrhundert* (Berlin, 1903), pp. 547, 528. Krause (*Werner Sombarts Weg*, p. 52) is probably not far off in concluding that in this, Sombart's most radical period, his hopes for the Socialist movement extended little beyond having it function as a protective and stabilizing force among the proletariat.

the Germans as "Huns," "Eastern Barbarians," "militarists,"
and "nonliberals," German intellectuals rallied to the defense of their homeland by publishing counterstatements in
which the uniqueness of Germany vis-à-vis the nations of
the West was proudly proclaimed.[32] Sombart published his
war book to answer the attacks on Germany formulated by
Herbert Spencer well before the war and revived once again
as British propaganda. Spencer had drawn a sharp contrast
between the commercial, peace-loving English and the aggressive, warlike Germans. The thesis of *Händler und
Helden* was simple: it accepted the Spencerian distinction
but asserted that the values German society embodied were
better than those of the commercial English society.

Speaking in behalf of his homeland engaged in a war he
characterized as a conflict of *Weltanschauungen*, Sombart
resorted once again to the method of ascribing ideological characteristics to ethnic groups. He depicted the English spirit as narrow and practical, poor in ideas, oriented
toward conflict, and motivated by the thought of gain and
profit. The strong economic values of Englishmen, together
with a long tradition in trade, had given this unique stamp
to the English character. The members of the merchant
society of England could conceive of the state only as "a
great trading organization [*Handelsgeschäft*]." The contract
theory of the state had originated in the same spirit. England's concept of a balance of power in international affairs
was clearly based on the image of the merchants' scales
on which traders measured out goods, just as her concept
of imperial dominion was cast on the model of a large business house, England being the home office and the colonies
(India, for example) outlying branches.[33]

The German spirit, in contrast, stood for everything that

---

[32] Cf., e.g., the sampling of such statements by the editors of the
Frankfurter Zeitung, Moeller van den Bruck, Max Scheler, and, of
course, Sombart, in Harry Pross, ed., *Die Zerstörung der deutschen
Politik* (Frankfurt-am-Main: Fischer Taschenbuch paperback, 1959),
pp. 189ff.

[33] Sombart, *Händler und Helden* (Munich, 1915), pp. 4-14, 22, 39,
35.

was antithetical to the merchant spirit. Repudiating the "ideas of the eighteenth century," those imbued with the German spirit remained loyal to the idea of *duty*. "To be German meant to be a hero"; only the soldier in wartime fully displayed heroic qualities. It followed for Sombart that the heroic spirit was a patriotic one. "The state is the mighty armor which the nation dons. . . ." Sombart accepted Western charges of German militarism. Militarism was the German spirit in action, "the manifestation of German heroism."[34] Sombart consequently saw as the most characteristic expression of the anti-heroic English spirit the safety razors which the English soldiers had taken with them into the trenches!

To his defense of the German heroes in their struggle against the English shopkeepers, Sombart added a critique of German Social Democracy, the "inner England." In what came to be a classic argument of social conservatives, an argument revealing the doctrine as a reaction of the societal strata most injured by the rapid social change produced by industrialism, Sombart stepped up his criticism of Socialists for their lack of revolutionary zeal. Socialism had been unable to stem the growth of the merchant spirit in Germany. It was ineffectual because it had accepted the commercial values of 1789; it sought to achieve liberty, equality, and fraternity. Like the merchant spirit, socialism was now merely another interest, not a living truth enveloping the whole Folk. Rejecting now even the methods and ideals of English trade unionism, Sombart attacked Social Democracy with one of the fundamental arguments of social conservatives: it was "nothing other than capitalism or commercialism with a different label."[35]

When Germany lost the war and the Revolution put the

[34] *Ibid.*, pp. 59, 64-65, 79, 84.

[35] *Ibid.*, pp. 110-13, 116. Sombart had made a lecture tour of Russia on the eve of the war, and, judging from the newspaper articles he wrote on his return, it is evident that his sympathies for Marxism had cooled remarkably. Waldemar Zimmerman, "Der proletarische Sozialismus ('Marxismus') von Werner Sombart," *Schmollers Jahrbuch*, LVI (1932), 125.

Social Democrats for the first time in a position to guide the destiny of the nation, Sombart's disillusionment with them grew still deeper. The activities of the natural child of the Social Democratic movement, the Communist Party, moreover, promised the acceleration of social disorder. In September 1924, some months after the runaway inflation had been brought to a halt and three months after the representation of the Communists in the Reichstag had been strengthened in the national elections, Sombart delivered a withering attack on the doctrine of class struggle in an address before the Verein für Sozialpolitik.

He joined issue first on the theoretical level. The doctrine rested on a theory of "social naturalism," which he identified as having been derived, not from the human sciences, but rather from the natural sciences. Thus, by implication, he brought into question the validity of applying so foreign a mode of thought to human society. Historically, the origins of "social naturalism" could be traced back to the dissolution of old communal bonds, the rise of capitalism, and the emergence of democracy in the French Revolution—in other words, to a period of accelerated economic and social transformation. The theory of class struggle (read proletarian socialism) was a serious menace, he charged, in that it endangered the souls of the masses, disrupted the development of a harmonious public life, and, worst of all, was "common," reducing man to the level of a *Schweinehund*.[36]

In place of the superstition of the doctrine of class struggle Sombart preached "true religion." Religion and love were now for him the ultimate values which had to inform any solution to the social question. The upsurge of religious and national feeling in the German people gave Sombart hope that the godless doctrine could be overcome.[37]

The storm that Sombart created in making his first extensive public attack on Marxism and in offering in its place God and the nation had not yet subsided when later that year he published a continuation of the polemic in the tenth edition of his book on socialism. The whole tone and

[36] "Die Idee des Klassenkampfes," *Verhandlungen des Vereins für Sozialpolitik, Stuttgart, 1924, Schriften,* **CLXX,** 12-13, 21-22.

[37] *Ibid.,* pp. 24-25.

substance of the 1896 work were altered. Hope had given way to bitter invective—a thorough, analytic invective sustained throughout two volumes totalling over a thousand pages.

In a new social conservative synthesis he defined socialism now simply as "anti-capitalism."[38] Marxism was corrupted socialism; it accepted modern industrialism, rejecting only the form, but not the essence, of modern civilization. Its values were bourgeois, although its twin roots were the Greek philosophy of decadence (*Verfallsphilosophie*) and the Jewish spirit.[39] And its great theorist, Karl Marx, was "the most rootless, and contradictory of all socialists, the most torn by conflicts."[40] Sombart accepted the validity of Othmar Spann's argument that Marx was not really a Hegelian.[41] Marxian socialism could engender only demagogic leaders; it was a mass movement of dissolution, lacking the national, statist, and racial components which determine the accession of a "genuine leader."[42] The democracy which socialism advocated would lead to a low intellectual and spiritual level of representation, for "the greater the mass, the more stupid it is as such."[43] Invoking the names of some of Europe's greatest conservative social critics of the nineteenth century—men such as Fichte, Schopenhauer, Tolstoy, Dostoievski, Nietzsche, Strindberg, and Stefan George—Sombart chided the Marxist for being incapable of appreciating their profound criticism of modern civilization and for dismissing their warnings as utterances of despair and as unjustified cultural pessimism.[44]

Employing a common mode of social conservative argumentation, Sombart contrasted German Social Democracy with the heroic Bolshevism of Russia. Bolshevism was not concerned with individual welfare, for it fought for the

---

[38] *Der proletarische Sozialismus* ("*Marxismus*") (2 vols.; Jena, 1924), I, 10.

[39] *Ibid.*, pp. 256, 84, 224.   [40] *Ibid.*, p. 59.

[41] *Ibid.*, p. 79.   [42] *Ibid.*, II, 279.

[43] *Ibid.*, p. 173.

[44] *Ibid.*, I, 256. As was common for such lists, Goethe, Kant, and Hegel were also included.

transcendental ideal of the nation. But even Bolshevism was corrupt: "The Jews had thought up the system, the Tartars had put it into practice, and the Slavs up to now [1924]— have endured it."[45]

Bolshevism ruled by means of terror. The Social Democratic movement had compromised with the civilization of industrial capitalism. On what evidence did Sombart base his expectation of a post-capitalist communitarian era? As far back as 1904 he had discerned the beginnings of a "transition from capitalist to communitarian modes of [socioeconomic] organization."[46] By the mid-twenties, after he had largely completed his critique of Marxian socialism, he turned to the elaboration of his theory of "late capitalism."

Modern capitalism, especially high capitalism, had turned Western and Central Europe into a great city, according to Sombart. It had increased the reserves of power, the number of goods produced, and the size of the population.[47] But now, since the years immediately preceding World War I, the capitalist spirit was on the wane. Business practices and leadership were becoming more and more questions of administration. The profit motive and the willingness to take risks, in sum the spirit of enterprise, were weakening. The form of capitalism was becoming more restricted; greater bureaucratization was producing greater rigidity. The number and size of cartels were growing. State restrictions and, primarily after the war, workers' restrictions (like factory councils and heightened union power) had multiplied. In the sphere of technic, capitalism was slowly losing the old free-market mechanism. Not market forces, but rather a pattern of price and wage regulation by the fiats of governmental agencies and of the monopolies in labor and industry ruled production and distribution in the era of late capitalism.[48]

---

45 *Ibid.*, p. 97; II, 517.   46 *Gewerbewesen*, II, 59.
47 "Entfaltung," p. 103.
48 Sombart, *Die Zukunft des Kapitalismus* (Berlin-Charlottenburg, 1932) , pp. 8-11.

Writing on the eve of the depression, Sombart described late capitalism as a new kind of feudalism; for it forced both factory and white-collar workers to live under conditions of dependency even greater than those of the nineteenth century. The power of money had reached new heights. "A plutocracy . . . of unprecedented magnitude had developed in the society and in the state. The economy, i.e., capital, i.e., large capital, i.e., finance capital, rules the world and makes our statesmen dance on strings like marionettes."[49]

The tempo of industrial life was slowing down all over Europe, Sombart asserted. Nor would the productivity of labor increase very much more, even if business rationalization and technical innovation were to continue. Industrial capitalism was being hemmed in on three sides. First, the free soil of the prairies and the opportunities for imperialist expansion were becoming increasingly exhausted in the years after the war. Sombart saw the beginnings of a youthful capitalism, "a colored capitalism," in postwar Asia and Africa. These peoples had begun to live from their own agricultural output. They were projecting their own industrialization, and they would resist European encroachments.[50]

Second, in the 1920s Sombart reevaluated his predictions of two decades before regarding the demise of pre-capitalist forms. He now was impressed at the tenacity of artisan industry and peasant farming. The 1929 revision of his *Gewerbewesen* concluded that artisan labor had held out and would continue to do so. With capitalism in decline the pre-capitalist styles of production and life which had survived the pressures of high capitalism could expect to experience a resurgence.[51]

The growth of post-capitalist modes of organization, finally, offered further evidence that Europe was living in an

[49] Sombart, "Wandlungen des Kapitalismus," *Verhandlungen des Vereins für Sozialpolitik, Zurich, 1928, Schriften,* CXXV, 30.

[50] *Zukunft des Kapitalismus,* pp. 25-29.

[51] *Ibid.,* pp. 40-41; *Gewerbewesen* (2 vols.; 2nd edn., Leipzig, 1929), II, 26ff.

age of late capitalism. The variety of economic styles prevalent after the war—superannuated capitalist enterprises
alongside cooperatives and mixed public-private and
state enterprises—foretold the beginnings of a new era.
The liberal economy of high capitalism was gradually yield-
ing before the normative, planned, and total economic order
of the future. The planned economy of the future would resolve the tensions between the high degree of planning within capitalist firms and the chaos of the national economy.
It would also open the way for values superior to those of
efficiency and profit. Although he did not surrender completely to an organic view, Sombart predicted that the new
economy would function *as if* the society were one organism. In the end, the spirituality so sadly absent during the
capitalist epoch would once more emerge.[52]

Living in the age of high capitalism, Sombart had accepted much of Marxist analysis as valid, had championed the
Socialist movement, and had heralded the doom of anti-
capitalist and anti-industrialist social groups. But by the
1920s the major economic features of the age of late capitalism seemed to him to give the lie to Marx. "We can no
longer believe in the creative power of capitalism as Marx
did . . . ," he wrote. "We know that, in spite of all the
noise, nothing of any cultural importance has come of it,
and nothing ever will. . . . Salvation can be sought only in
turning away from it." On the eve of the depression
he clothed his differences with Marx in the armor of historical inevitability. "The difference in the whole plan of our
system and the conclusions at which we arrive result, with a
certain inner necessity, from the different times in which we

[52] *Zukunft des Kapitalismus*, pp. 19, 38-39; *Ordnung des Wirtschaftsleben* (Berlin, 1925), p. 63. Addressing a convention of civil
servants in 1927, Sombart invited this group to join the rest of the
old Mittelstand in awaiting the post-capitalist order: "The bureaucratization which is now upon us is nothing less than the return to
the natural ordering of human society ordained by God, to the subordination of the economy to the higher and the highest purposes
of the universality of *Kultur* and the salvation of man's soul." *Beamtenschaft und Wirtschaft: Vortrag gehalten auf dem Mitteldeutschen
Beamtentag am 11. September 1927* (Berlin, 1927), p. 20.

wrote our books. . . . When Marx conceived his ideas, capitalism was new land. . . . Then it was morning and the skylark sang; today the evening draws nearer and the owl of Minerva has begun her flight."[53]

By the depression, then, Sombart had assembled and ordered the principles for his social conservative ideology. He had systematized his nationalism and identified it with the aspiration for a new community. He had suspended the death sentence of the old Mittelstand and had promised its members an important place in the new society. Having rendered the past comprehensible and having indicated the direction of future economic and social change, Sombart, like German society in the early 1930s, arrived at a crossroads. Two intellectual paths lay before him: he could next treat the means of bringing about the new order, or he could elaborate the features of the post-capitalist society.

It was characteristic of social conservatives in the period of the Republic, in sharp contrast to the Socialists and Communists, that they proceeded directly from a critique of the existing society to a remarkably detailed projection of what the new order would be like. The left, in general, also started from a criticism of contemporary society but speculated on the future utopia less extensively. The left emphasized, rather, the technique of change, the method of revolution, the program of reforms, and the ways of altering society. In part because they were still ensnared by the myth of progress but also because of their greater sophistication about the problem of predicting social change, the Socialists and Communists of the Weimar period concen-

---

[53] *Der moderne Kapitalismus* (3 vols.; 7th edn., Munich, 1924-1928), III, Part 1, xxi. The owl of Minerva metaphor is from Hegel's *Philosophy of Right*. It refers to Hegel's contention that, by the time theorists have become aware of a state of affairs, the phenomenon is already passing. It is in this context: "When [philosophy] paints its grey upon grey, a form of life has already become old: and in grey and grey it can no longer be made young again but only understood. The owl of Minerva begins its flight when the shades of twilight have already fallen." The translation is Sidney Hook's, *From Hegel to Marx: Studies in the Intellectual Development of Karl Marx* (Ann Arbor: Ann Arbor paperback, 1962), p. 23.

trated their thoughts on the *means* of bringing about social change. Social conservatives like Sombart, on the other hand, had a picture of a pre-industrial society as their guide. Their theoretical problem was essentially that of selecting threads from the contemporary economic fabric to weave into the old linen of the past in such a way as to yield a sturdy, finished social order.

A more important, and related, difference between the style of thought of socialists of all hues and Sombart, as well as the social conservatives who followed in his wake, was their unequal success in explaining social and economic change. Marxism may be interpreted as a theory of social and economic change resting on the assumption of the continuation of technological and organizational progress. On the basis of Marxist assumptions, socialists felt they could predict the future developments of capitalist society. The question here concerns, not the correctness of such Marxian predictions, but rather their theoretical orientation to the future "moment in history." Sombart could not account for economic change with the same degree of *theoretical* success. Assuming, as he did in his theoretical work, the unity of an economic epoch and the uniqueness of the spirit of that epoch, he could not explain coherently the transition from one economic epoch to the next. A consequence of this deficiency in his system was his designation of medieval trade as a handicraft; for otherwise he would have had to admit the existence of capitalist activity in a noncapitalist age.[54] This same weakness caused him to write of the

[54] Cf. the mode of argument of his *Moderner Kapitalismus*, I, Part 1, 279-309, with, e.g., that of the Marxist Fritz Sternberg, *Der Niedergang des deutschen Kapitalismus* (Berlin, 1932). Otto Hintze, too, charges Sombart with failing to offer anything more than a metaphor (in this case, the biological metaphor of youth, maturity, and old age) in his explanation of the transition from the age of high capitalism to that of late capitalism in the era of World War I. See Otto Hintze's two elaborate critiques of Sombart's theory of capitalism, "Der moderne Kapitalismus als historisches Individuum. Ein kritischer Bericht über Sombarts Werk" and "Wirtschaft und Politik im Zeitalter des modernen Kapitalismus," both written in 1929 and both reprinted in Hintze's

means of achieving German Socialism in a vague and ambiguous language not characteristic of his analytical writings. In his pamphlet *Die Zukunft des Kapitalismus* (*The
Future of Capitalism*) written in 1932, for example, he
stated:

> The bearer of the resolute will to a new order in eco-
> nomic life can vary. It can appear as the will of an indi-
> vidual as in the case of Lenin, Kamal Pascha, Mussolini;
> but it can also be a collective will. This depends on the
> contingencies of history, or probably also on the individ-
> uality of the peoples in whom it is operative. However,
> this will must be strong; [it must be] completely conscious
> of its goal, and yet clear-sighted. Our whole desire is that
> our Fatherland might also be granted the grace of such a
> will, for we know that without it we will be swallowed up
> in chaos.[55]

Although social conservatives like Sombart could offer an
elaborate critique of what offended or injured the old middle classes in industrial capitalist society, although they
could describe the outlines of the future society for which
they longed, nevertheless, the advent of Nazism threw them
into confusion. Were the Nazis the "bearers of the resolute
will"? Would they act decisively to end the "chaos"? The
sheer dynamism of the movement cast a spell over many
social conservative thinkers. The Nazis seemed to be the
most active and most successful of all the competing groups
working for the conservative revolution. The vulgar Nazis
offered themselves to social conservative intellectuals as the
agents for reconstituting society. Sombart was one of those
social conservative intellectuals who, in effect, permitted

Gesammelte Abhandlungen, II: *Soziologie und Geschichte*, ed. Gerhard
Oestreich (2nd expanded edn., Göttingen, 1964), 374-452, and, on
the specific point, 411-12.

[55] *Zukunft des Kapitalismus*, p, 45. This passage also appeared in
his article on "Die Zukunft der Weltwirtschaft," in Othmar Spann's
periodical *Ständisches Leben*, II (1932), 290.

Nazi deeds to fill in a proposition missing from their systems.

In 1934, a year after the Nazis had come to power, Sombart spelled out what he anticipated from German Socialism. In what we may describe as the eleventh edition of his original book on socialism, Sombart tried to align his doctrines of German Socialism with what he believed were reasonable expectations for a National Socialist reconstruction of society. His *Deutscher Sozialismus*[56] should not be evaluated as a surrender to National Socialism. The courage and independence Sombart had displayed as a young man in maintaining unpopular views excludes any explanation of this action in terms of careerism or opportunism. The autonomy of the work and of the man, especially his rejection of the thoroughgoing racism of the Nazis,[57] would tend, rather, to indicate that the promises of National Socialism coincided with his expectations. In the face of a movement which pledged to bring about the long-awaited transformation of German society, Sombart proved willing to blur the sharp edges of his image of the new social and economic order. For one hundred and fifty years, the great age of the capitalist era, Germany had been following a false path. He believed that so great a historical detour could be explained as nothing less than the work of the devil! He was satisfied that, under National Socialism, Germany had at least started back on the right path.[58]

Sombart now defined German Socialism succinctly as "anti-capitalism." It implied "nothing less than the rejection of the economic age in its entirety." If economic license and caprice were typical of capitalism, then socialism, he reasoned, meant adherence to "obligatory norms." Thus,

---

[56] *Deutscher Sozialismus* (Berlin-Charlottenburg, 1934). The English translation by Karl F. Geiser is entitled *A New Social Philosophy* (Princeton, 1937). All references are to the American edition, which, because of frequent inaccuracies in translation, I have compared to the original and modified if necessary for any citations used.

[57] *Ibid.*, pp. 175-79.

[58] *Ibid.*, p. 5.

Every punishment for murder according to the law is socialism, in contrast with impunity for murder or with revenge for bloodshed; all compulsory education in the public schools is socialism, in contrast with conditions in which there is no public education at all or where it is carried on by means of private instruction; every law for the protection of labor is socialism, in contrast with unbridled exploitation by the employer; yes, every prohibition: "No Smoking!" "Do not open the door before the train stops!" "Do not pick the flowers!" is the same kind of socialism as that of public exhortation: "Turn to the right!" "Pay your taxes!" "Silence!"[59]

German Socialism was uniquely suited to contemporary conditions in Germany. It was an ideology appropriate to an era of long-term transition from late capitalism to socialism. Yet Sombart did not expect an early demise of capitalism. Revolutionary changes could not reasonably be projected. "We must renounce the idea of building a completely new structure for our society and be satisfied with reshaping and completing the existing structure," he wrote.[60] The most immediate means of ending the anarchy of capitalism, he thought, would be to introduce regulation of the process of production.

Sombart believed it possible to build upon the existing structure of cartels and monopolies of late capitalism to the end of creating "a sort of capitalist gild-constitution." At first allowed to regulate itself, this arrangement might eventually flower into a fully corporative system of the kind advocated by the Viennese professor Othmar Spann. Although they differed in minor respects, both men agreed on giving economic values the lowest priority in the organization of society. Within the economic order Sombart gave first place to agriculture. He also valued small business more highly than big business. The coming of the Nazi era, however, had made him more patient. "Big business, especial-

59 *Ibid.*, pp. 41, 58-59, 146.
60 *Ibid.*, pp. 113, 151-52, 209.

ly big industrial enterprises in their modern intellectu-
alized form, are in every case to be regarded as an evil,
even if under certain conditions, a necessary evil."[61] Service to the state formed the basis of the scale of values by
means of which Sombart ranked his hierarchy of estates.
And this state he wished isolated from the rest of the world
and kept autonomous for strategic, national, and economic
reasons.[62]

The full emergence of German Socialism would be
hastened by the introduction of planning into the economy.
Planning would serve a double purpose. It would make for
a more orderly economy and society. And, more important,
it would permit the salvation of the middle classes. To insure this outcome, Sombart proposed surrounding the economic world of the peasants and artisans with legal barriers
to protect them from the penetration of the capitalist
spirit.[63] Since he believed that the agrarian population was
vital to the welfare of the state, he proposed to guarantee
its continuation by the institution of reforms in the distribution of land. These reforms were not to be so radical,
however, that large landowners would be deprived of their
hereditary estates. By the reduction of mechanization in
agriculture, he felt, Germany's rural population might be
restored to a sound forty to fifty percent of the total
population.[64]

At the turn of the century Sombart had acquiesced in
predictions of the economic and social decline of the artisan
and peasant population. In the 1920s his prognosis of the

[61] *Ibid.*, 200-209, 277, 285.

[62] *Ibid.*, pp. 257-58. Regarding economic autarky, he eschewed detailed development of the argument with the advice: "Those who are
especially interested in removing the chains of a world-economy from
our own political economy, may be referred to the work on *Autarkie*
(1932) by Ferdinand Fried, who has judiciously compiled all of the
material figures on this subject."

[63] *Ibid.*, p. 283.

[64] *Ibid.*, pp. 259-60, 265, 287. This was the percentage of the population which lived on the land sometime after the turn of the century,
at the height of the Agrar- oder Industriestaat debate. *Deutsche
Wirtschaftskunde*, pp. 8-9.

incipient decline of capitalism gave him hope for the durability of the Mittelstand. Now, after the depression and the advent of National Socialism, it was these classes which Sombart unequivocally designated as the beneficiaries of German Socialism. For "the interests of the individual, as well as those of the state, [would be] best guarded by the middle classes. . . ."[65] In contradistinction to the drabness of proletarian socialism, Sombart painted a picture of an idyllic middle class socialism:

> Nothing is farther from German Socialism than a proletarian culture. We desire a gradation based on affluence and have also a thought for the cultured prosperity of a few. We wish to extend the number of the well-to-do. A comfortable dwelling of one's own in a well-kept garden which is more than a pasteboard box or a cell in a honeycomb, with more rooms than are necessary for merely sleeping and cooking, in which the members of the family may also be separated; means to cultivate a decent conviviality: good wine, fine linen, old silverware for the table; festive baptisms and weddings in a circle of friendship; room and appreciation for old family portraits; a select library—all these things we regard as also having a cultural value which we would not deny. Call it "bourgeois" if you will. It merely shows that the bourgeois class is in no sense destitute of culture. In addition to the bourgeois estate, there should be a rooted, permanent, well-to-do, great peasant class, maintained and encouraged in their unique habits. What a loss it would mean to our culture if instead of the stately peasant houses . . . , the rich peasant costumes, the colorful folk-festivals, there were nothing to be seen but the uniformity of a grey proletarian poverty![66]

It is not recorded to what degree Sombart was disappointed with the failure of the National Socialists to create a genuine German Socialism. For the Nazis discovered what

[65] *A New Social Philosophy*, p. 262.
[66] *Ibid.*, pp. 247-48.

Sombart should have realized: that a socialism for artisans, peasants, civil servants, and small businessmen would have been too costly to appeal to any segment of German society but those groups most immediately injured by the spread of large-scale enterprise. The National Socialists could not afford to alienate the established and real community of big business just to propitiate enthusiasts of a romantic anti-capitalist people's community.

As a young man Sombart had known intimately both the old agrarian Germany and the new industrial society. Early in his intellectual career he took sides with the victims of the rapid industrial development of Germany, while at the same time endorsing the general economic trends of his age. He pitied the poor marginal peasant and artisan, and he applauded the Socialist movement for organizing the economic protection of the industrial working class. But, just as he believed that special protection for the pre-industrial classes was hopeless and reactionary, so he also believed that the revolutionary claims of the Socialist movement were undesirable. For all his endorsements of modernization in the years before World War I, Sombart nurtured deep in his psyche a revulsion for the culture and the works of industrial capitalism.

The war and the Revolution marked the true turning point of the ideology we have termed social conservatism. Whatever further aid the Imperial government might have given the Mittelstand was now out of the question. And yet the source of the social conservative impulse, loyalty to the Imperial social and power structure (if not to the Empire per se), was still very much alive. Sombart, having made clear his rejection of both capitalism and socialism before 1918 but also having refrained from sterile public opposition to modern forms of economic organization, was ideally suited to tell the tale of the old Mittelstand in a new setting and in a new language. This was his major intellectual achievement in the 1920s and early 1930s. In this period his vague animosities crystallized into militant ideology. His rejection of democracy, Marxian socialism, big business, and the main components of twentieth-century industrial society, we shall see, were to become hallmarks of social conservative thought in the years of the Weimar Republic. By means of his theory of late capitalism and its corollary, the ideology of German Socialism, Sombart sought both to revitalize a socially conservative outlook for the circumstances of Republican life and, at the same time, to disarm the criticism that he was a social reactionary. But, as evidenced by his 1934 *Deutscher Sozialismus,* his willingness to make his peace with the society of modern industrialism masked a deeper and older ideal—his dream of conservative social order protecting the old Mittelstand and in turn supported by them.[67]

In *Der proletarische Sozialismus* Sombart had written of the "tragic dissolution" which had begun to affect European society at the close of the Middle Ages.[68] When he addressed the Verein für Sozialpolitik in 1928, he reported to his audience of professional economists that the age of capitalism was finally drawing to a close, that the tragic process of dissolution was coming to a halt. Edgar Salin, professor of economics at Basel, rose to voice his agreement. Salin drew attention to the wave of anti-captialism in the world, which gave him hope that "it could come to pass that the primacy of economics . . . will thereby come to an end . . . , that the living Being itself, suppressed in the century of high capitalism, will strike off its bonds and take command."[69]

Salin shared with Sombart a tendency to describe and to evaluate the processes of social and economic life in language that was highly aesthetic.[70] The judgments of both were informed by an outraged morality. A strong moral

[67] For a somewhat different interpretation of the sources of Sombart's hostility to progress, see Arthur Mitzman, "Anti-Progress: A Study in the Romantic Roots of German Sociology," *Social Research,* XXXIII (1966), 65-85, esp. 83-85.

[68] *Der proletarische Sozialismus,* I, 31.

[69] *Schriften,* CLXXV, 115-18.

[70] It is worth noting that even the main categories of Sombart's economic history—early, high, and late capitalism—suggest the values and methods of the art historian more than those of an economics scholar.

sensibility such as Salin's, articulated in tones of moral anguish or exaltation, cannot be explained merely by reference to the unique personality quirks of the individual. This mode of perception and of statement was, indeed, highly characteristic of social conservative thinkers as a whole. An examination of the thought of Edgar Salin offers us access into this realm of the social conservative vision.

III. Edgar Salin

THE LONGING
FOR A NEW MORALITY

EDGAR SALIN belonged to two
worlds. As a student he discovered the vision of the poet
Stefan George. He remained loyal to the poet's ideal of the
"beautiful life" even after he had become a respected professor of what Thomas Malthus called "the dismal science." His search for the "beautiful life" influenced his economic thought; at the same time, his training as an economist disciplined his moral nature. In Salin we see combined in heightened form both the sensitivity and the this-
worldly sophistication of many thoughtful academic youths
of middle class origin. The poet George and the economist
Salin alike could express the *anomie* which so many middle
class young men and women felt in the first three decades
of the twentieth century. But, whereas George preferred the
intimacy of a circle of loyal followers, Salin lived and worked
successfully in the troubled world of Weimar Germany.

Salin was born in 1892 in Frankfurt-am-Main, the son of
a well-to-do Jewish industrialist. He graduated from the fa-
mous Goethe Gymnasium of that city in 1910. He attended
the Universities of Munich, Berlin, and Heidelberg where
he studied economics, law, philosophy, and literature. In
Munich he heard the eloquent Lujo Brentano fulminate
against the injustices of industrial society; in Berlin the agricultural economist Max Sering introduced him to the problems of that sector of life; and in Heidelberg the brother of
Max Weber, Alfred Weber, taught him economic analysis.[1]
Salin's career as a professional economist started at Heidel-

[1] "Lebenslauf," in Salin's doctoral dissertation, *Goldwäscherei und
Goldbergbau im Klondike und in Alaska* (Tübingen, 1914).

berg. He then moved to Kiel and, finally, in 1927 was called to a professorship at the University of Basel.

What set Salin apart from other academic economists was his life-long commitment to the ideals and values of the "beautiful life" of the poet Stefan George. It was in Frankfurt that Salin first came in contact with people close to the literary organ of the circle around George, *Die Blätter für die Kunst* (*Pages for Art*). As a student in Munich he attended gatherings at the lodgings of Karl Wolfskehl, a man in the inner circle of the Georgians.[2] But only while walking along a street in Heidelberg on a warm spring day in 1913 did the student Salin finally meet the poet himself. Thirty-five years after the event Salin's vivid description of this first encounter still revealed that awe which true members of the inner circle felt in writing about the poet. Salin described himself as having been rooted to the spot. He had caught a glimpse of a being from a higher world, clad in a yellow silk jacket, his thick brown hair showing under a large broad-brimmed hat, a thin walking stick in his hand. After the poet had passed without noticing the young man, Salin hurried after him to catch just one more glimpse. Half a year later young Salin and two of his friends, Wolfgang Heyer and Norbert von Hellingrath, met George in the room of their teacher, Friedrich Gundolf.[3] From that time Salin, the student of economics, the German professor, the shrewd man of the world, became also a loyal disciple of George and an adherent of the ideals of his world.

A great poet is rarely a person typical of the society in which he lives. He is an outsider in his own society, although vitally linked to its language and culture. This special status allows him to express, if not the most commonly held values of his countrymen, at least their deepest longings and their most sacred and cherished values. If he is a poet of discontent and a poet of skill, he is in a position to give voice to frustrations and malaise shared by many men yet only dimly perceived by them. Such a poet can thus have great influ-

---

[2] Salin, *Um Stefan George: Erinnerung und Zeugnis* (2nd expanded edn., Munich, 1954), p. 16.

[3] *Ibid.*, pp. 11-12.

ence as a reflector and reinforcer of what others only sense vaguely. Influence of this sort is difficult to determine. If, however, such a poet has a coterie, which absorbs his message and passes it on in other forms to the rest of society, he is a fit subject of historical study and perhaps a valuable source of insights into the society.

Stefan George was such a poet. There can be no doubt of his great gift for lyric poetry. Yet his tightly constructed poetry, with its disregard for the conventional rules of punctuation and capitalization and with its private and obscure language and symbols, could be read—indeed, was meant to be read—only by a small circle of initiates.[4] George had his poems set in a typeface copied from his own handwriting, which in turn bore a loose resemblance to German calligraphy styles of the twelfth century. Characteristically, these poems often first appeared in privately printed limited editions. The poet shunned success in the usual sense of the word. He selected his intimates carefully, keeping their number small. This exclusivity did not deter people who had only met George and spoken to him for a few moments from calling themselves members of his circle, however. On the small band of intellectuals who had entrusted to him their education for beauty and for life, George produced a deep impression. In his circle were assembled men who were to go on to become important students of literature and history, poets, men who gave their lives in opposition to Hitler—and some who became rabid Nazis. He tended to recruit his followers from among the sons of

[4] Information on George and his circle is difficult to obtain. Most works of primary value are by his followers and seem as intent on proving his greatness as they are on obscuring his activities and doctrines. Each Georgian had his own "George," often differing widely from portrayals by other followers. I have found most useful the book by Salin; Claude David, "Stefan George: Aesthetes or Terrorists?" in *The Third Reich*; Friedrich Wolters, *Stefan George und die Blätter für die Kunst* (Berlin, 1930); Robert Boehringer, *Mein Bild von Stefan George* (Munich, 1951); Dominik Jost, *Stefan George und seine Elite* (Zurich, 1949); Hansjürgen Linke, *Das Kultische in der Dichtung Stefan George und seiner Schule* (2 vols.; Munich, 1960); Franz Schonauer, *Stefan George* (Reinbek-bei-Hamburg: Rowohlt Taschenbuch paperback, 1960).

the lower nobility and Jewish youths of the upper middle class.[5]

In his earlier years the poet George had sought to find
his way out of the meanness and ugliness of the world
through art alone. Like his French masters, George had believed that the poet could create an alternate world of
beauty, shutting out the sordid present. To share his world,
he had assembled around himself the young men who were
to learn from the Master, much as Socrates had taught the
youth of Athens. Infused with his teachings, the "friends"
were then to go out into the world and, in their various sta-
tions, were to continue to spread the ideal of the "beautiful
life." The Georgians, to varying degrees, became bearers of
George's realization of degeneration and the harbingers of
renewal.

George was typical of the men of letters, philosophers,
writers, and poets whose names are associated with the mood
of cultural pessimism in Germany and elsewhere in Europe
around the turn of the century.[6] The concept of cultural
pessimism represents a complex psychological, aesthetic,
and moral reaction of hostility to the flatness of life in
the twentieth century, to large industrial centers with their
soulless masses, and to the despoiling of the countryside. To
many cultural pessimists, life and the world were no longer
beautiful, and heroism was dead. Their tone was one of anguish, the redemption, they awaited chiliastic. Thus a disciple of George, Friedrich Wolters, cried out: "Does there
exist no force to halt the all-powerful corruption which has
already pulled down the whole earth with claws of iron,
and which threatens to grind down human nobility under

[5] "George's circle, in Germany, was a meeting place for conservative
Jewish intellectuals." David, *The Third Reich*, p. 298. "He consorts
with people who live from their investments" was Brecht's harsh
judgment; quoted in Schonauer, *Stefan George*, p. 169.

[6] See the good study of Paul de Lagarde, Julius Langbehn, and
Moeller van den Bruck in Fritz Stern's *The Politics of Cultural
Despair* (Berkeley, 1961), esp. pp. 267ff.; for France, see Michael Curtis,
Three Against the Republic: Sorel, Barrès, and Maurras (Princeton,
1959).

the rolling mill of mass society?"[7] The implications of this mood for social and political thought were generally conservative. The Georgians rejected the philistinism and sterility of bourgeois life, into which most of them had been born. They hated the masses, as well as modern democracy and the institutions closely associated with it. In their views of education, society, and politics they championed a thoroughgoing elitism.

This, then, was the intellectual climate in which Edgar Salin spent his formative years. As a professional economist he ventured beyond the aesthetic universe of the poet, but, even in his doctrinal and political writings, strong traces of the message of George may be discerned. For Salin, too, reacted aesthetically and morally to contemporary national misfortunes. The Georgian context of his critique of unpropitious economic events will become clearer if we examine briefly some of the themes of the poetry of George.

As a young man George had left his native Rhineland to travel in Europe. In Paris he had met the symbolist poets Villiers de l'Isle-Adam, Verlaine, and Mallarmé.[8] He then returned to Germany to do battle against naturalism in literature and the radical social ideal informing it, having become imbued with the credo of *l'art pour l'art* of French symbolism. The poetry he published in the early issues of his newlyfounded periodical *Die Blätter für die Kunst* was characterized by its obscurity, by its glorification of the artificial, and by its blindness to values beyond the realm of art. Art was the only reality for the young George; the world beyond held no meaning for him.[9] In the struggle against naturalism George sought out and maintained contacts with kindred spirits throughout Europe.

But his pure aestheticism was an inherently unstable doctrine. It created a meaningless universe for the poet to inhabit. Words no longer had reference beyond the context

[7] *Stefan George und die Blätter für die Kunst*, p. 302.

[8] David, *The Third Reich*, p. 289.

[9] *Ibid.*, p. 190; Wolters, *Stefan George und die Blätter für die Kunst*, p. 433.

of the poem. There was ultimately nothing left in the poet's universe about which he might write. Aestheticism can easily lead to nihilism. The terrible implications of George's aestheticism may be seen in his early poem *Algabal*.[10]

Algabal is a nihilist ruler, a man of both tenderness and cruelty. He lives in artificial palaces built of stone under the ground. His garden needs neither air nor warmth. The birds in it have never seen springtime come. Out of ennui Algabal commits acts of great cruelty. At his worst he wants to see his people groaning and dying and "every mocker . . . nailed to the cross." This last act he hopes will bring renewal through its cataclysmic impact.

Artistically, George grew beyond this early experiment in the ramifications of complete decadence, although many elements in *Algabal* (such as the figure of renewal through catastrophe) he retained in his later thought. George passed from the primarily literary ethic of *Algabal* to poetry in which he pictured himself as an educator for the beautiful life.[11] With a growing sense of poetical mastery and a longing for the moral rejuvenation of his homeland, he gave up the cosmopolitanism of the French symbolists in order to become a *German* poet.[12]

The catastrophic appeared once again in the *Stern des Bundes*,[13] published just before the outbreak of the war. Here he spoke of the "holy war" which the gods demanded as a blood sacrifice.

[10] George wrote this poem while still under the strong influence of similar French efforts of this sort. E. K. Bennett, *Stefan George* (New Haven, 1954), p. 36. The text of this poem, written in 1892, may be found in George's *Hymnen, Pilgerfahrten, Algabal* (Berlin, 1905).

[11] Cf. his poem *Teppich des Lebens* (*Tapestry of Life*) in *Der Teppich des Lebens und die Lieder von Traum und Tod. Mit einem Vorspiel* (Berlin, 1932).

[12] This transition occurred sometime between the composition of the *Teppich des Lebens* in 1898 and that of the *Stern des Bundes* (*Star of the Covenant*) in 1914; cf. David, *The Third Reich*, p. 292. George saw himself as a seer, as "the leader of the youth of his Folk and the shaper of the future." Jost, *Stefan George und seine Elite*, p. 60.

[13] (Berlin, 1914).

Zehntausend muss der heilige wahnsinn schlagen
Zehntausend muss die heilige seuche raffen
Zehntausend der heilige Krieg.

When war broke out in the summer of 1914, many of George's disciples considered it to be the "holy war" the Master had preached.[14] Salin was among the enthusiasts. In the course of the war he mailed back a piece written at the front entitled "Volk und Heer" ("The Folk and the Army"). George's criticism was quite harsh. When Salin next saw the Master, he was still in uniform. George asked him angrily whether he believed that "the Burger [was] perhaps different today from what he had been before 1914?" Did Salin believe that a few moments of war could change a "degenerate people"? Nothing of lasting value had occurred during the war, George explained to the young soldier, except perhaps Tannenberg.[15]

The war had been an opportunity for greatness, but it had degenerated into merely a bloody slaughter, according to George. The enemy, too, was proving capable of sacrifice and strength. It was a mass war, without goals, formless. In his poem *Der Krieg*, published in 1917, George castigated both sides in the war: the Germans for seeking to hawk their wares where others now traded, the enemy for seeking to regain lost distinctions while at the same time seeking profits.[16] The war would end ingloriously:

[14] Linke, *Das Kultische*, I, 179.

[15] Salin, *Um Stefan George*, pp. 27-28. In the battle of Tannenberg German armies under Hindenburg and Ludendorff stopped the Russian advance into East Prussia in late August 1914. The Germans fought a brilliant battle, the Russian commander committed suicide, and the myth of the titanic General Hindenburg was launched.

[16] ". . . Hier: sorge nur zu krämern
Wo schon ein andrer krämert . . . ganz zu werden
Was man am andren schmäht und sich zu leugnen
Ein volk ist tot wenn seine götter tot sind.
Drüben: ein pochen auf ehmaligen vorrang
Von pracht und sitte, während feile nutzsucht
Bequem veratmen will . . . im schoss der hellsten
Einsicht kein schwacher blick, dass die Verpönten

Zum jubeln ziemt nicht: kein triumph wird sein
Nur viele untergänge ohne würde. . . .

George rejected that meaningless butchery and repudiated
its identification by his less discriminating disciples with
his "holy war." Yet what if the whole war had been a series
of Tannenbergs? George rejected the ugliness of *that* war,
its destruction of heroism, its lack of style, but not its
cruelty. Nor did he abandon his belief in the value of
catastrophe.

The war only confirmed for George that a radical change
in society was necessary. The German people had to be
freed from philistinism and the weight of the masses. He
rejected the liberal notion of progrsss, as well as the values
of Prussia and of Prussian conservatism, so stark and
empty of culture. He championed a "new Germandom
against the deteriorating [*zerfallende*] Germandom of the
Imperial state, as well as that of the newly created Republic."[17] Individualism was unacceptable; capitalism was the
rule of money; socialism was spineless.[18] Only the artistic
nature, who led the beautiful life, and the peasant, who
was bound to the soil, fitted into George's ideal of a cultural
elite exercising moral leadership in a hierarchical, nonmo-
bile, agrarian society. The cult around George was the
"secret Germany," a state within a state, each member a
transmitter of the ideal to the rest of the society.[19]

Salin's vision was more than a mere translation of the values of the George circle into economic thought and policy.
Nevertheless, the Georgian language was there: the emphasis on the ugliness and demoralization of modern society,

---

Was fallreif war zerstören, dass vielleicht
Ein 'Hass und Abscheu menschlichen geschlechtes'
Zum weitren male die erlösung bringt."
                          Der Krieg (Berlin, 1917) , p. 7.
[17] Wolters, *Stefan George*, p. 443.
[18] David, *The Third Reich*, pp. 297-99.
[19] For the cultic features of the circle, see Linke, *Das Kultische*, Vol.
I, *passim*.

and the search for a redemption and a redeemer. To understand the strong psychological and ethical rejection of industrial society so typical of social conservative thinkers, it is important to appreciate Salin's point of view. All the thinkers under examination would have agreed with Salin's anguished judgment that "this lofty mode of life [of pre-industrial Germany] has been succeeded by a style whose sole binding characteristic has become stylelessness. In place of an organically constructed [gegliederten] society in which each has his estate [Stand], his status, and his vocation, and only the soldier as the guardian and the official as bearer of the state, and, in rare instances, the genius rise from a lower to a higher estate—in place of this, a disjointed, formless mass in which each presses forward and upward, each wants to appear as more than he is, each wants to acquire more than he has."[20] Salin, however, realized the nature and the immensity of the transformation for which he longed. He did not envision a return to the conditions of life prevalent before industrialism and the World War. Anyone who wanted to be an architect or worker for a Third Reich, the Reich of Stefan George, had to forego this sort of naive romanticism.[21]

Only a great statesman could lead Germany out of its evil days, hearten the timid, unite a fragmented people into a Folk, and cause even mavericks to place themselves under him voluntarily.[22] With Plato, Salin desired a ruler uniting wisdom and authority.[23] Germany once had had such a

[20] Salin, *Wirtschaft und Staat* (Berlin, 1932), p. 64.

[21] Salin, *Die deutschen Tribute: Zwölf Reden* (Berlin, 1930), p. 9.

[22] *Ibid.*, p. 215.

[23] *Ibid.*, p. 234. The influence of classical models was great in the George circle; cf. the section on George in E. M. Butler's *The Tyranny of Greece over Germany* (Boston: Beacon Press paperback, 1958), pp. 322ff. Salin wrote extensively on the classical world. Of special interest for this study is his view that for classical Greece not the economy but rather politics was crucial. He took exception to the thesis of the classicist Poehlmann that the Polis fell under the weight of radical socialism and argued instead that it was stifled by the plethora of parties in it. "Der 'Sozialismus' in Hellas," in Salin, ed., *Bilder und Studien aus drei Jahrtausenden: Eberhard Gothein zum siebzigsten Geburtstag als Festgabe* (Munich, 1925), pp. 19-58.

statesman in Bismarck, whose dismissal drove from politics
"the noblest German bonds and forces, mutual loyalty of
leader and follower, magnanimity and manly courage...."[24]

Instead of promoting the vigorous political life, with its
partisan disputes and its parties, which, Salin believed, prepared statesmen of other nations for roles as rulers of great
powers, Germany had sunk back into the morass of petty
politics among the states in the Empire.[25] Although Germany was now emerging as a great power, she still lacked
the requisite leadership. Salin fell into a dilemma frequently encountered by neoconservatives in the Weimar period.
He bemoaned the passing of the greatness that was Bismarck's while chiding the Germans for not having the political life capable of producing other great leaders, on the
example of England; yet he silently passed over the
equally true fact that Bismarck had been the gravedigger
of parliamentary life in the Empire. According to Salin, the
emergence of Germany as a great economic power was
weakened by the absence of adequate political backing for
it. Since Germany had to depend on raw materials from
abroad for her industries and much of her food supply, England's mastery of the sea made Germany dangerously dependent. Germany's lack of economic autarky had proven
to be a great political liability because of her isolation from
the sources of necessary supplies during the war.[26]

The war had destroyed the balance of power in Europe,
the balance of forces in every nation, and, indeed, the equilibrium in the souls of men.[27] The youths who had
marched off to war were free of the gold-lust of their fathers,
but not even their bravery could save the declining Wilhelmian Empire.[28]

The questioning of the tottering old social order of the
Empire, although justified, had now grown into the belief,
dangerous to both state and society, that "all men are equal,

[24] *Die deutschen Tribute*, p. 11.
[25] *Ibid.*, p. 12.   [26] *Ibid.*, pp. 18-19.   [27] *Ibid.*, p. 36.
[28] *Ibid.*, p. 21.

that every individual is born to rule, that greatness is im-
posture, and that service dishonors."[29] Salin saw this internal danger to capitalistic societies aggravated by the example of the successful revolution in Russia. Only a saving
leader, a giver of a new law, a leader "who sanctified authority [Herrschaft] and ennobled service . . ." could properly
bring about the rejuvenation of the Reich.[30] The absence
of this "magic" in Germany made Communism a major
threat. For the German bourgeoisie had no values of its
own, "no banner," to oppose to the ideals of militant Communism. It cultivated only the idolatry of material posses-
sions. It was capable only of heaping up wealth.[31]

Salin extended his attack to the politics of the bourgeoisie, its "liberal-democratic pseudo-religion." In England,
with a parliamentary tradition growing out of aristocratic
origins, the two-party system could serve for a time as an
institution conducive to the ascent of the best of society to
the heights of political life. The twentieth-century decadence of English political life he deduced from the fre-
quency of coalition governments. No one party was able
any longer to speak for the whole people, and demagogues
like David Lloyd George could become prime minister.

The mystic faith in the God of Reason, the raison d'être
of liberal democracy, was dying, according to Salin. Yet
often the empty shells of institutions remain on the political scene long after their informing spirit has died. In this
sense, the faith in democracy was irrevocably dead. Salin
agreed with the Marxist prediction that the evolution toward fuller capitalism meant the demise of older forces
and ties. Socialists were as much responsible as capitalists
for the decline of the old. The connection of democracy
with capitalism gave Salin grounds for prophesying the im-
manent destruction of the democratic order.[32]

The schemes advanced by political reformers were, he
believed, superficial in the light of political reality. Never-

[29] Ibid., pp. 49-50.   [30] Ibid., p. 51.   [31] Ibid.
[32] Wirtschaft und Staat, pp. 145-59.

theless, Salin could offer only the usual platitude of the narrow traditionalist: a better political order was possible only
through a transformation of men's souls.[33] But democracy, he held, was inadequate to the tasks of the day.
"Defending, conquering, organizing states, winning and
pacifying the world, was never, and is also not today, the
affair of democracies but always the affair of Caesars."[34]

German youth sensed the country's need in the time of
her distress. "In all its yearning, albeit strained and hoarse,
calls for the true leader and in all its bitter, albeit already
rigid and empty, indictments of modern democracy and
the rule of the parties [Parteiregierung], the correct, incon-
trovertible insight emerges that in the years of German
distress no statesman arose to infuse the whole structure of
the state with new spirit. . . ." Stresemann, who had freed
Germany from foreign occupation, and Hindenburg, who
once had saved her in battle, both deserved the thanks of
the nation; yet Salin could not blame the youth for being
unwilling to recognize in either of these men the awaited
savior, the leader who would free Germany from internal
and foreign subjugation and bring a final solution for her
reparations burden.[35]

The moralistic strain in Salin's thought emerged, improb-
ably enough, even in the fields of economic philosophy and
public policy. His economic philosophy might almost be
described as Georgian, if his technical competence did not
prohibit such an easy formula. He sought to raise the level
of economic thinking above questions of mere technical
interest (such as those related to the exchange of goods
and services) to an appreciation of the eternal, the universal, and the organic—in short, the nonscientific. He emphasized the political in economics, characterizing the
"science" of economics as an invention of modern times.
He traced its roots back to the rise of the individualistic
spirit, the emergence of the nation-state, and the victory of
capitalism. "The economy" as an object of study, he

[33] Die deutschen Tribute, p. 47.
[34] Wirtschaft und Staat, p. 165.
[35] Die deutschen Tribute, pp. 126-27, 229-30.

claimed, was in reality a tool of liberalism; for the physiocrats had turned the study of economic relations into economic theology.[36] The end of economics as a scientific discipline on the model of the natural sciences would facilitate the realization of the ideal of all social conservatives and the chief aim of Salin: the disappearance, both in theory and in practice, of the deadening cleavage between the economy and the state. The notion of mechanical causality, the prime unifying principle of economics as a science, was already weakened, according to this George disciple, and would soon have to give way to the "newly arising or revitalized old bonds of universal-religious origin."[37]

In the tradition of Sombart, Salin judged the French and the English to have come to their own peculiar and appropriate styles of economic individualism in the nineteenth century. Germany, however, still had before it the task of building its own unique economic doctrine. Salin argued that the spadework had already been done by Adam Müller, Friedrich List, and Karl Knies. He assigned to himself and his contemporaries the task of constructing a German theory, one resting upon organic and historical fundaments. It would be not merely economics but "a genuine doctrine of *political* economy [Volks*wirtschaftslehre*]."[38]

The achievements of contemporary German economists notwithstanding, Salin found more of a supranational element in their work than anything specifically German. On the other hand, the brilliant English economist John Maynard Keynes, he believed, devised theories compatible with English interests. The Englishman viewed things from the standpoint of a creditor country.[39] But Schumpeter's

[36] *Wirtschaft und Staat*, pp. 176-77.

[37] Salin, *Geschichte der Volkswirtschaftslehre* (1st edn., Berlin, 1923), p. 1. The twin foundations of European civilization, in Salin's eyes, were the classical heritage and the Christian aspiration which supplemented it. See his *Civitas Dei* (Tübingen, 1926), *passim.*

[38] *Geschichte der Volkswirtschaftslehre*, p. 42 (italics mine). See also *Wirtschaft und Staat*, pp. 186-87.

[39] Salin, "Die Entthronung des Goldes (Bemerkungen zu Keynes 'A tract on monetary reform')," *Schmollers Jahrbuch*, XLVIII (1924), 95-112.

works, Salin asserted, could as well have been written by
an American economist. Only in the doctrines of Othmar
Spann did Salin see an extension of the great nineteenth-
century heritage of uniquely German economic doctrine.
Spann was attempting to place the economy in its proper
perspective, not as an end-in-itself, but as the servant of the
society and its true ideals.[40]

In the work of the Friedrich-List-Gesellschaft, Salin
hoped to carry forward the development of German economic doctrine and at the same time exert influence on public life. Late in 1924 Salin and one of his former students
Arthur Sommer, broached the idea of founding such a society to Professors Arthur Spiethoff of Bonn and Friedrich Lenz of Giessen. Lenz was close to the neoconservative
periodical *Vorkämpfer*, which followed a National Bolshevik line. Spiethoff had for a long time been an assistant to
Schmoller. He was a "pure" economist and a student of
business cycles. The two men reacted enthusiastically to the
suggestion, and the Society was accordingly constituted in
1925, with the preparation of a definitive edition of the
works of its namesake as its first task.

The List Society proposed to differ from the Verein für
Sozialpolitik in at least two ways. First, whereas the
Verein had by the 1920s become the society of all academic
economists irrespective of doctrinal persuasion, the founders of the List Society decided to emulate the earlier pattern of the Verein by creating a large executive committee
comprising not only scholars but also many representatives
from political life, public administration, and the business
community. Salin and his friends hoped thereby to increase the involvement and, therefore, the influence in public life of economists with social conservative leanings. Second, on the pattern of the Verein of the nineteenth century,
Salin intended the List Society to guide the important de-
cisionmakers of the society in the direction of the kind of
social and economic thought we have termed social con-

[40] Salin, "Deutsche volkswirtschaftliche Theorie im 20. Jahrhundert,"
Zeitschrift für schweizerische Statistik und Volkswirtschaft, LVII
(1921), 87-134, esp. 129ff.

servative. Starting with a definitive edition of the works of Friedrich List, the Society, Salin hoped, would go on to create a "universalist" consciousness among an elite.

The List Society, in Salin's eyes, even bore traces of a halting attempt to establish a circle of the like-minded on German economic problems similar to that of the like-minded friends around George. Salin had first offered the chairmanship to Werner Sombart, hoping to gain for the infant Society the prestige of the Berlin professor, who was then the most distinguished social conservative economist in Germany. But Sombart was not interested in the proffered honor.[41] The chairmanship finally went instead to Salin's good friend and patron, Bernhard Harms. This remarkable man headed an international trade institute at the University of Kiel and was responsible for organizing some of the most valuable efforts of collective economic research produced during the Republican era. He was the same man, however, whom Lujo Brentano had denounced as a dilettante and who had once challenged Max Weber to a duel. It is significant that many years later Salin wrote of his friend in language which could have been applied as well to his relationship to the poet George: "The narrow and even the wider directorate of the List Society was at bottom a circle of friends with Harms at its center...."[42]

The List Society fell short of Salin's full expectations. There were few members who could accept completely the philosophical direction Salin and Lenz sought to give it. The number of overt social conservative economists in Germany was relatively small, and the group around Salin was never able to dominate the councils of the Society, whose membership in April 1932 was 1,100. A society with scholarly pretensions, of course, could scarcely exclude candidates for membership on the basis of their economic

[41] Hermann Brügelmann, *Politische Ökonomie in kritischen Jahren: Die Friedrich List-Gesellschaft e.V. von 1925-1935* (Tübingen, 1956), p. 22—hereafter cited as Brügelmann, *FLG*. It may be that Sombart felt acceptance of the offer would have been below his dignity and might perhaps hurt his chances for election to the chairmanship of the more prestigious Verein.

[42] Salin, "Bernard Harms in Memoriam," *ibid.*, p. xvi.

philosophies. But not even Harms saw eye to eye with Salin on all matters. Harms was, for all his unique qualities, an academic without the intense interest in politics that Salin manifested. He was, also, an advocate of free trade. In statements and correspondence about the Society, Salin frequently expressed disappointment and dissatisfaction with the large numbers of business liberals in the Society and the direction which discussions took as a consequence. Finally, although the List edition was a fine piece of work, the contemporary generation of economists and intellectuals showed little interest in it.[43] In a letter to Harms, Salin expressed his hope that the *next* generation would find the List edition valuable.[44] The lack of interest, together with a lack of financial resources during the depression, limited the sales among academicians. The radical parties, however, bought many copies. In February 1930, for example, ninety percent of the orders came from the Communist Party, the National Socialists, and the trade unions. In Düsseldorf alone the Communists ordered nine sets and the Nazis eleven.[45]

The Society had comparatively little difficulty in financing its work. The German Academy and the *Notgemeinschaft der Deutschen Wissenschaft* (Special Aid Association of German Scholarship) both supplied funds. Money flowed in from German industry, and Secretary of State Johannes Popitz of the Finance Ministry proved very sympathetic. Gustav Stresemann had backed the work of the Society from its early days.[46]

Carrying its work beyond the List edition, the Society sponsored a series of conferences on economic questions of contemporary concern. The most important of these were two conferences on reparations, a conference on the agrarian question, and one on currency problems.[47]

[43] Erwin von Beckerath, Karl Goeser, Friedrich Lenz, William Notz, Edgar Salin, Artur Sommer eds., *Friedrich List. Schriften, Reden, Briefe* (10 vols.; Berlin, 1927-1935).

[44] Brügelmann, *FLG*, p. 59.

[45] Letter of Salin to Harms, cited *ibid.*, p. 36.

[46] Brügelmann, *FLG*, p. 32.

[47] After the elections of September 1930, in which the Nazis gained 107 seats in the Reichstag, the Society planned a conference on National

The first reparations conference, the conference of Pyrmont, held in June 1928, dealt primarily with the problem
of transferring German reparations payments to the Allies.[48] The ideological fronts came to a confrontation
at Pyrmont. The followers of a modified classical theory,
primarily business liberals, led by Walter Eucken (himself
an "Ordoliberal" and one of the architects of the post-
World War II economic recovery), saw no transfer problem involved in the reparations payments. The automatic
workings of the foreign exchange markets, Eucken believed,
would effect the transfer. Wilhelm Röpke seconded him in
arguing that there would be no problems in getting German goods into foreign countries. The economists grouped
around Salin held to the more pessimistic viewpoint that,
if difficulties for Germany were to be avoided, transfers
would have to be "protected" in the manner specified in
the Dawes Plan. They did not believe that export of German goods to creditors with high customs barriers was as
easy as Eucken and Röpke made it seem.

Although the transfer of reparations payments had in
practice involved few difficulties (as may be recalled from
the discussion of reparations in Chapter I), the protection
of transfers—that is, the American agent-general's mandate
to regulate the transfers *in behalf of Germany*—did pose a
great psychological problem. This fear was reflected in the
statements of pessimists at the Pyramont conference. Moreover, as it turned out, the sale of German goods to the countries of the West, with their high customs barriers, was not
as easy as the neoclassicists had thought it would be.

The surprise event of the conference was the address
given by the president of the Reichsbank, Hjalmar Schacht,
in which he denounced the neoclassicists and reaffirmed his
belief in the difficulty of the transfer of reparations payments. Using the language of a street-corner orator, he
closed his harangue with the defiant statement: "Gentle-

Socialism. The conference was never held because of disagreement on
the focus of the topic and on whether the Nazis themselves were to be
invited. *Ibid.*, pp. 120ff.

[48] Salin, ed., *Das Reparationsproblem*, I: *Verhandlungen und Gutachten der Konferenz von Pyrmont* (Berlin, 1929).

men, I tell you I do not want to pay, and therefore I will
accept no theory which proves to me that I have to pay."
Schacht negotiated the Young Plan, then repudiated his
work in a published memorandum and during a lecture
tour of the United States. Both acts were embarrassing to
the government and hurt Germany on the international
money market.[49]

The reopening of the discussions on the Young Plan
prompted the List Society to call a second conference on
reparations in the fall of the same year. The members
hoped thereby to brief the German delegates to the discussions in the intricacies of the German reparations position. At this second conference, held in Berlin, the social
conservatives came out in greater force. Friedrich Lenz
launched the social conservative attack by rejecting the
widespread view that the Dawes Plan had taken reparations
out of the political arena and had translated the question
into one of sound commercial relations among the concerned nations. He agreed with the Nazis and the Communists that the Dawes Plan was still very much a political
issue. He saw in the Plan simply a slight rearrangement of
the European power structure; its negotiation appeared to
him as merely the subordination of French imperialism to
that of Britain and the United States. The reparations
tribute in his eyes, then, was basically a superprofit paid by
Germany to the capitalist economies of the victorious
powers.[50]

Salin took the stand next to give a report in which he
lashed out at the views of the neoclassicists with great
venom and with more substantial arguments than Lenz
had employed.[51] The neoclassicists had continued to cham-

[49] Because of the sensitivity of the topic and of Schacht's position,
the executives of the Society chose not to print the address in the
volume on the conference. Most of it may be found quoted in Brügelmann, *FLG*, pp. 81-85.

[50] "Der Reparationstransfer im Rahmen der gesamten Zahlungs-
bilanz," *Das Reparationsproblem*, II: *Verhandlungen und Gutachten
der Konferenz von Berlin* (Berlin, 1929), 273-88.

[51] The neoclassicists tended to be somewhat more willing to accept
reparations as a necessary evil. They had set the tone of the discussion

pion the view that the normal functioning of the international goods and money markets would create the conditions necessary to permit the automatic transfer of German reparations. This theory Salin castigated as "cosmopolitan." But his meaning was not too different from the meaning of Lenz's remarks. Such a transfer of payments was automatic only in those instances where the debtor nation, in this case Germany, was to a large degree in the power of its creditors and could be forced to adjust its fiscal policies to meet the payments.

Turning to the question of the methods of raising the tribute sum, Salin analyzed two basic approaches to realizing the necessary surpluses. The money could come either from reduction of wages or from curtailment of profits. If a drop in German export prices were to be achieved by the depression of wages, there would then be two further, and equally draconian, alternatives. Either the restoration of a free economy could be achieved by abolition of existing wage contracts, the arbitration apparatus of the state, unemployment insurance, and other welfare programs—in conjunction with the dissolution of the organizations of entrepreneurs and labor unions—or it could be written off and a command economy instituted by so strengthening the state as to give it enough power to enforce all its demands. It is not surprising that, having presented the alternatives in this way, Salin could envision no likelihood of the immediate implementation of either approach.

On the other hand, achieving price reductions by slashing the margin of profits was, in Salin's opinion, also out of the question. The profits of the export industries, he believed, were already down to the narrowest margins possible. But, even if profits could be cut further, the sacrifice would mean only that the sums available for dividends to the stockholders or for direct reinvestment by the firms would be correspondingly diminished. Pursuit of such a policy could not but intensify Germany's serious capital shortage.

---

at Pyrmont to such a degree that Salin had commented ironically at the time on the pressing need to found a List Society. See *ibid.*, p. 340.

Salin could correctly point to the fact that, even if Germany somehow managed to depress her price level, there was no guarantee that the low-priced German goods could penetrate the tariff walls raised against them. Thus the solution to the reparations question, Salin was arguing, could not proceed on the basis of any automatic "economic" theory. On that level Germany was lost. She would have to find a political way out of the tangle.[52]

The German experts sent to Paris to discuss the revision of the Dawes Plan and the contents of the Young Plan had available to them the two volumes published by the List Society. The papers they contained comprised the most complete and careful treatments of reparations in the German economic literature. But it is unlikely that the work of Salin's Society influenced the outcome of the negotiations to any significant degree. The volumes contained all the views presented at the two reparations conferences of the Society; hence, along with the reports of Salin and Lenz, were to be found those of Röpke and Eucken. The German representatives had little freedom of action in any case. Although they had clear instructions on the broad policy aims of their government, the Allied powers were not apt to show much inclination to follow German suggestions in anything but minor details. Since the two chief German representatives were Dr. Albert Vögler of the Vereinigten Stahlwerke (United Steel Works) and Hjalmar Schacht, the role of the List Society volumes could at most have been that of reinforcing the "hard" line on reparations, to which these men were already personally and politically committed. Even so, the volumes offered the German delegation scientific support for all aspects of their presentation, which probably helped avert blunders that might otherwise have been committed owing to poor preparation on the part of the German participants.[53]

[52] "Die Bedeutung des Transferschutzes," *Das Reparationsproblem*, II, 291-98. Salin preferred to use the more value-laden word "tribute" when discussing reparations.

[53] Salin himself had little use for Schacht, even though he agreed with him on his strong stand against reparations. Salin accused

In the most serious phase of the depression, when the gravity of the error of Chancellor Brüning's deflationary policy was manifest to all, the List Society had a final opportunity to exercise a direct role in the planning of national economic policy. In the middle of September 1931 Hans Luther, a former chancellor and at this time president of the Reichsbank, called a hurried conference on state fiscal policy. As the director of the central bank Luther felt it incumbent on himself to act to ease the crisis. In broad terms, Luther invited the thirty economists he had called together to discuss an alternative to the policies of the Brüning government. What role, he wished to know, could the Reichsbank play in the policy shift? To start the discussion, the participants were given for their evaluation a memorandum composed by Dr. Wilhelm Lautenbach of the Economics Ministry.

The memorandum represented the kind of approach to national economic policy that we associate with the name of Keynes in England and with the program of the New Deal in the United States. The Lautenbach plan advocated an end to the administrative and contractual restrictions on the fluctuations of wages. Lautenbach expected that the resultant decline in wages would be five percent annually on the average. At the same time, administered prices in the highly monopolistic iron and steel industries were to be forced down. This action, he was confident, would permit reduction of costs and, hence, prices in those industries dependent on these primary raw materials. Finally, credit expansion through state action, reinforced by the lowering of interest rates and supplemented by a program of public works putting approximately half a million of the unemployed back to work, would, he hoped, stimulate investment.[54]

Schacht of abusing his power as a central bank director, as well as of acting on the basis of erroneous theories. He did not, however, specify what the abuses and errors were. See Salin's address *Theorie und Praxis staatlicher Kreditpolitik der Gegenwart* (Tübingen, 1928).

[54] Brügelmann, *FLG*, pp. 133-39. After the war Wolfgang Stützel and Wilhelm Röpke collected a number of Lautenbach's articles and

A great majority of the economists meeting with Luther
were in agreement on the need for some sort of plan on the
order of Lautenbach's proposal to reverse Brüning's deflationary policies and help the German economy climb out of
the trough.[55] Inherent in the Lautenbach plan, as well as
in most of the other proposals for combatting the depression in that time of crisis, was the potential unleashing of
inflationary tendencies.[56] But public fear of the possible
repetition of the inflation of 1924 and governmental fear of
the political consequences of inflation paralyzed the policymakers. So greatly did the irrational slogans of street politics dominate economic and political life that, even when
two such diverse thinkers as Salin and Eucken agreed on
the general direction state economic policy ought to take,
it proved impossible to go in that direction. The Lautenbach proposals were not to influence the Brüning regime
very extensively. They played a greater role in the actions
of the von Papen government, but not until the Nazi era
were public works undertaken on any scale commensurate
with the social and economic needs of the country.[57] In this
sense, the conference with Reichsbank President Luther was
a failure. Politics had come to dominate economic considerations completely, too completely to allow the voices of
experts, independent or partisan, to be heard.

So dissatisfied was Salin about the fate of his List Society
and the plight of Germany under reparations that he devoted a series of essays to elaborating his views further.[58]

Salin charged the United States with having taken advan-

---

memoranda from the depression years under the title *Zins, Kredit und
Produktion* (Tübingen, 1952) ; see esp. "Gutachten über Arbeitsbeschaf-
fung und Defizitpolitik," 28 Aug. and 9 Sept. 1931, pp. 137ff.

[55] Brügelmann, *FLG*, pp. 133-39; Walter Eucken, *This Unsuccessful
Age* (London, 1951) , p. 65.

[56] Wilhelm Grotkopp's *Die Grosse Krise* contains discussions and
evaluations of the most important of these proposals; see esp. pp.
231-62.

[57] Cf. *ibid.*, p. 38, n. 4.

[58] It is interesting to note the play on Fichte's *Reden an die deutsche
Nation*, also written to hearten Germans against a foreign menace, in
the title of Salin's book, *Die deutschen Tribute, Zwölf Reden.*

tage of its special economic position to profit from the distress of others. Instead of cancelling Allied debts, the
United States had used the capitalistic spirit as the cement
of its alliances.[59] Thus, according to Salin, had Wilson
kept faith: the United States received all the reparations
monies extracted from Germany, excluding funds used for
reconstruction purposes, in the form of repayment of inter-
Allied loans.[60] He denounced the Young Plan as the imposition of two generations of slavery on the German people, a slavery made worse by the fact that it took the form
of a "normal commercial obligation."

Speaking less ambiguously in this more popular work
than he had at the Berlin conference of the List Society,
Salin advocated a reduction in real wages as the method of
depressing prices so that Germany could pay off its tribute
through export surpluses. The going politically determined
wage level, he felt, was too high. It could be maintained
only if entrepreneurial talent and inventiveness could increase productivity. Since the Young Plan operated within a capitalist framework, the German capitalist should be
hemmed in by neither economic nor political restrictions.
What Salin was saying here was that reparations and capitalism were structurally linked. He intimated that the
demise of capitalism would solve the reparations question,
too.[61]

The Young Plan, he believed, was itself unworkable; Germany could not pay. He nevertheless advised bending Germany's energies to the task of carrying it out—even though
this action would inevitably lead to an economic crisis.
Echoing Stefan George's mystical vision of cataclysm, Salin
welcomed the crisis of capitalism. Although a collapse was
not in itself a purification, collapse was the necessary condition for purification. For "the fearful effort cautiously
to avoid every serious crisis is not a path to the healing
final solution, but rather only a means by which the infect-
ing germs are allowed to continue to exist." The task of

---

[59] *Die deutschen Tribute*, pp. 69-70.
[60] *Ibid.*, p. 72; cf. also pp. 166-67.
[61] *Ibid.*, pp. 204-6.

the statesman, in Salin's view, would be to formulate a political goal and to prepare the Folk and the Nation for the
unavoidable "healing crisis" (*Heilungskrise*) that would
finally bring reparations to an end.[62]

The fact of reparations and the economic and political
situation of Germany vis-à-vis the other major powers led
Salin to the conclusion that, if she were not to become a
French or English colony, she would have to strive to
achieve economic autarky. She had to be in a position to
procure her food supply, to as great a degree as possible,
out of her own resources.[63] As a professional economist
Salin could not but realize that complete autarky for an industrialized nation of sixty-five million men was impossible.
He sought primarily the termination of the predominance
of industry in the German economy and society; much
like Sombart, he longed for a return to the balanced "agri-
cultural-industrial-commercial state" of which Friedrich List
had written.[64]

Salin considered a policy of encouragement and protection for agriculture necessary for the nation for several reasons. First, with the collapse of the world economy, which,
like Sombart, he anticipated, Germany would have to be
able to stand alone or would go down ignominiously with
the rest of the West. The "back to nature" movement of
the Romantics, Salin urged, had become an economic
necessity.[65]

Second, East German agriculture, as the part of the
economy most in danger, deserved special protection, "even
if these [aid measures] occasionally should accrue to the
advantage of particular groups."[66] He believed, also, that it

[62] *Die deutschen Tribute*, pp. 202-3; *Wirtschaft und Staat*, p. 33.

[63] "Am Wendepunkt der deutschen Wirtschaftspolitik," *Wirtschaft
und Staat*, p. 86—expansion of a paper first printed in the List Society study of German agriculture, Harms, Salin, et al., eds., *Deutsche
Agrarpolitik* (2 vols.; Berlin, 1932), II, 684ff.

[64] *Ibid.*

[65] *Ibid.*, p. 106.

[66] *Ibid.*, pp. 108-9. The East Elbian Junkers were the greatest beneficiaries of government subsidies to agriculture, subsidies which were
uneconomically employed—in several cases, as far away as the Riviera.

was important to aid the peasants who had been settled in East Prussia and Silesia by the governments of both the Imperial and Republican eras. Heavy German settlement of these borderlands, he maintained, would help limit Polish penetration of this part of Germandom.[67]

Third, the peasants, along with artisans and small businessmen were, in Salin's opinion, mainstays of the state. They still represented living forces, for otherwise, he argued, they would have been swept away long ago. Viewing the peasantry with the eyes of a Georgian, Salin saw them as the last remnant of "primordial nature" (*dumpfer Natur*) defending itself with "that desperate courage which the sensing of incurable infection, of imminent violation, of incipient destruction by the evil and mediocre confers."[68]

"The Enlightenment and the money-calculating sickness" would die with the end of the "liberal-democratic economic-state."[69] The new order would give the state priority over the "economy"; it would be the *true* state.[70] Under what conditions could such a state come into existence? How would it be organized? Would it be repressive and dictatorial? Salin answered these questions with the archaic rhetoric and political obscurantism of a Georgian: "In such times [of crisis and renewal] the particulars of constitutional arrangement and the degree of freedom remaining automatically become unimportant; in such times the strength of creative action grows and in the innermost heart of German man, rediscovering himself, there occurs the birth of the new founder of the Reich."[71]

---

[67] "Am Wendepunkt . . . ," *Wirtschaft und Staat*, pp. 110, 122.

[68] "Von der Wandlung des Staatswesen und der Wirtschaftsordnung," *Wirtschaft und Staat*, pp. 162, 193. This passage—"jenem Mut der Verzweiflung, den das Gefühl der heillosen Ansteckung, der drohenden Schändung, der beginnenden Überwältigung durch das Böse und Minderwertige verleiht"—defies accurate translation.

[69] *Ibid.*, p. 196.

[70] *Ibid.*, pp. 196-99.

[71] "In solchen Läuften werden von selbst die Einzelheiten der staatlichen Bindung und die Grade der verbleibenden Freiheit ungewichtig, in solchen Läuften wächst die Kraft des schöpferischen Handelns und

Through a union of the demands of economic necessity,
interest of state, and a highly sensitized moral vision of an
ideal society—all encompassed within a German economic
theory—Salin sought to bridge the gap between the vision
of a seer and the realities of the German situation. At the
center of Salin's critique of Weimar Germany lay a feeling of despair for a society in which the beautiful was tech-
nologically outmoded and epic heroism stifled by the
crowd. Germany was led, not by the wise, the creative, and
the heroic, but rather by the efficient, the ambitious, and
the mediocre. Salin retained the Georgian contempt for the
rule of quantity. He could not accept an individual as a
man of worth if his only qualification was the ability to
heap up money. He could not accept a movement as legiti-
mate just because it could attract to its banner large numbers of followers. Indeed, Salin believed that, precisely because during the depression Germany was weak and in
danger of collapse while her enemies were strong, there was
greater reason to press the search for men of quality and
excellence. The overthrow of the rule of number—of democracy, liberalism, and socialism at home, and of sub-
mersion in a world economy and reparations externally—
would prepare the way for the true state. Salin awaited
a healing crisis that would signal the beginning of Germany's liberation.

Writing with the partisan fervor of a moral visionary,
Salin described as the rule of the good and the beautiful a
future society with a rigid social structure headed by a small
elite under the direction of a wise dictator. The mainstays
of this society were to be the classes most endangered by
the direction of social and economic change in the twentieth
century—the firmly rooted peasantry, the artisan class, and
small businessmen. In Salin's good society those seekers
after wealth of the business world and those radicals who
had made of vulgar envy an economic and political creed

---

in dem innersten Kern des zu sich selbst heimfindenden deutschen
Menschen vollzieht sich die Geburt des Neubegründers des Reiches."
Ibid., p. 200.

would find themselves powerless. Salin was too good a Georgian and too careful an economist to offer specifics on the form of the ideal economic system. But, surely, the economy would be clearly subordinate to the political structure. It would not be capitalistic in any of the senses in which members of the business community understood the word. The balance which Friedrich List championed for the German economy in the early nineteenth century would be restored, but urbanism and industry would have to be deemphasized to the advantage of agriculture and rural life. Certainly, Germany would not be paying reparations to her enemies, and she would be buffered by protectionist economic policies from the vicissitudes of international affairs. Then, after being put in order, the economy would gradually be relegated to the secondary position it deserved—as the means of supporting high culture, permitting the practice of morality, and making possible once again the conduct of heroic political life.

Many of Salin's criticisms of the quality of life in the twentieth century, if not novel, were in some measure justifiable. German industrial society did have its seamy aspects. The malfunctioning of democracy in Germany and the naked conflicts of interest in that society caused many men to long for some better constitution of the social order. The *anomie* felt by the middle classes that had been engendered by the radical alterations in their position in society was well suited to arouse pity in the hearts of those with a finely attuned moral sense. The failure of the democratic governments of the Weimar period to solve the agrarian question was a serious shortcoming, too, although during the depression the peasantry and the owners of large estates were able to avenge themselves by putting their influence and votes at the service of the destroyers of Weimar democracy. The constant political irritation of the high reparations sums and the shortsightedness of the Americans and Allies in their approach to the question, finally, understandably provoked moral indignation in Germany.

In the years between World War I and the great depression Salin managed to combine in himself both a longing

for the coming of the Reich envisioned by the poet Stefan
George and an interest in the technical and more mundane
problems of economic life. On the one hand, he still seemed
to believe that a new morality and a putative lost beauty
could be, or at least should be, realized in twentieth-century
society. On the other hand, he displayed a strong practical
sense. He wrote prolifically on complex theoretical and
technical questions. He advanced his career ably, becoming a professor at Heidelberg at an uncommonly young age,
gaining an important chair at Basel at the age of thirty-
five, and finally acceding to the honor of the rectorship
of that Swiss university which had once harbored Jacob
Burckhardt and Friedrich Nietzsche from the philistines of
the nineteenth century.[72]

Perhaps nothing reveals the double nature of Salin so well
as his attitudes toward the depression and the political un-
rest associated with it. As an economist he was aware of
the common interpretation of downswings in the business
cycle as moments of beneficial economic disaster which permitted the readjustment of wages, interest rates, and production and which drove inefficient firms from the marketplace. Yet he wrote of the great depression as the final crisis
of capitalism. For Salin believed, as did other social conservative writers, that the German depression was not just
another serious cyclical downturn but a total crisis of the
liberal state and of the liberal philosophy behind it. He
wrote of the depression in the wild and vague language of a
Georgian, rather than in the cool, precise terms of a social
scientist.

---

[72] See the evidence of the broadness of Salin's interests, both in the
realm of technical economics and in those of literature and culture, in
the *Festschrift, Antidoron; Edgar Salin zum 70. Geburtstag*, ed.
Erwin von Beckerath, Heinrich Popitz, Hans Georg Siebeck, and Harry
W. Zimmermann (Tübingen, 1962), "Bibliographie," pp. 297-305. The
late Sigmund Neumann, who had studied under Salin briefly, once
expressed his perplexity about the paradoxical coexistence in one
personality of a snobbish aesthete and a hardheaded economist. I
am indebted to Walter Struve for allowing me to read the notes of
his interview with Professor Neumann in Middletown, Connecticut, in
the winter of 1959.

Just as Salin had been wrong about the power of renewal which World War I would generate, so George and a great number of his followers had worked to prepare Germany for the wrong catastrophe in 1933. In that year George himself had once more to deny that this was *his* crisis. He refused the Nazi offer of the presidency of the German Academy, as he had refused all marks of honor from the Republic. His Jewish disciple, Ernst Morwitz, conveyed his reply.[73] George left for Switzerland to begin his voluntary exile from the Third Reich. He died later in that same year.

The coming of Nazism posed no moral problem for Salin, a Jew and a Swiss university professor since 1927. The Nazis' anti-Semitism, their vulgarity, their recruitment of elements of the society Salin considered rabble doubtless all offended him. Salin's political sympathies in the last years of the Republic are a matter of conjecture. He was attracted to the economic thought he read in the pages of the periodical *Die Tat*. Extrapolation of the political line of *Die Tat* and the trend of Salin's own political thought point in the direction of General Kurt von Schleicher, the proponent of a third-force government made up of the left wing of the Nazi party and the trade unions. Salin, however, never concerned himself sufficiently with daily political struggles to take any clear-cut position on parties or politicians. Thus what he desired specifically in German politics must remain obscured in the ambiguities of a mode of expression more appropriate to a visionary poet than to an *engagé* economist.

Intermixed with all that was reprehensible in Salin's works was an aggrieved moral sensitivity, a true love of beauty, and a strong loyalty to his German homeland. The moral aesthete in Salin caused him to long for, and argue for, the beautiful life of pre-industrial Germany. The competent analyst and man of hard reality in him tended to serve the paradoxical end of making his visionary utterances more acceptable to his contemporaries. Because of his own revulsion with many of the paramount features of indus-

[73] David, *The Third Reich*, p. 311.

trial society, Salin was an able and articulate spokesman for
what many of his fellow middle class Germans only dimly
felt. He could express a longing, a feeling of loss; but he
offered no positive principles of social organization to replace the hated modern system.[74] It remained for Othmar
Spann to outline the organization of the "true society."

[74] John Harrison's judgment of the linkage between the politics and
the aesthetics of Yeats, Pound, Wyndham Lewis, and Eliot is surely
overstated. Yet it might with some justice also be applied to the main
political illusion of Georgians like Salin: "What [they] wanted in
literature was bareness, a hard intellectual approach ruled by the
authority of strict literary principles. They rejected the humanist
tradition in literature, and in society, the democratic humanitarian
tradition. The same principles governed their social criticism as
their literary criticism. . . ." *The Reactionaries: A Study of the Anti-
Democratic Intelligentsia* (New York, 1967), p. 33.

IV. Othmar Spann

CORPORATISM
IN INDUSTRIAL SOCIETY

CORPORATISM was the most significant blueprint for the society of the future within social conservatism.[1] While Sombart and Salin offered essentially negative critiques of existing capitalist society and the socialist opposition, Othmar Spann supplied the positive vision of the new society. As an attempt to solve the social question by means of structuring social disharmony within more or less rigid estates or occupational divisions, twentieth-century corporatism appealed to the groups of middle income and status within European society. Corporatism offered the middle classes social stability and social peace. Its advocates proposed to confer certainty of social position on members of the old middle class, who were presently adrift in a fearfully unpredictable industrial world. Corporatism further supplied a definition of the new middle class of white-collar workers which did not relegate them to the ranks of the proletariat, as Marxism did.

Most corporative doctrines prized the peasantry highly, assigning them a very important, if somewhat paradoxical, place in the urbanized society of the twentieth century. Corporatism has always found adherents among old upper class landowning elements of European society, for its proponents contemplated no radical rearrangement of the social hierarchy. It did not seek to lop off "historically irrelevant" classes. Even some industrialists recognized the value of the corporate state as an arrangement which, at its

[1] For the range of such theories, see Ralph Bowen, *German Theories of the Corporate State: With Special Reference to the Period 1870-1919* (New York, 1947).

worst, might limit some of their past freedom but which, at the same time, would perform the vastly beneficial tasks of ending the class struggle and of making their hold on their property secure. For most corporative philosophies, even Catholic varieties, did not contemplate a social order led by workers or their representatives. Corporatism was, rather, an attempt by conservative elements of the European population to build an alternative to the system of industrial society and to Marxism, much as European conservatives earlier had sought to employ nineteenth-century corporatism and romanticism as a dam against, and as alternatives to, militant liberalism and commercial society.

In an age which had come increasingly to question the value of capitalism and democracy, and even industrial society itself, corporatism offered a relatively coherent way out. It presented a new order that would curb capitalism and destroy (or at least antiquate) Marxism, with only minimal rearrangements in the existing structure of contemporary society. In the 1920s and 1930s corporatism exercised a fresh appeal in conservative and fascist circles. It served as the ideology of Franco's Falange—insofar as the Falange possessed an ideology—and greatly influenced Oliveira Salazar, who became the dictator of Portugal in 1926.[2] In France the men of Vichy clothed themselves in French corporative ideas to cover their political nakedness.[3] In Italy Mussolini championed an early experiment in, or —more accurately—the promise of, the corporate state.[4]

As the old feudal estates were rendered increasingly obsolete by the newer political forms of the nineteenth century, experiments in compromise were tried. One was the

[2] See Stanley G. Payne, *Falange* (Stanford, 1961) for the Spanish movement. There is a Salazar apologia by Freppel Cotta, *Economic Planning in Corporative Portugal* (London, 1937).

[3] See Mathew H. Elbow, *French Corporative Theory, 1789-1948* (New York, 1953), for a sympathetic treatment of corporative thought and experiments in Vichy France.

[4] See G. L. Field, *The Syndical and Corporative Institutions of Italian Fascism* (New York, 1938), and the relevant sections of H. Stuart Hughes, *The United States and Italy* (rev. edn., Cambridge, Mass., 1965).

compromise between the feudal aristocracy and the aggressive bourgeoisie, which was institutionalized in the three-strata voting procedure of the Prussian parliament after 1850. Since this system apportioned one-third of the parliamentary seats to each third of the income pyramid, the land-owning aristocracy, in the course of the nineteenth century, had to give way to the new men of wealth. Vastly underrepresented in relation to their numbers, the workers of Prussia fought the three-class voting procedure until they managed to exact the *promise* of its destruction from an unwilling government in the midst of World War I. In the twentieth century the workers of Prussia would not have tolerated its reintroduction, had social conservatives made the attempt.

But social conservatives also were dissatisfied with this kind of corporate arrangement. As the analyses of Sombart's and Salin's views have shown, social conservatives felt that the mere possession of wealth was insufficient justification for claims to political leadership. After 1848 it became evident to the conservatives who favored a corporate organization of the state that the old feudal estates were irrevocably dead. Increasingly in the years after the political upheavals of the middle of the century advocates of corporatism advanced schemes for a corporate order based upon occupational representation.[5] In the second half of the nineteenth century, however, plans for a total corporative reconstitution of society slipped into the background, and reformist ideas of a broadly corporative nature dominated the discussions of social philosophy in both old conservative and Catholic circles. It was only after World War I, when the forces of stability of the nineteenth century had been disarranged and ideas of soldiers' and workers' councils, emanating from the wave of leftist revolutions, had forced conservatives to reevaluate their principles, that schemes for the construction of the corporate state based upon occupational estates came once more to the foreground.[6]

[5] Justus Beyer, *Die Ständeideologien der Systemzeit und ihre Überwindung* (Darmstadt, 1941), p. 36.

[6] *Ibid.*, p. 25. Cf. also the proposal for a "corporative socialism"

After the war Austria became a center for German corporative theorizing, owing in part to its character as a Catholic country (corporative strains have long been prevalent
in Catholic social doctrine) and in part to the militancy
and ideological sophistication of Austrian Socialists. Geo-
graphical proximity to Fascist Italy also acted as a stim-
ulant on corporative currents of thought in Austria. Not as
highly industrialized as Germany, Austria still had significant numbers of independent artisans, farmers, and small
shopkeepers, as well as superfluous civil servants and military officers left over from Imperial days,[7] for whom corporatism could serve as an intellectual shield against
Marxism and as a vision of a utopia projecting their conceptions of an idealized past into the future.

Austria in 1932 was a land suffering from economic depression, irreconcilable political conflict, and social disintegration. Now only the rump of a once great empire, her
capital city, Vienna, contained almost one-third of the population. Here the major political currents of the land met,
representing a microcosm of Western European politics in
the interwar period.

In 1932 the right-radical novelist Ernst von Salomon arrived in Vienna. The man who had been in the inner circle
of the assassins of the German (social) liberal foreign
minister Walter Rathenau had come to study at the university on the invitation of Professor Othmar Spann. At the end
of his stay, a year later, von Salomon was intoxicated by the
beauty and intricacies of Spann's social philosophy, but he
had to confess in his last interview with his teacher that he

---

in *Das Dritte Reich*, ed. Hans Schwarz (3rd edn., Hamburg, 1931),
pp. 164ff., by the influential theoretician of the new German conser-
vatism, Moeller van den Bruck, and the provision for a National
Economic Council in the Weimar Constitution's economic clauses,
Section V. Brunet, *The New German Constitution*, pp. 297-339. The
Council proved of little political importance in the history of the
Republic.

[7] Emil Januschka, *The Social Stratification of the Austrian Population*, United States WPA Foreign Social Science Monographs, No. 21
(New York: Columbia University, 1939).

did not understand it.[8] Nor, for that matter, could the North German comprehend, or follow, Spann's involvement in the tangled web of Austrian politics. When one day von Salomon asked Spann's sons, Adelbert and Rafael, what their father and his associates were trying to do in the arena of Austrian-German politics, what the meaning of their writings and negotiations was, he received the cryptic answer that they *packlten.*

Packln is an Austrian word that is quite difficult to translate or define. It designates a special kind of negotiating skill, a talent for getting on with irreconcilable opposites, a diplomacy of the highest order. The English word "politicking" conveys only part of its meaning; the American phrase "wheeling-and-dealing" is perhaps closer. The Spanns were referring to their father's ability to keep a finger in every (right-wing) political pie in Austria. Spann and his followers had entrance to the circles of the Christian-Socials, the Nationalists, the Heimwehr (Home Guard), and the Nazis. Spann's version of the corporative ideology, which he called "Universalism," appealed in some way to all of these groups—even though they themselves were often at loggerheads with one another. Whereas Werner Sombart and Edgar Salin operated in an academic situation, working out social conservative theories in isolation from the hard realities of street politics, Spann assumed a middle position, mediating between the high intellectual tradition of social conservative ideology and the leaders of the political and the street movements. He contributed a major link in the chain of thought which made social conservatism into an ideology of political activism.

Spann was born in 1878 in Altmannsdorf, a village at the edge of the spreading metropolis of Vienna. His father plied his artisan trade in the family home. He was sufficiently prosperous to send his son to a gymnasium and then to the University of Vienna. Between 1898 and 1903 Spann stud-

---

[8] Von Salomon confessed to Spann that he still did not understand the meaning of the Professor's concept of "corporative articulation" *(ständische Gliederung)*. Ernst von Salomon, *Der Fragebogen* (Reinbeck-bei-Hamburg: RoRoRo paperback, 1961), pp. 165ff.

ied at Vienna, Zurich, Bern, and Tübingen. In 1903 he was awarded a Ph.D. for his dissertation, "Examinations of the Concept of Society as an Introduction to Sociology." In the fall of 1903 he took a position at the Zentrale für private Fürsorge in Frankfurt-am-Main. There for six years he conducted statistical studies of the problems of unwed mothers and illegitimate children. In 1909 he was named professor of economics at the Technische Hochschule at Brünn; in 1911 he was promoted to *Ordinarius*. When the war broke out, Lieutenant Spann was posted to the front. Wounded in action, he soon recovered, but, rather than return to battle, he spent the rest of the war working for the Wissenschaftliches Komitee für Kriegswirtschaft (Scientific Committee for the War Economy) of the War Ministry. In 1919 he reached a pinnacle of Austrian academic life: he was named professor of economics and sociology at the University of Vienna. From 1919 until 1938, when the National Socialists removed him from his post, Spann lectured, wrote, and propagandized prolifically in behalf of his philosophy of Universalism.[9]

This philosophy was ideally suited for *packln* in Austrian and German politics. Its metaphysics was sufficiently erudite and obscure to be both intellectually respectable and still clearly offensive neither to Nationalists nor to Christian-Socials. Spann's social and economic proposals were indefinite enough to elicit both praise and censure from most of the major conservative political groupings, while in the short run they often proved useful as political propaganda. In short, Universalism offered an ideal vehicle for the transmission of social conservative ideology to various captains and tribunes of the armies of the dissatisfied middle classes. It was *packln* turned into a metaphysic.

Spann's metaphysics amalgamated scholastic philosophy and the German tradition of philosophic idealism. Starting from the age-old metaphysical problem of the relationship of the whole to its parts, Spann argued for the logical

[9] Hans Riehl, *Das philosophische Gesamtwerk von Othmar Spann im Auszug* (Vienna, 1950), p. 324; Otto Hausmann, "Othmar Spann und seine Schule" (Ph.D. diss., University of Vienna, 1962), pp. 1-11.

priority of the whole. Without the whole the parts would have no meaning; they only assume meaning and reality in the context of their appropriate incorporating whole. So, too, in the study of man, Spann, confronted by the polarities of the individual and his society, assigned priority to society. There were, Spann postulated, two alternatives open to the student of society: he could view society as a "pile of stones," made up of many separate, autonomous individuals standing in external and mechanical relation to one another; or he could see society as a whole, an organism like the human body, having different members, each member with its own unique function and value.[10] Spann labelled the method and value system which began with the individual "Individualism"; the organic approach he designated "Universalism." Individualism was, for him, nonmetaphysical, empirical; it employed the concept of cause. Universalism, on the other hand, was teleological and irrational; it worked intuitively from a priori premises. Resorting to the most damning criticism drawn from the heritage of social conservatism, Spann condemned Individualism because it promoted "civilization" and impaired the development of *Kultur*, of true spirituality.[11]

Spann argued that Individualism had proved incapable of answering the question of the relationship of the individual to society; it could not show the individual his place in the cosmic order, the universal whole. Experience, he felt, contradicted the assertion of absolute individual autonomy. "Individualism makes the individual alone and poor."[12] By obliterating the distinction between "is" and "ought," between fact and value, Spann managed to shift his discussion away from the disparate ways of studying man in society to an evaluation of Individualism and Universalism as

[10] *The History of Economics*, p. 59—hereafter cited as *HE*. All references are to the English translation of the 19th German edition (New York, 1930).

[11] *Der wahre Staat: Vorlesungen über Abbruch und Neubau der Gesellschaft* (3rd edn., Jena, 1931), pp. 89-98—hereafter cited as *WS*. All references are to this edition, unless otherwise noted.

[12] *WS*, pp. 26-29.

better or *worse* principles of social organization.[13] Society was, for him, a "spiritual entity, *sui generis*, a necessary precondition of the life of the individual, and for this reason, perforce, an entirely ethical and not merely 'utilitarian' structure." "Society," he continued, "stands on a higher plane than do individuals. . . ."[14] Without differentiations of rank, status, and function society could not exist; consequently, he advocated social stratification according to principles of value and function. It followed that, in an ethically organized society, the best should rule.[15]

Spann defined justice, the first political principle of Universalism, in the language of Aristotle and St. Thomas Aquinas: justice meant "giving everyone his due."[16] In an interpretation reminiscent of Sombart's *Händler und Helden* Spann traced the Individualist idea of justice—that equals are individuals who exchange things of equal value —to the marketplace. The prime political value of Individualism, however, was not justice but freedom, a freedom of autonomous beings, which Spann found especially repellent because of the spiritual impoverishment it engendered in the individual.[17]

Spann found the egalitarianism of Individualism unacceptable as well. To view men of varying aspirations and talents as equals, he felt, was to contradict experience. Egalitarianism as advocated by democracy, socialism, and— in modified form—by liberalism represented "the rule of the lower over the higher."[18]

The state, according to Individualism, was a mechanical union of individuals. It took the various forms of the strong exercising their freedom to dominate the weak, appeared in the guise of social contract and natural law schemes employed to curb the absolute freedom of the in-

---

[13] Cf. Max Weber's criticism of Spann's confounding of science and values, *Wirtschaft und Gesellschaft* (Tübingen, 1922), pp. 8-9.

[14] *HE*, p. 61.

[15] *WS*, pp. 201, 212-13.

[16] *HE*, pp. 62-63.

[17] *WS*, pp. 56-57.

[18] *WS*, pp. 60-61.

dividual for the sake of the political order, or, in its most extreme manifestation, existed with no ruling force or authority at all.[19] Spann drew up the usual social conservative indictment of liberalism and democracy, the political embodiments of Individualism, but he added a few characteristic flourishes of his own: Aristotle had opposed democracy; democracy had caused the fall of Athens; true democracy could not endure; it tended to degenerate into radicalism and dictatorship; it was inconceivable that a genius like Nietzsche, for example, should have a vote carrying no more weight than that of his bootblack; voters do not know their own wills, leaders must tell them what they really want; and so on.[20]

In the tradition of political romanticism Spann identified the Universalist state with the Folk, the Folk as a spiritual entity and a unique whole. Folk and state were the largest possible political units Spann believed to be worthy of consideration; for, contrary to the fantasies propagated by the theorists of Individualism, there existed no significant political organizations encompassing all of mankind.[21]

By identifying the state with society Spann opened the way for the drift into totalitarianism. For, if politics is viewed as the arena in which social and economic conflicts are defined and resolved, the equation of state and society can only lead to surrendering society and social relations to political domination. In such a situation, as Alfred Diamant has pointed out, the mediating role of political parties becomes unnecessary.[22] Unless other institutions serve the approximate function of the parties, totalitarianism is almost certain to ensue. Votaries of corporatism, especially some of the more democratically oriented Catholics, proposed to avoid this homogenization of society by the creation of corporate bodies, or estates, throughout the state-society. The effective operation of many autonomous, yet

[19] *HE*, p. 62; *WS*, pp. 20-22.
[20] *WS*, pp. 106-23.
[21] *WS*, pp. 96-97.
[22] Alfred Diamant, *Austrian Catholics and the First Republic* (Princeton, 1960), p. 69.

interdependent, occupational estates working from the bottom up in society would, according to corporatist arguments, take due account of occupational and regional diversities while blocking the levelling and homogenizing tendencies of democracy and socialism. It is not unreasonable to conclude that a properly functioning corporate state might thwart totalitarian forces within a society.[23]

The historical evidence, however, seems to contravene such a conclusion. In the ventures in the corporate organization of society undertaken during the twentieth century in early Nazi Germany, Austria, Italy, Spain, and Portugal, the degree of control over the society exercised by the rulers of the state apparatus and their minions increased greatly. An explanation for this apparent contradiction is not hard to find. Insofar as corporatism in the twentieth century was anything more than an ideology revived to counter Marxian radicalism, its effective functioning depended upon the attainment of some semblance of balance among competing social and economic interests through the creation of many relatively small pockets of self-administration within the society. But such a reconstitution of society would have slowed down the decisionmaking process and would have proved unwieldy in times of economic and political crisis. Without an authoritarian central power, in fact, corporatism would have been only a poor screen covering the fierce and open social struggles in the land. The establishment of corporatism—or, rather, the seizure of power by conservatives bearing the banner of corporatism—thus required the suppression of a significant segment of the population hostile to the new rulers and their ideology. But, without the cooperation of working class elements organized in free corporate bodies, corporatism was an unworkable and even superfluous ideology. Authoritarianism

[23] Both the Nazi specialist on corporatism, Bever (*Ständeideologien*, p. 86), and the dispassionate student of political philosophy, Eugene O. Golob (*The "isms": A History and Evaluation* [New York, 1954], pp. 541 ff.), agree on drawing a distinction between totalitarianism and corporatism.

and totalitarianism (where necessary) proved to be more effective instruments of political order.

As basically a vision of a pre-industrial social harmony, corporatism was ill-adapted to deal with the complexities of modern economic reality. It is difficult to envision a smooth-running corporate communications and distribution system in a society industrialized to any significant degree. Here, too, planning and authority from above proved to be simpler and more predictable modes of economic decisionmaking and control.

As a sociologist and economist Spann was well aware of the tensions between a corporative vision and the modern industrial societies of Europe, with their need of economic efficiency, their rebellious working classes, and their defensive business communities. But, like other social conservatives, Spann shrank back, in theory at least, from drawing the full totalitarian implications of his ideology. He equivocated, wavering between a corporative ideal and totalitarianism. He pictured society as a collectivity (*Ganzheit*) composed of hierarchically ordered subwholes (*Teilganzen*), or estates. The estates that Spann distinguished were, in ascending order, (1) the workers, (2) the craftsmen and representational artists, (3) the economic leaders (who were creative but still enmeshed in the world of the senses), (4) the leaders of the state (headed by warriors and priests), and (5) the Wise (also called the "creative teaching estate").[24]

The exercise of internal and external political power within the Universalist corporate order would devolve upon the political estate, which would have as its functions the leadership of the Folk and the supervision of the other estates.[25] But if, as Spann desired, the best were to be the

[24] *WS*, pp. 227-28. Since Spann and his followers considered the Wise creative geniuses, the Wise were not included in the hierarchy of estates —making the political estate the supreme one in the mundane world. Cf. Walter Heinrich, "Universalismus," *Staatslexikon der Görres-Gesell-schaft* (5th edn., 1932), cols. 543-44.

[25] *Ibid.*, col. 545.

rulers of the moral state-community (*Staatsgemeinschaft*), it is difficult to see how the doctrine of the rule of a political elite within the political estate could be avoided. In the first two editions of his chief work, *Der wahre Staat* (*The True State*), published in 1921 and 1923, Spann resisted drawing the conclusions of his own logic. But by 1931, when the third edition appeared, he was beginning to write of politics in terms of a "state-bearing stratum" (*staatstragenden Schicht*). Ultimately, then, Spann's Universalism entailed that, from a concentration of authority and political power at the top, power and authority would be delegated downward, thereby destroying genuine self-administration on the lower levels and rendering corporate autonomy largely meaningless.

The economic doctrines of Universalism revealed similar ambiguities.[26] Spann carried through his basic distinction between the one and the many in his characterization of the history of economics as the history of the theoretical opposition between Individualism and Universalism. Like most other social conservatives, Spann traced the origins of his economics back to Adam Müller. He also praised Friedrich List and the historical school for working in the right direction.[27]

[26] The delineation separately of Spann's theory of society, political philosophy, and economic thought is necessary for coherent analysis. It must always be kept in mind, however, that Spann sought to formulate a total, organic, and logically closed vision of the activities of men in society. Because of their irrelevance to the issues under consideration in this study, I have refrained from elaborate treatment of Spann's metaphysics, set forth in *Die Kategorienlehre* (Jena, 1924) and in *Der Schöpfungsgang des Geistes: Die Wiederherstellung des Idealismus auf allen Gebieten der Philosophie* (Jena, 1928), his theory of history, formulated in *Geschichtsphilosophie* (Jena, 1932), and his sociology, presented in *Gesellschaftslehre* (Leipzig, 1923). These aspects of Spann's thought are summarized at length in Hausmann, "Othmar Spann und seine Schule," pp. 20-332. Hausmann also offers a coherent roadmap through Spann's economic ideas on pp. 305-21.

[27] Spann, *Tote und lebendige Wissenschaft* (2nd edn., Jena, 1925), p. 91—hereafter cited as *TW*. Spann had early in his career accepted the doctrines of the marginal utility school because of what he con-

In company with Sombart and Salin, Spann rejected the view of economic activities that made them ends-in-themselves. Economics was for him an intermediary activity, a means (*mittelbeschaffendes Handeln*) of creating the necessities of clothing, shelter, and production and consumer goods that were prerequisites for the realization of the spiritual ends existing in a higher realm.[28] He mirrored Sombart and Salin, too, in placing economic institutions lowest on the scale of social values. The economy, in Spann's definition, was the "sum total of things, which serve some end, but which are in themselves without value."[29] Like the Romantics, he refused to view the meeting of buyer and seller at the marketplace as the starting point of economic activity, assuming instead the existence of a prior agreement on goals, a community of values. Not exchange, but rather function (*Leistung*) lay at the foundation of economic life.[30] Explicating this concept, Spann distinguished between a higher leadership function and a subordinate function charged with the execution of policies formulated by the leadership. He defined further a consumption function, encompassing those activities directly involved in the achievement of the final end, a capital function, which included intermediate activities aiding in the performance of consumption functions (such as machinery and tool production), and a capital function "of higher order," comprising the activities of the state in the economy—the maintenance of public order, the conclusion of trade treaties, the construction of arteries of travel and communications, and the like. A final, preliminary function (*Vorleistung*) consisted of the contributions of invention and education to economic activity.[31]

---

sidered its organic view of the interdependence of values. Its tendency in the direction of an atomistic picture of economic behavior, however, soon caused him to reject them. See his *HE*, pp. 240-69; Hausmann, p. 2.

[28] *WS*, p. 75.

[29] Spann, *Fundamente der Volkswirtschaftslehre* (4th end., Jena, 1929), p. 25: ". . . Inbegriff von Dingen die zu etwas dienen, die aber nichts Wertvolles sind."

[30] *Fundamente*, p. 76; *TW*, p. ix.   [31] *Fundamente*, pp. 91-104.

An economy is constructed of various interdependent functions, some higher, some lower, but all essential to the achievement of society's moral ends. In this sense, Spann believed, trade would be better described as a process in which various goods and services are integrated into an economic whole[32] than as one in which buyer and seller meet at the marketplace. In Spann's system it was the relationship of the economic functions to one another that determined the level of prices. Since price expressed organic interconnection and articulation, the price of a commodity, relative to the prices of other goods, mirrored the position of that commodity in the total economic system. Shifts in prices, consequently, reflected both the changes and the direction of the changes in the structure of the economy. If a given price performed its function well—that is, if it correctly mirrored the economic situation of a particular commodity—Spann termed it a "just price."[33] The construction of Spann's theory of prices was rather ingenious. He managed to state it in such a way that it seemed to occupy an intermediate position between the theory of the free-market mechanism of capitalism and the doctrine of the planned economy of socialism. And it could be modified in either direction.

His conception of property also struck the mean between state and private ownership. Private property he accepted with the justification that complete equality in goods was impossible, even within the same estate. Spann advocated that property be viewed as a form of trusteeship, a sort of feudal tenure, an idea consistent with Catholic social teachings on property. Although he suggested restrictions on the completely free use of private property, his writings offered no clear picture of the nature of these restrictions, beyond the vague references to trusteeship. He also allowed for the possibility of property held in common by estates, communities, and the state.[34] Universalism permitted all forms of property ownership short of absolute private property, on the one extreme, and thoroughgoing communism, on the other.

[32] *TW*, p. 17.   [33] *TW*, pp. 68-79.   [34] *WS*, pp. 261-67.

Spann's conceptions of pricing and property did not log-ically exclude an organization of the economy along the lines of the late capitalism of his day. Indeed, like Sombart, he expected the corporate society to develop from the regu-lated capitalism of that era.[35] The emergence of corpo-ratism, Spann averred, would lead to the gradual extinction of capitalism and, more important, to the thwarting of So-cialism and Communism.

Spann rejected the capitalist economy as he had rejected Individualism in politics. Capitalism meant to him "the un-curbed freedom of the economically strong to exploit the economically weak. . . ." Despite the wealth it had con-ferred upon the economy and the contributions it had made to the advancement of productive processes, capital-ism was "in fact . . . a barbaric life form. . . ." It was "the same sanguinary Individualism which had first made its ap-pearance in the Renaissance with poison and dagger."[36] Echoing Sombart and Salin, with whom he shared a strong moral and aesthetic sensibility, Spann criticized capitalism for its spiritual shortcomings. In the Middle Ages the jour-neyman had had a definite place in society; he could, more-over, aspire to be a master craftsman some day. Under capi-talism, in contrast, the worker was uprooted and denied his due place in society (Standlos). Unable to rise in the social hierarchy, he was doomed to spend his life as an "eter-nal worker," a man constantly at the mercy of the vicissi-tudes of an Individualistic economy.[37] In turning to Marx-ism the industrial worker had worsened his predicament, for he had embraced an ideology that was both "untrue" and pernicious.

When Spann denounced Marxism in 1920 in the course of a lecture series, later published as his *Wahrer Staat*, the students of then Red Vienna pelted him with rocks. The experience must have intensified the intellectual antipathy he already felt toward left-wing radicalism. Marx, his venomous attack read, was wrong or superficial and, at any

[35] *WS*, pp. 128-30.
[36] *WS*, p. 126.
[37] *Ibid.*

rate, not at all original. Marx was a vulgar materialist who
had perverted Hegel and thereby abandoned the great tradition of German idealism. Spann withheld the designation
of "genius" from Marx on the ground that a genius was by
nature a metaphysician. The core of Marxian economics,
the theory of surplus value, was completely inadequate, according to Spann, for it neglected the creative role of capital and the contributions of entrepreneurs to the economic
process. Marxism erred in not appreciating the economic
contributions of white-collar staffs of factories, tradesmen,
and all those involved in the economy who did not work at
machines. Marxism was also mistaken in disregarding the
contributions of the state and the state administration,
Spann's "capital of a higher order." Since these nonpro-
letarian elements added their share to the value of a good,
they deserved a portion of its price in return.[38] Spann repudiated any construction which equated the totalistic approach to economic policy of communism with his own Universalism. Under communism, Spann argued, the elements
of the economy were first atomized—not *articulated* in a
truly corporative fashion—and then highly centralized.
Communism was, therefore, really a unique form of the
false doctrine of Individualism.[39]

In concert with Sombart and Salin, Spann discerned a
crisis of Individualism in postwar society. Capitalism was in
the throes of atomistic disintegration. Only the continued
existence of older corporate forms was keeping the unstable regulated capitalism of the day alive.[40] The classic
capitalist ideal of the nineteenth century was being buried
in the plethora of restraints imposed by business monopolies, trade unions, and labor legislation. In creating a degree of economic consolidation unknown in nineteenth-century business, capitalism was implanting in itself the seeds
of corporate organization which were to grow out from it
and destroy it.[41]

In the second edition of the *Wahrer Staat* Spann reck-

---

[38] The critique of Marxism in his *Wahrer Staat* is Spann's most
elaborate formulation; see pp. 141-75, esp. pp. 141-48.

[39] *TW*, pp. 21-22.   [40] *TW*, p. 34.   [41] *WS*, pp. 127-28.

oned with the power of the trade unions by postulating the labor contract arrived at by collective bargaining (*Gesamt-arbeitsvertrag*) as the foundation of the future corporate order. Collective bargaining would force entrepreneurs into trade organizations. The subsequent industry-wide agreement on labor costs would, in effect, make the labor contract the determinant of price levels. Spann expected this system of corporate pricing to eliminate price determination by free-market forces.[42]

There is little need to elaborate on the degree of naïveté Spann displayed in inflating the importance of labor costs for *all* modern industry. One has only to point to examples of industry-wide bargaining (in the American automobile industry, for instance) to refute Spann's claim that such an arrangement would eventually abolish the market mechanism and start the economy on the road to corporatism. It is important to observe that, at the same time as Spann was trying to fit the labor unions into his corporate order, he was exhorting German businessmen to make their trade organizations the basis for the corporative reconstruction of society.[43] Ten years later, in the midst of the depression, as social conflict in both Austria and Germany reached new heights of intensity, he reprinted his 1922 appeal to the business community.[44] Even in 1938, after Hitler had come to power in Germany and Austrians had been living for four years under a new corporate-fascist constitution, Spann continued to call for the creation of the true society; but now he directed his appeals primarily to the large corporations and the cartels.[45] Like Sombart, Spann could not present a completely clear theoretical formulation of the process by which late capitalism was to be transformed into the societal ideal of social conservatism. He named only possible agencies of change and even for these left no instructions on how to proceed.

[42] *WS* (2nd edn., Jena, 1923), pp. 268-70.
[43] "Von Interessenverband zum Berufstand," *Der Arbeitgeber*, XIV (1922), 467.
[44] In his periodical *Ständisches Leben*, II (1932), 72ff.
[45] *Der wahre Staat* (4th edn., Jena, 1938), p. 210.

It is clear that the goal of Spann's corporatism did not
lie in the direction of greater economic efficiency. That was
a capitalist value. What Spann's scheme promised, rather,
were social harmony and sufficient security for the full articulation of the subwholes of the economy. The problems of
the peasantry—low and unsteady prices, low agricultural
wages, and high land values—would all be solved, he believed, if only agriculture were organized "in appropriate
compulsory gild-like organizations."[46]

Similarly, Spann admitted that free trade was economically more efficient than autarky yet opposed it nonetheless on
the ground that, to the degree that the national economy
was involved in international trade, it was subordinate to
the requirements of the world market. Only under autarky,
he contended, was the complete realization of a genuine totality (*Ganzheit*) possible. The benefits accruing to
parts of the economy from extensive international trade
were, in Spann's view, cancelled out by the risks of harm
to the whole that exposure to the dealings of international
financiers and to international market forces presented: extensive international trade might easily lead to an increase
in urban population, to the growth of social uprootedness,
to intensification of the misery of large cities, and to higher
prices. Spann believed that relative economic isolation
would go a long way toward preventing economic crises and
that, even if a crisis did erupt, autarky would permit
a speedy recovery. Left alone, the corporate order could develop freely into its ideal form.[47]

Spann entered the political arena equipped with an elaborate vision of a new society. Highly abstract, it neverthe-

[46] *TW*, pp. 143-44; "Ein ständisches Programm der Agrarreform,"
Schmollers Jahrbuch, L (1925/26), 39-42, esp. 42.

[47] *TW*, pp. 113, 135-39; *HE*, p. 298. In fairness to Spann it must be
emphasized that such conceptions of the relationship between depres-
sions and international trade were widespread in the once classically
orthodox circles of economic thought throughout Western Europe and
the United States, especially after the eruption of the depression of
the 1930s. See, e.g., the data on the decline of international trade
in the interwar period in Shepard Clough and Charles Cole, *Economic
History of Europe* (Boston, 1941), pp. 791 ff.

less spoke to the condition of the Austrian and German middle classes living in societies incapable of sheltering them from a harsh social and economic environment. For all its complexity and polemics, Spann's philosophy of Universalism rarely rose above the level of obscure mundanity. But Spann did not really aim at novelty, as Andree Emery points out in his apt summary of Spann's contribution to social conservative thought:

> There is nothing new in Spann's economics, not even its confusion. But the significance of the trend of thought he typifies can not be underestimated. It is a search for a coordinating principle, something which has the semblance of the new but does not entail radical changes. His is a philosophy which apologizes for the *status quo* in spite of all unfamiliar expressions.[48]

Postwar European society suffered from the lack of a principle of order which would keep the conflicting social forces within it in equilibrium. In Austria and Germany in the late 1920s it became increasingly doubtful whether any kind of dynamic equilibrium within the existing societies could be attained. The gulf separating the left and the right had grown too wide to be bridged peaceably. In recognition of this fact most of the major political groupings of Germany and Austria organized and equipped paramilitary units to continue civil strife by other means. In Germany the Nazis finally imposed their order on society. In Spann's Austria the principle of order came in the form of a corporate constitution promulgated after the Heimwehr (Home Guard), supported by conservative elements of political Catholicism, defeated the socialist Schutzbund (Defense League) in bitter fighting in the streets of Vienna in February 1934.

The political scene in Austria was dominated internally by four major blocs and further influenced by Austria's powerful neighbors to the south and to the north, Italy and

[48] Andree Emery, "The Totalitarian Economics of Othmar Spann," *Journal of Social Philosophy*, I (1936), 276-77.

Germany. Austria's Christian-Social conservatives, German Nationalists, the Heimwehr, and Social Democrats shared an intense preoccupation with the social question. They also all (with the possible exception of the Social Democrats) opposed liberalism, which they accused of having engendered the social disruption of the past century.[49] It was in this context that Spann *packlte* with Christian-Social conservatives, Nationalists, and the Heimwehr, with Italian Fascism and German Nazism.

His influence among the Christian-Social conservatives was great. Because of its extrapolitical source, Catholic social thought could tolerate greater flexibility in its approaches to social questions than other social philosophies based on narrow principles of economic and social interest. Thus, even while some Catholic social philosophers in the twentieth century were advocating improvement of the existing society through piecemeal reforms, others could still work for a fundamental reconstruction in the direction of a society resting on a form of order and harmony akin to that which they claimed had existed in the Middle Ages.[50] The general state of society and the peculiar position of Catholics in a country determined which tendency predominated in Catholic circles at any given time. German Catholic social philosophy seemed to be slowly meeting the challenge of early industrialism when the ideas of radical reconstruction (dominant in the 1870s and the 1880s) championed by writers like Karl von Vogelsang[51] began to be superseded

[49] Peter G.J. Pulzer, *The Rise of Political Anti-Semitism in Germany and Austria* (New York, 1964), p. 135, writes: "By 1914, practically nothing was left of Liberalism in Austria." See further Adam Wandruszka, "Österreichs politische Struktur: Die Entwicklung der Parteien und politischen Bewegungen," in Heinrich Benedikt, ed., *Geschichte der Republik Österreich* (Munich, 1954), p. 293.

[50] Heinz Herberg, "Eine wirtschaftssoziologische Ideengeschichte der neueren Katholischen Soziallehren in Deutschland" (Ph.D. diss., University of Bern, 1933), was the first to distinguish these two trends in social Catholicism; Diamant employs the distinction to good effect in his study (*Austrian Catholics*, p. 16 and *passim*).

[51] "[Vogelsang's] scheme for reform is, in fact, as complete a return as possible to the principles of medieval society." Pulzer, *Political Anti-Semitism*, p. 134.

by programs of piecemeal reform. But by the turn of the century, as the Center Party's role in the Agrar- oder Industriestaat debate and the party's opposition to traditional German political authoritarianism both show, the Catholic faithful still had no clear guide on the path of modernity. Despite this vacillation, however, it is fair to say that German Catholics were making a better peace with the modern world than their Austrian coreligionists. The Center joined with the SPD and the Democratic Party to become early supporters of the Weimar Republic after 1918. But in Catholic Austria neither democratic instincts born of persecution nor the restraint that minority status confers held back the Christian-Socials from projecting better "Christian" societies for the future. They were therefore amenable to the lures of Spann's corporatism.

To be sure, Spann's Universalism placed the state above the church; still, it esteemed religion above political power. Similarly, on the question of marriage, a sensitive one for Catholics, it ranked the state higher than the family; yet it gave marriage precedence over both the state and the family.[52] Catholic conservatives, without insisting on the resolution of these paradoxes, encouraged the diffusion of Spann's ideas in Catholic circles. In an address before the Leo Society, with Cardinal Piffl in attendance, and in articles in Catholic journals Spann argued for an appreciation of his philosophy of Universalism as a continuation of the heritage of the Church.[53] When Karl Pawek wrote a dissertation proving that Universalism was not inconsistent with Catholic scholasticism, it received the approval of the Catholic Institute for Scholastic Philosophy in Innsbruck; Spann himself readily assented to such a reading of his work.[54] The corporatist ideas contained in the 1931

[52] Hausmann, "Othmar Spann und seine Schule," pp. 112-13.

[53] The address was reprinted in the semi-official *Die Leuchte*, 12 Dec. 1928, pp. 13ff.; see also his article "Die politisch-wirtschaftliche Schicksalstunde der deutschen Katholiken," *Schönere Zukunft*, VIII (1932), 821ff.

[54] Karl Pawek, "Spanns Universalismus der Scholastik gegenübergestellt: Das Untersuchungsergebnis einer Innsbrucker Diss.," *Schönere Zukunft*, VIII (1932), 935ff.

Encyclical *Quadragesimo Anno,* together with a growing repudiation of the Austrian Republic and democracy on the part of the Catholics, further served to increase Spann's prestige in the Catholic social conservative camp. The depression revived reconstructive tendencies in social Catholicism and impelled them to a new intensity. Catholic social conservatives saw in the economic crisis the long-sought end of liberalism and capitalism. Consequently, they listened to the philosopher of corporatism with renewed interest.[55]

Whereas Spann worked to convince Catholics that his philosophy was compatible with their faith, his relation to the Heimwehr was of a different kind. Founded after the war as primarily an anti-Marxist defense organization, the Heimwehr had no positive ideology in its first years. Its heterogeneous membership, composed of workers and businessmen, Jews and anti-Semites, friends of *Anschluss* and enemies of *Anschluss,* made agreement on a positive program quite difficult.[56] Spann's influence penetrated Heimwehr circles initially only to the extent that it was received as a viable anti-Marxist ideology. But by 1930, when Heimwehr leaders decided that the overthrow of the Republic was both necessary and possible, the absence of a positive ideology had made itself felt. The leadership began giving voice to projects for corporative reconstruction in support of their claims to political power in Austria. At an important Heimwehr gathering in Korneuburg in Lower Austria in May 1930, Richard Steidle exacted an oath from the men "in the double columns" which read in part:

> We want to renew Austria root and branch. We want the people's state of the Heimwehr. . . . We want to seize the power of the state and to remodel state and economy to

---

[55] Wandruszka, *Geschichte der Republik Österreich,* p. 336. An attempt to compromise between Individualism and socialism in the doctrine of solidarism, developed by the Jesuit student of Adolf Wagner, Heinrich Pesch, came under especially vigorous attack from Spann's school. Solidarism was the chief rival of Universalism in Catholic circles. Spann's analysis reduced it to another unworkable form of Individualism. "In eigener Sache," *Ständisches Leben,* II (1932), 330-33.

[56] Wandruszka, p. 362.

the benefit of the whole people. We reject Western democratic parliamentarianism and the party state. We want to replace it by the self-administration of the estates [Stände] and a strong leadership of the state which will be formed not from representatives of the parties, but from the leading persons of the large estates and from the ablest and best men of our movement. . . .[57]

So pervasive was the influence of Universalism on the Heimwehr's leadership, if not on the rank and file, that Adam Wandruszka termed Spann and his disciple Walter Heinrich the chief ideologists and "intellectual advisors" to the movement.[58]

The union of conservative Catholic corporatists with the Heimwehr in the Fatherland Front produced the overthrow of republican government in Austria. Spann's intellectual influence on the destroyers of Austrian democracy is difficult to overestimate. When the Austrian people "received" its new constitution in 1934, Spann's ideas bore political fruit. The preamble read: "In the name of Almighty God from whom all justice emanates, the Austrian people receives for its Christian, German, Federal State on corporative foundation this Constitution."[59]

Elements of German and Austrian business saw in movements like the Heimwehr and National Socialism a defense against militant Marxism.[60] Spann also *packlte* with the leaders of big business. In an address before the Vereinigung der Deutschen Arbeitsgeberverbände in Cologne in

---

[57] Charles A. Gulick, *Austria from Habsburg to Hitler: Fascism's Subversion of Democracy* (2 vols.; Berkeley, 1948), II, 894-95. See also Steidle's address before the Industriellen-Klub on 6 March 1930, the pertinent passages of which are cited in Wandruszka, pp. 364-65.

[58] Wandruszka, pp. 364-65.

[59] A German text may be found in *Bundesgesetzblatt für die Republik Österreich*, I (1934), No. 239. I have used the translation by Gulick from his illuminating treatment of the document, *Austria from Habsburg to Hitler*, II, 1403-56.

[60] For the Heimwehr and Austrian business, see Wandruszka, *Geschichte der Republik Österreich*, p. 363; on National Socialism and industry, see the concluding chapter of this work.

March 1922 Spann proclaimed the failure of socialism to the assembled magnates. He exhorted them to action. "This moment in history is the right time to act. If, gentlemen, you all do your duty, if you work along, not letting the appropriate moment pass by, we could restore our German Folk once more to health. . . ."[61] He chided German businessmen for thinking in Marxist terms: their acceptance of concepts such as "class struggle" and "surplus value" weakened their position in the struggle with Marxism. He advised entrepreneurs to give up their Individualistic outlook and urged them to embrace instead an organic-Universalistic economic philosophy.[62]

The industrialist Fritz Thyssen was sufficiently impressed by Spann's corporatism (which he learned about from Dr. Klein, who was social welfare secretary of I. G. Farben in Düsseldorf) that, shortly before the NSDAP came to power in 1933, he agreed to head a National Socialist Institute devoted to the study of corporative reconstruction. He also faithfully attended the daily sessions of an experimental Chamber of Corporations which existed for a short time before 1933 in Düsseldorf. He had found corporatism appealing because he believed it would allow the factory owner the requisite freedom to run his business well but "would at the same time avoid excesses."[63]

With the German Nationalists Spann took yet a different tack. He wrote of the "open wound on the German body

[61] "In diesem geschichtlichen Augenblick ist der rechte Zeitpunkt um einzugreifen. Wenn Sie, meine Herren, alle ihre Pflicht tun, wenn Sie mithelfen, diesen rechten Augenblick nicht versäumen, dann können wir unser deutsches Volk wieder gesund machen. . . ." Reprinted as "Die wissenschaftliche Ueberwindung des Marxismus," in *Stahl und Eisen*, XLII (1922), 822.

[62] "Vom Interessenverband zum Berufstand," *Arbeitgeber*, XIV, 467.

[63] Fritz Thyssen, *I Paid Hitler* (New York, 1941), pp. 124-26. One of Spann's disciples, Hans Riehl, was also involved with the Düsseldorf institute and, before that, with the Heimwehr. Hausmann ("Othmar Spann und seine Schule," pp. 385-86) considers his ideas of some importance in the spread of corporatist ideology: "Riehl's corporatist ideas were taken up by German industry to bind Hitler to a program."

politic [*Volkskörper*]," the suffering of millions of Germans under foreign subjugation. "We clearly understand today why Poland, Bohemia, Hungary, Jugoslavia (even Greece) were once German fiefs. They must once more become so [*So muss es wieder kommen*]." He predicted for his eager Nationalist readers a return to the splendor of the old, medieval Empire.[64]

Spann greeted the advent of the Nazis in 1933 as the dawn of that new age. Speaking before the National Fascist Confederation of Commerce at Rome in June 1933, he emphasized the need of the corporate economy, like the corporate state, for "enthusiasm." As Mussolini had aroused the Italian people, so Hitler had kindled the fire of enthusiasm in the German people.[65] Spann was probably the only academic economist who had taken the schemes of the Nazis' economic "expert" Gottfried Feder seriously.[66] Now, in 1933, he fitted the Nazis into his system by seeing in their ranks his "state-bearing stratum." To him they represented the beginnings of a "corporate gild of leaders."[67]

Spann was prepared with advice for the reconstruction of Germany. The political legislature would have to yield its prerogatives in economic legislation to a new House of Economic Estates (*wirtschaftliches Ständehaus*). The ministries would be given new supervisory duties, and the burdensome bureaucracy would be relieved of some of its functions, as well as reduced in size. Outdoing himself in intellectual diplomacy, Spann emphasized the full veto power that the state, as the highest estate, would have over this economic self-administration.[68] The Nazis seemed prepared to listen. Spann was invited to lecture in Berlin and in other

[64] *WS*, pp. 102-4.
[65] Reprinted as "Die Bedeutung des ständischen Gedanken für die Gegenwart," in *Ständisches Leben*, III (1933), 361.
[66] *HE*, pp. 238-39.
[67] Reprinted as "Die Bedeutung des ständischen Gedanken für die Gegenwart," in *Ständisches Leben*, III (1933), 7ff. (He wrote two articles with that title in 1933.)
[68] "Die politische Wendung ist da—Was nun?" *Ständisches Leben*, III (1933), 67-69.

parts of Germany. For a time he was considered for a professorship at Berlin. After the Nazis came to power, one of
Spann's students, Walter Heinrich, took over the direction
of the same institute in Düsseldorf that Thyssen had
headed.[69]

But, as we have seen, corporatism (even Spann's version)
and totalitarianism are incompatible, at least in theory.
Seeking total political authority, the Nazis found the reser-
vations of Spann's corporatism a hindrance. From early interest in corporatism they passed over to strong rejection
of it. Alfred Rosenberg attacked Spann's distinction between Universalism and Individualism for neglecting the
factor of race.[70] Max Frauendorf, who in 1933 ran the Nazi
bureaus for the Labor Front and for Corporative Organizations, criticized Spann for not recognizing sufficiently the
supreme authority of the state and for allowing the estates
too much autonomy. Nor was Frauendorf satisfied with the
reduction of the state to being merely the most important
of the estates.[71] E. H. Vogel labelled Universalism a tool of
reactionary absolutism.[72] Finally, even Dr. Ley, head of
the Labor Front and one of the leading advocates of corporatism in high Nazi circles, publicly took issue with Spann's
corporatist ideology and expressed as well his disapproval
of the workings of the actual systems in Austria and
Italy.[73] The party could not tolerate the slowness with
which a true corporate state operated. Hitler, moreover,
most likely feared that the corporate estates—the Labor
Front, for example—might gain enough independence and

[69] Emery, *Journal of Political Philosophy*, I, 264-65.

[70] *Der Mythos des 20. Jahrhunderts* (12th edn., Munich, 1933), pp.
695ff. Rosenberg, of course, had made this charge as long before as the
first (1930) edition of his book.

[71] J. Roloff, "Der Begriff des Ständestaates," *Ständisches Leben*, IV
(1934), 93.

[72] Roloff, "Misverständnisse über den Universalismus Othmar
Spanns," *Ständisches Leben*, V (1935), 43.

[73] Taylor Cole, "Corporative Organization of the Third Reich,"
Review of Politics, II (1940), 450. The wording of Ley's statement
may be found in the *New York Times*, 2 Jan. 1935, p. 2.

power to serve as viable foci of resistance to party plans and directives.

Probably the most important reason why the corporatist scheme was, in substance, abandoned in Nazi Germany, however, was the strong opposition to it in business circles. Corporatism was taken seriously by the radical elements of the party, and German business saw itself threatened by the possibility of a social revolution going beyond the national revolution. Businessmen also feared that such estates might impose restrictions on their managerial and entrepreneurial prerogatives, not imagining that the Nazis would later impose even greater restrictions upon them. As F. Ermath correctly concluded, "The tenacious resistance of business, particularly big business, to a well-planned gild organization with unlimited powers of control over production and distribution [was] chiefly responsible for the government's abandoning . . . the project to build up a corporative mechanism."[74] By 1940 it was no longer reasonable—if it ever had been—to look for corporate organization within Nazi Germany.[75]

Spann sought to defend himself against his attackers. In a final twist he tried to introduce the missing element of racism into his philosophy, but he could only bring himself to a description of Folkdom (Volkstum) as a "spiritual community . . . bound together by race." He reminded the Nazis of the intensity with which "Marxist and Masonic writers of all kinds and colorations" hated him. He claimed credit for having been one of the precursors of National

[74] F. Ermath, The New Germany (Washington, D.C., 1936), pp. 86-87.

[75] This is also the conclusion of Cole (Review of Politics, II, 461) and, by implication (it is not even mentioned in the index), of David Schoenbaum, Hitler's Social Revolution: Class and Status in Nazi Germany, 1933-1939 (Garden City, N.Y., 1966), e.g., pp. 91ff., 108ff., and passim. Cf. also Wilhelm Rössle, Ständestaat und politischer Staat (Tübingen, 1934), pp. 42-43; Rössle based his explanation of the Nazis' rejection of corporatism on their desire to free the state from the pressures of social and economic interests.

Socialist thought.[76] The Nazis responded by arresting him
when they marched into Vienna in 1938.[77]

Spann was aware of the tension between the essentially
pre-industrial ideal of a corporate society and twentieth-
century industrial society. His philosophy of Universalism
sought to modernize corporatism, but in the process it fell
into the pattern we today call totalitarianism. By obliterating the essential distinction between state and society, by
envisioning no autonomy for the corporate estates, by accepting the forceful imposition of a rule describing itself as
corporatist, and by *packln* with his own principles, Spann
turned the social conservative doctrine of corporatism
into a useful tool for clerical fascist domination in Austria
and for early Nazi rule in Germany.

If Spann had been a mere opportunist, his political gyra-
tions would be of only limited interest. Spann's intellectual
problems, however, to a great extent mirrored other European experiments in corporatism in the 1920s and 1930s.
Where corporatism was advocated by the ruling groups of
social conservatives and fascists, as in Italy, Austria, Germany, Spain, and Portugal, a totalitarian political order resulted. Only in the more industrialized of these countries,
though, did all vestiges of corporatism disappear. Thus in
Portugal and Spain, still primarily agrarian lands, the elimination of all intervening bodies and forces from the gov-
ernors down to the governed was not required. In Austria,

[76] "Leidlicher Austrag unleidlicher Dinge, Eine Erwiderung auf
aberwitzige Angriffe," *Ständisches Leben*, VI (1936), 122-23. He concluded his defense in a spirit typical of social conservatism (p. 125):
"Der Geist echter Erneuerung ist doch dauernd, frischblühend und
doch reif für grosse geschichtliche Aufgaben. Diese Aufgabe liegt im
Gesellschaftlichen . . . , in der Lösung der sozialen Frage; im Geistigen
in der Wiederherstellung des Idealismus, des echten metaphysischen,
gottsuchenden Idealismus, dieser wahrsten urtümlichen Form des
deutschen Geistes, wie er in Wolfram von Eschenbach, in gotischer
Baukunst, in Dürerischer Malerei, in Bachs und in Mozarts und
Beethovens Musik, wie in der deutschen Romantik und der deutschen
klassischen Philosophie unsterblich hervorgetreten ist. Das ist die
deutsche Aufgabe."

[77] Frederick D. Rodeck, "Obituary of Othmar Spann, 1878-1950,"
American Sociological Review, XV (1950), 803.

Italy, and Germany, on the other hand, corporatism gave way to totalitarian control when it became evident to the rulers that corporate organization and industrial society were incompatible.[78] For farmers, artisans, small businessmen, and—to a lesser degree—the white-collar middle classes, the backward-looking ideal of corporatism may have offered some hope of the alleviation of hard economic conditions; but, for Nazi leaders, corporatism proved to be too unwieldy, too outmoded, and too strongly opposed by big business to serve well the function of keeping dissatisfied elements of the population in check while at the same time offering effective machinery for the execution of party policy decisions. Spann's failure was due, ultimately, less to his personal shortcomings as a thinker or tactician than to the inherent weaknesses of social conservatism. Corporatism could not work in an advanced industrial society; or, rather, none of the powerful groups that determined the shape of the society—neither labor nor capital—wanted it to work.

When Spann attacked the Christian Corporate State in Austria for having no foundation of corporate estates, the authorities removed his *Haupttheorien der Volkswirtschaftslehre* from the municipal libraries of Vienna.[79] It is said that, when the Nazis marched into Vienna in 1938, Spann was in the midst of working out his ideas on a Fourth Reich.[80] He had offered the Nazis and the Austrian right an elaborate ideology forged within the social conservative tradition. They had accepted it as long as it proved useful in recruiting members of the middle classes into their ranks, as long as an ideology to counter Marxism was needed, and as long as it did not hinder the achievement and maintenance of political power. They cast corporatism aside, along with Spann himself, when it no longer served any politically useful function.

[78] Cf. Gulick, *Austria from Habsburg to Hitler*, II, 1403ff.; Hughes, *The United States and Italy*, pp. 65-92; and Schweitzer, *Big Business in the Third Reich*, pp. 142-46, 156ff.

[79] Spann, "Unleidlicher Austrag unleidlicher Dinge . . . ," *Ständisches Leben*, VI (1936), 122.

[80] Cole, *Review of Politics*, II, 450-51.

With the discussion of Spann's corporatism the treatment of the high intellectual tradition of social conservatism is completed. We must now turn to an examination of the propagandists and the popularizers of social conservative doctrines. Sombart, Salin, and Spann worked primarily in the environment of the academy. Even Spann considered himself first of all a social philosopher and only secondarily a political activist. With Ernst.Niekisch, Oswald Spengler, and Ferdinand Fried we come to an evaluation of the arguments and activities of intellectuals who counselled immediate political action. These three also spoke in behalf of the middle classes, but to a degree much greater than Sombart, Salin, and Spann they aimed their writings at the problems and at the politics of the new middle classes. Let us first consider the National Bolshevism of Ernst Niekisch, who tried to move the members of the middle classes to the left, and the Prussian Socialism of Oswald Spengler, who sought to push them to the right.

V. The Uses of Social Conservatism

ERNST NIEKISCH CONFRONTS NATIONALISM OSWALD SPENGLER DISCOVERS SOCIALISM

THE PROPONENTS of social conserva-
tism offered it as a middle way between capitalism and socialism. In the 1920s and 1930s adherents of the far right,
and even of the far left, paid tribute to the propaganda
power of social conservatism by borrowing from its rhetoric
and its doctrines. Oswald Spengler, at heart a nineteenth-
century reactionary, and Ernst Niekisch, first and always a
Marxist revolutionary, both framed their exhortations in
the language of social conservatism. Neither man was a true
believer. But both men adorned their own theories with the
trappings of social conservatism, and each was so taken by
the effect that, for a time, he seemed to lose interest in dis-
tinguishing between the substance of his prime outlook and
its ornamentation.

Spengler, of all the theorists and propagandists discussed
in this study, was emotionally and intellectually the most
sympathetic to the prewar Imperial Establishment.
Niekisch, in contrast, looked back to the days of the Empire only with distaste. Yet in the years of the Republic both
men were alike in their preoccupation with reconciling
the divergent ideologies of nationalism and socialism. Spengler worked to save what was salvageable from the prewar
German past and, as a result, arrived at a position very
close to Nazism; Niekisch, as a leftist, sought the overthrow
of bourgeois society and, in consequence, fiercely opposed
Hitler. Yet each in his own way tried to direct what he con-

sidered the vital forces of the nation to the task of freeing
Germany from domestic conflict and from the oppressive obligations imposed by the victorious Western powers.

ERNST NIEKISCH: A SOCIALIST GLORIFIES THE NATION

Up to the outbreak of World War I, the international
solidarity of the working class had been an ideal of the German Socialist movement.[1] When the Socialist members of
the parliaments of Germany, France, and Britain voted
war credits to their governments, the solidarity of the Second International was broken. Nationalism had proved to
be a more powerful force than "an artificial sympathy"
among "the most downtrodden people," to recall the words
of Werner Sombart.[2] The national humiliation of Germany
by the great powers at Versailles forced the SPD to reckon
with nationalist sentiments within its own ranks and among
the middle classes, whom they sought to recruit into their
ranks.[3] Nationalism posed a problem for the Socialists, but
the German Communists proved quite willing to exploit
nationalist sentiments when there was a chance for political
gain from such tactics.

The flirtation of the German Communists with nationalism was quite calculated and opportunistic. It was merely
another strategy for winning over middle class youth and
other segments of the newly politicized middle classes.[4]
Niekisch, however, was probably an exception among leftist

[1] See Max Victor, "Die Stellung der deutschen Sozialdemokratie zu
den Fragen der auswärtigen Politik, 1869-1914," *Archiv für Sozialwissenschaft und Sozialpolitik*, LX (1928), 147-79; also Hermann
Heidegger, *Die deutsche Sozialdemokratie und der nationale Staat,
1870-1920* (Göttingen, 1956).

[2] *Socialism and the Social Movement*, p. 167.

[3] On the small, but vocal, group of democratic nationalists within
the SPD, see Hunt, *German Social Democracy*, pp. 238-40. Kurt
Schumacher, a member of these "Young Turks," was to become the first
leader of the SPD in 1945 after his release from a concentration camp.

[4] Arthur Spencer advances a most unconvincing argument that this
line was more than just a tactic, that it won real acceptance in Communist circles, and that it led to the serious errors in their evaluation
of the political situation in the last days of the Republic. See his
"National Bolshevism," *Survey*, Oct. 1962, pp. 133-53.

radicals. He was a socialist who hoped to effect a genuine reconciliation between the values of nationalism and those of the German left. He wished to organize resistance against both the domestic and the foreign exploiters of the German people.

Three themes may be distinguished in Niekisch's ideology of resistance. He was above all a Marxian socialist. Second, as a result of his disappointment with the outcome of the German Revolution and because of his Eastern orientation in foreign policy, he warmly championed German emulation of, and cooperation with, the Soviet Union. And, finally, shaken by Germany's defeat in the war and the obligations this defeat had placed upon her, he embraced an exceptionally militant form of nationalism. During the years of the Republic these strands became tightly intertwined to form an ideology of national resistance. Perhaps meaningful separately, together they appeared somewhat bizarre. Because it united basically incompatible ideas, Niekisch's ideology of resistance could not bear the heavy strains put upon it in the last days of the Republic. The origins of these weaknesses may be traced directly to the introduction of social conservative elements into his ideology.

Ernst Niekisch was born of working class parents in 1889 in Silesia. He moved with his family to Bavaria, where the outbreak of the war found him teaching in a primary school. In October 1917, when it became obvious to him that Germany would lose the war and when he learned of the revolutionary ferment in Russia, he joined the SPD. At the outbreak of the Bavarian Revolution in November 1918 he was elected head of the Augsburg Soldiers' and Workers' Council. First as a delegate to Munich and then as head of the Bavarian Soldiers' and Workers' Council he engaged actively in furthering the Revolution in Bavaria, but now as a member of the more radical USPD (Independent Social Democratic Party of Germany). Niekisch, however, shrank back from active participation in the proclamation of an independent Republic of Bavaria, in an early instance of his opposition to particularism and national fragmentation, and was replaced in office by the young playwright Ernst Toller. Niekisch's participation in the Revolution nonetheless earned him a two-year prison term (1919-1921) after its suppression. Following his release from prison Niekisch returned to the SPD. He entered the bureaucracy of the Textile Workers Union in 1922 as director of its youth program. From 1923 to 1926 he served as secretary of the union.[5]

Prior to 1926 Niekisch's career bore no marked traces of action or thought that would distinguish him from the vast majority of contemporary socialist politicians and trade union officials. To be sure, the dynamism of the Russian Revolution and the lack of radicalism in the SPD made him critical of his party; nevertheless, he remained within its ranks.[6] By 1926, however, he had so aroused the ire of the party leadership with his nationalist agitation to arouse a "revolutionary people" to resist "proletarianization by Western capitalism" that he was expelled. These twin concepts were to become the signature of Niekisch's ideology of resistance. They also lay at the core of his broader propaganda for a National Bolshevism.

In 1919 the conservative academician Professor Paul Eltzbacher had published a desperate pamphlet in which bolshevism was held up as a fate infinitely more desirable for Germany than Western enslavement.[7] An Eastern orientation in foreign policy had been the dream and goal of many North German conservatives since the nineteenth century. The enmity of the Allies for the new government of Lenin was skillfully, if unsuccessfully, exploited by patriots like Count Brockdorff-Rantzau, the German representative at Versailles. He viewed Soviet Russia as another

[5] For biographical data on Niekisch, I have drawn primarily from his autobiography, *Gewagtes Leben: Begegnungen und Begebnisse* (Cologne, 1958) , pp. 11-169. I have also used information elicited by Otto-Ernst Schüddekopf in extensive correspondence with Niekisch and his associates of the Republican era. *Linke Leute von Rechts: Die nationalrevolutionären Minderheiten und der Kommunismus in der Weimarer Republik* (Stuttgart, 1960) , p. 510, n. 1—hereafter cited as *LLR*.

[6] Niekisch, "Republikanisches Hoffen," *Der Firn*, VI (1924) , 4-6.

[7] *Der Bolschewismus und die deutsche Zukunft* (Jena, 1919) .

outsider nation with whom Germany might cooperate to regain her lost diplomatic leverage; at the same time, he recognized that the *threat* of Russo-German amity might produce milder peace terms for his defeated country.[8] The German military also saw advantages in keeping the line to Moscow open, if the visits in 1919 of Admiral Hintze and Colonel Bauer to the cell of the imprisoned Soviet representative, Karl Radek, may be accepted as evidence.[9]

On the left, two dissident Communists, Heinrich Laufenberg and Fritz Wolfheim, issued in November 1919 a National Communist manifesto advocating a "revolutionary party truce." They demanded a German Red army led by members of the old military caste whose nationalist hatred of the Versailles powers would link them to their proletarian soldiers. The soldiers, for their part, would be motivated by anti-capitalist sentiments to create a united people, which would be supported by Soviet Russia in its conflict with the West. The domestic class struggle would yield to a revolutionary foreign policy. Communist leaders in Germany condemned the Hamburg deviation, while Lenin characterized the doctrine of National Communism as a kind of "childhood disease" of Marxism.[10] But the deviation of 1920 became the new party line in the midst of the Ruhr crisis of 1923. The KPD now decided to try to exploit the aroused nationalism of all elements of the population in order to gain new adherents. The conservative nationalist Count Ernst von Reventlow was asked to contribute an article to *Rote Fahne*, the party organ. The Communists competed with the Nazis in honoring Albert Leo Schlageter, the nationalist who had been shot as a saboteur by the French invaders.[11]

[8] See his *Dokumente und Gedanken um Versailles* (2nd edn., Berlin, 1922), pp. 54ff., 82-87.

[9] E. H. Carr, "Radek's 'Political Salon' in Berlin, 1919," *Soviet Studies*, III (1951/52), 411-20.

[10] Karl Radek and August Thalheimer, *Gegen den Nationalbolschewismus* (Leipzig, 1920); Lenin, *Der Radikalismus, die Kinderkrankheit des Kommunismus* (Leipzig, 1920).

[11] The new Schlageter Line took its name from the eulogistic speech entitled "Albert Leo Schlageter, der Wanderer ins Nichts"

The intensity of French animosity and the weakness of Germany five years after the end of the war shocked Niekisch. He felt himself compelled to reevaluate his political principles. He was not yet ready to go against the policy of the SPD by publicly denouncing the Dawes Plan and German entrance into the League of Nations. And the founding of an organ for a policy of revolutionary resistance was still two years off. But he would not accept Germany's manifest impotence meekly; nor did he believe other Germans should. "Germans would betray their future," he wrote in 1924, "if they stopped being a revolutionary people, [a people] which works for the overthrow of contemporary international power relations with a burning passion and a tenacious will."[12]

The negotiation of the Locarno Pacts in 1925 seemed to mark a new era of conciliation in Europe. The fruit of Gustav Stresemann's "policy of fulfillment" of German obligations under the Treaty of Versailles, the Locarno Pacts were a series of regional nonaggression and arbitration agreements signed by Germany, France, Britain, and Italy. Stresemann reiterated German acceptance of the territorial settlement in Western Europe as laid down at Versailles in exchange for the Allies' promise of an early withdrawal of the troops occupying the Rhineland. The happy conclusion of the negotiations elicited statements from the patriotic German foreign minister on the reality of a supranational "European idea."[13] It was at this moment of restoration of

---

given by Karl Radek, its chief advocate in the Communist International, before the Executive Committee of the International meeting in Moscow on 20 June 1923. Reprinted in the *Internationale-Presse-Korrespondenz*, 21 June 1923, p. 869.

[12] *Der Firn*, VI (30 Aug. 1924), cited by Schüddekopf, *LLR*, p. 355. His two pamphlets of the same year may be described as more exploratory than exhortatory; see *Grundfragen deutscher Aussenpolitik* (Berlin, 1924), and *Der Weg der deutschen Arbeiterschaft zum Staat* (Berlin, 1924).

[13] British indifference to the security of the lands to the east of Germany (the British made no commitments involving the Eastern successor states) made Locarno an inadequate solution to the problems of European security. This inadequacy was clearly evidenced when

international stability that Niekisch chose to speak out forcefully.

Since the end of 1924 Niekisch had worked closely with the Young Socialists assembled in the Hofgeismar circle. The men of Hofgeismar had dedicated themselves to the work of breaking down the intellectual barriers separating socialism and nationalism. The very moderate 1925 Heidelberg Program of the SPD drew the criticism of these Young Socialists. They despaired of the party; they were especially disappointed by the lack of the kind of firm commitment to national values they claimed to find in the Erfurt Program of 1891.[14] Niekisch's position was becoming awkward. His maverick nationalism was embarrassing to the party. His contacts with Count Reventlow also hurt his prestige. His insistence on the formation of a right-wing coalition government in Red Saxony to include the SPD, the DDP, the DVP, and the DNVP led, finally, to his expulsion in 1926.[15] At the same time, the national leadership of the Young Socialists effected his expulsion from the youth group, and then the party disbanded the organization.

In January 1926, writing in the last circular letter of the Hofgeismar circle, Niekisch launched his attack on the philosophy and the politics of the Locarno era. He castigated the German negotiation of the Locarno Pacts as a betrayal of the East, of Russia. European stability could not but redound to Germany's disadvantage. Only by keeping European politics unstable and complicated could Germany hope to find room for maneuvering, for bringing about a restoration of her great power status.[16] Rather than interpret Locarno as a German diplomatic coup, Niekisch preferred to view it as a crime against the German people.

Germany, under Hitler, broke out in the East, as Hajo Holborn has pointed out in his *Political Collapse of Europe* (New York, 1957), pp. 124-37.

[14] On the Young Socialists, see Bruno Neumann, "Wandlungen des Jungsozialismus," *Die Gesellschaft*, III (1926), 514-20.

[15] For the particulars of the Saxon conflict, see Hunt, *German Social Democracy*, pp. 210-21.

[16] Schüddekopf, *LLR*, pp. 170-75.

Two years later he continued his war on Locarno. By voluntarily recognizing the Versailles settlement and giving up German claims to Alsace-Lorraine and Eupen-Malmedy, Stresemann had, in Niekisch's opinion, more firmly enchained Germany; he had bartered off Germany's vital interests for the friendship of Germany's Western oppressors.[17]

No longer having any publication or group to propagate his idea of radical national resistance to the Versailles powers, Niekisch founded his own periodical in July 1926. He called it *Widerstand: Blätter für sozialistische und nationalrevolutionäre Politik (Resistance: Pages for Socialist and National Revolutionary Politics)*. Niekisch hoped to assemble a group of readers who might make up the core of what he termed "the national opposition." He stated the basic premise of his theory quite succinctly: "Either the German people acts [*ist*] as a revolutionary people, or it will be suffocated in the swamp, and eliminated from the ranks of the free peoples."[18] Niekisch's task, as he saw it, was to bring about the liberation of the German worker by *first* liberating his homeland—"liberation from social oppression, which is impossible without emancipation from national slavery."[19]

By 1926 Niekisch found himself politically isolated. He had been purged from the SPD for his first hesitant nationalist writings and contacts, and yet he had not gained the satisfaction of seeing his nationalist activities bear fruit. By means of his periodical, *Widerstand*, he hoped to organize the elite of the "national minority." He first experimented with the idea of forging an alliance of nationalists (*Völkische*) and Communists to agitate for national liberation. Was not bolshevism Russia's rejection of the West? And

---

[17] "Sammlung zum Widerstand," *Widerstand*, III (1928), 162.

[18] *Gedanken über deutsche Politik* (Dresden, 1929), p. 249—hereafter cited as *Gedanken*.

[19] "Befreiung," in the "Zeitschau," *Widerstand*, I (1926), 40. Although this portion of the magazine was unsigned, Niekisch claimed in correspondence with Hans Buchheim to have written the "Zeitschau" in most issues; see Hans Buchheim's article "Ernst Niekischs Ideologie des Widerstands," *Vierteljahrshefte für Zeitgeschichte*, V (1957), 334-61.

was that not the meaning of Mussolini's domestic and foreign policy? Both fascism and bolshevism, he argued, were social and yet national—the difference being merely that bolshevism had started with the social issue and only subsequently arrived at a true valuation of the nation, while fascism had followed the reverse order.[20] In the same year Niekisch prevailed upon the nationalist Count Reventlow to write his view on "the Workers and the Future of Germany," in a column headed "From the Other Camp." Reventlow proved sympathetic to liberal reforms for the German worker.[21]

Niekisch's dissent produced no political consequences in the relatively quiet years of 1926 and 1927. In the summer of 1928 he left Dresden to expand his activities. He decided to found a Resistance Press and to continue the publication of his periodical from Berlin.[22] In Berlin Niekisch's organization of the "national minority" took on its greatest scope. He elaborated his ideology of resistance at length in the pages of *Widerstand* and in several books written between 1929 and 1930. To his gratification his ideas began to meet with acceptance in nationalist circles.

Niekisch's thinking on national liberation was conditioned, in the first instance, by his socialism. When the French and Belgians marched into the Ruhr, the Germans put up a spirited passive resistance which completed the destruction of their finances. Niekisch accused the Cuno government of being a tool of big business: instead of making the large industrialists pay the costs of the resistance, the government had allowed the burden to fall on those who could least afford the expense. "The plundered Mittelstand,

[20] "Russland, Italien, Deutschland," *Widerstand*, I (1926), 53-58.

[21] Graf Ernst von Reventlow, "Die Arbeiterschaft und die Zukunft Deutschlands," *Widerstand*, I (1926), 58-60. Starting as a member of the Pan-German League, Reventlow turned to propagating a Germanic Christianity by the late 1920s. He ended as a Nazi.

[22] In Dresden he had sought in vain since 1926 to win over the Saxon Old Socialist Party, a right-wing splinter party of the SPD, to his nationalistic ideas. Lack of success probably prompted his resignation from that party in 1928 and his removal to the more fertile climate of Berlin. Cf. Schüddekopf, *LLR*, p. 511.

the betrayed working class—at the end they were the ones who alone had to bear the burdens of the resistance. The great industrialists and the bourgeoisie of finance capital made money and revealed not a trace of civic responsibility [*Staatsbürgersinn*]."[23]

The Treaty of Versailles, reparations, the Ruhr invasion, the Dawes and the Young Plans were all, in Niekisch's eyes, evidence of national enslavement. The principle by means of which Germany's enemies held her in subjugation was the Western and cosmopolitan concept of private property. The Dawes Plan's conversion of the political debt of reparations into a commercial debt outraged Niekisch's national pride, for it placed every single German in the position of a debtor to the recipients of German reparations. German *unwillingness* to pay thus took on the appearance of sharp business practice, the breach of a commercial contract. The German people were not a bourgeois people. Germany was, in the phrase of Moeller van den Bruck, a "proletarian nation." If Germans would only reject the un-German idolatry of unrestricted private property, Niekisch argued, they would strike a crucial blow in the cause of their own domestic and international liberation. To deny the sanctity of private property, in Niekisch's synthesis, was to deny at the same time capitalism and the Versailles order.[24]

To this end the German worker had to become a "soldier of the state." He had to display those great Prussian virtues of obedience, discipline, self-subordination, loyalty, and willingness to serve and to sacrifice.[25] As will be seen, it is difficult to distinguish this aspect of Niekisch's "proletarian nationalism" from Spengler's Prussian Socialism—except that such ideas are less jarring coming from the pen of a conservative nationalist than from that of a revolutionary socialist.

Niekisch's attempt to provide a historical justification for his proletarian nationalism required an attack on the cosmo-

---

[23] *Gedanken*, pp. 108-10.

[24] "Privateigentum als Tributfessel," *Widerstand*, V (1930), 260-63; *Politik des deutschen Widerstandes* (Berlin [1932?]), pp. 13-15—hereafter cited as *PW*.

[25] *Gedanken*, p. 293.

politanism of both Marxian socialism and liberalism. Such
foreign ideas as "humanity" and "internationalism" were
embraced by Germans, he thought, only because of his
countrymen's lack of "Germanness." As a socialist he asked
in whose interest such ideas were promoted; and he concluded that they served only his nation's Western oppressors.[26] To justify his position, Niekisch had to convince
his socialist and nationalist readers that socialists of importance in the past had not been hostile to national values and
that the state was not a committee of the bourgeoisie to administer its common affairs—to paraphrase Marx—but
rather a politically neutral and necessary structure.

On the first point he adduced Ferdinand Lassalle as a
true "national socialist." Lassalle, according to Niekisch,
had striven to put the workers at the vanguard of the movement for national unification with the aim of gaining for
them the leadership of the new state. How different,
Niekisch asked rhetorically, would the development of
socialism have been had the Lassallean course borne fruit?[27]

Niekisch invoked Bismarck for the benefit of the nationalists. He argued that Bismarck had led Germans to renounce
the liberal "night-watchman state." Bismarck had created a
"pure state," that is, one above class interests. He had removed questions of foreign policy from domestic interfer-
ence. Niekisch applauded the Machiavellism he ascribed to
the founder of the German Empire. Ethical limitations
should not be allowed to bind the foreign policy of a nation, for the sole aims of German foreign policy, Niekisch
believed, should be the connected goals of military security
and national freedom.[28] These foreign policy goals could
not, in his opinion, be implemented as long as Germany
was limited in her sovereignty by her subjugation to the

---

[26] *Politik und Idee* (Dresden, 1929), pp. 64-65, 74.

[27] *Gedanken*, pp. 182-83. Niekisch claimed to hear the echo of the
great Fichte in Lassalle's "national socialism."

[28] *Gedanken*, pp. 164-65, 169; *Politik und Idee*, p. 52. The latter work
especially was larded with allusions to, and expressions of, admiration
for Machiavelli. His *Widerstand* Press published the writings of
Machiavelli.

Treaty of Versailles and as long as she bound herself to membership in the League of Nations.[29] "The German nationalist," thundered Niekisch, "that is the German who would rather smash the whole world to pieces rather than be guilty of an act of disloyalty to his own German self."[30]

It would take a certain kind of national ethos for Germany to achieve her foreign policy goal of liberation. "The German will achieve the power state [*Machtstaat*] only if he acts like a 'Prussian,'" Niekisch asserted.[31] But Germans had lost their Prussian qualities. The Weimar Republic stood only for the idea of—J. P. Morgan.[32] Niekisch contrasted the "idea of Potsdam" to the features of Western politics and society which he, like Spengler and Sombart before him, blamed for Germany's predicament. Germany would have to give up her Carolingian roots, her Western features, and once again embrace the idea of dominion that had originated in the Prussian experience. "The realization of the idea of Potsdam is . . . the total state, within which the economy, the society, and the culture take the place which the state, taking into account its life-needs, assigns them."[33]

Niekisch used the theme of Potsdam versus the West as the bridge to his third major thesis: "In her gravest moment of danger Russia seized on the idea of Potsdam, elevated it to its greatest height . . . , and created that absolute warrior state, which forces even the features of everyday life under the rule of the field camp, whose citizen knows how to hunger, and when he has to fight. . . ."[34] By becoming Prussian once again Germany, in alliance with Soviet Russia, could free herself from domestic and international slavery.

As we have seen, this idea was not a new one. The form and persuasive powers Niekisch imparted to it, however, gave it a new intensity. Had the Germans taken the oppor-

[29] *Gedanken*, pp. 137-41, 155.
[30] *PW*, p. 20.
[31] "Entpreussung," *Widerstand*, IV (1929), 106-7.
[32] *Ibid.*
[33] *PW*, pp. 5-6.
[34] *PW*, p. 7.

tunity at Brest-Litovsk of making Russia their ally instead of imposing such draconian peace terms, he continued, both nations could have made common front against the English.[35] Niekisch was no crypto-Communist working to hook unwary Germans on the Schlageter Line. His conception of Russian Communism belies that interpretation, for he saw Russia as a peasant state in which Communist thought played but a small role. It was rather, he argued, a rhetoric used to win over the Russian masses to a sense of national loyalty. It was merely the form in which Russian nationalism clothed itself. What appealed to Niekisch in Communism was its "intransigent anti-Roman, anti-European fanaticism." Such fanaticism, if matched by that of eighty million Germans, could tear the Versailles order to shreds.[36]

It was with this potpourri of ideas that Niekisch tried to recruit a resistance movement in Germany. He claimed to see men of the right sort in all political camps, but especially among the nationalists of the Bünde, the National Socialists, and the Communists.[37] In his path, however, stood the stubborn facts that he had been expelled from the SPD and that the Communists treated him at best as a sympathetic outsider. His only recourse in his search for a following was to turn to the various nationalist groups. To woo them he proved willing to move in their direction. He opened the pages of *Widerstand* to racist nationalists like Reventlow and to Ernst Jünger, their intellectual gadfly.[38] Niekisch composed an extremely laudatory appreciation of President Paul von Hindenburg on the occasion of his eightieth birthday. The old soldier, he wrote, embodied the best traits of the German people.[39] Niekisch even went a

---

[35] *Gedanken*, pp. 47-48.

[36] *Ibid.*, p. 240; *PW*, p. 23.

[37] *Gedanken*, p. 370.

[38] See Jünger's article "Revolution um Marx," *Widerstand*, IV (1929), 144-46, in which he advanced the thesis that a strong state could not exist unless work was meaningful to the worker, that the social and national dimensions implied one another. For a more elaborate, but no less murky, development of this thesis, see his *Der Arbeiter: Herrschaft und Gestalt* (Hamburg, 1931).

[39] "Zeitschau," *Widerstand*, II (1927), 102.

long way toward condoning the assassinations by enraged
nationalists of the Catholic trade unionist and leader of
the Center Party, Mathias Erzberger, and of the liberal head
of the AEG, Walter Rathenau, on the grounds that the former represented the Roman, that is, Western element so
dangerous to Germany and the latter the "Shylock grip of
international finance capital."[40]

Niekisch's literary and organizational efforts finally bore
fruit in the spring of 1928 when he gained the following
of a wing of the Bund Oberland, the action group which had
helped overthrow the Bavarian Soviet Republic and had
taken part in the Hitler Putsch of November 1923. Between 1921 and 1925 the Bund Oberland had suffered a
series of splits and changes in political orientation. When it
was reconstituted in 1925, a wing under the leadership of Dr.
Österreicher and Beppo Römer refused to cooperate any
further with the National Socialists, turning instead to National Bolshevism.[41] Niekisch attended the annual Easter
meeting of the Bund in that year. He continued to court
the Oberlanders for the next three years. By November
1928 the leaders of the Bund were ready to drop their
newly started periodical, Der Führer, and adopt Niekisch's
Widerstand as the organ of the Oberlanders. Several of the
members of the Bund joined the editorial board of
Widerstand.[42] Soon afterward, in 1929, Niekisch organized
a Kameradschaft des Dritten Reiches, made up of members
from the Bünde Oberland and Wehrwolf, Saxon Old Socialists, and the Jungdeutsche Orden. This organization soon fell
apart, and Niekisch turned back to the Widerstand circle
as his main arena. The total membership of his circle probably never exceeded four thousand, and the active member-

[40] Gedanken, pp. 100-101.

[41] Schüddekopf, LLR, p. 366. On the action leagues of the Republican
era, see Ernst H. Posse, Die politischen Kampfbünde Deutschlands (2nd
edn., Berlin, 1931). and the excellent work by Robert G.L. Waite, Vanguard of Nazism: The Free Corps Movement in Postwar Germany,
1918-1923 (Cambridge, Mass., 1952).

[42] This faction reconstituted itself again in 1931 as the Oberlander-
kameradschaft des Widerstandskreis. Schüddekopf, LLR, p. 367.

ship could not have been an eighth of the total.[43] The circle met annually between 1930 and 1932, but there is no evidence that its activities went beyond reading *Widerstand* and putting on such meetings.

Niekisch actively circulated among right-wing groups in the hope of gaining a hearing. He once spoke before the Herrenklub, but his presentation of bolshevism as the way of independence for the Russian people and his call for social revolution in Germany were not well received. The important conservative intellectual Heinrich von Gleichen stormed out in anger.[44] Niekisch seemed to have somewhat better success with the officer corps of the Reichswehr, some of whom apparently read *Widerstand*. His speech attacking the Western orientation of German foreign policy evoked a mildly favorable response from his audience at the infantry school in Dresden in 1928. On the appearance of his *Gedanken über deutsche Politik* General Seeckt wrote him to express concurrence with his foreign policy proposals regarding the need for an Eastern orientation.[45]

Niekisch also involved himself in the cause of the radicalized peasants of Schleswig-Holstein. He arranged a conference of representatives of Otto Strasser, the Communists, and other national revolutionary groups in the hope of gaining support for the candidacy of Claus Heim, the peasant leader, in the 1932 presidential elections. If Heim ran, it would take the peasant vote away from Hitler. Niekisch received no support, and in the end he dropped the idea himself. Hitler won most of the Schleswig-Holstein peasant vote.[46]

[43] Niekisch, *Gewagtes Leben*, pp. 160-64; Schüddekopf, *LLR*, p. 368; Buchheim, *Vierteljahrshefte für Zeitgeschichte*, V, 337.

[44] *Gewagtes Leben*, p. 133.

[45] *Ibid.*, pp. 170-71. Niekisch claims that from the 1928 speech onward he maintained unbroken contact with members of the Reichswehr.

[46] *Ibid.*, p. 169. Even Niekisch was caught up in the peasant romanticism of social conservative writers. See "Bauer und Bürger," *Widerstand*, V (1930), 293-95, wherein he offered the judgment that "Rootedness to the sod is the womb of heroic bearing [*Die Schollgebundenheit ist der Mutterschoss heroischer Haltung*] . . . ," and *Gedanken*, pp. 275-77. See also the excellent study by Rudolf Heberle of the conversion

Niekisch was primarily an organizer and activist; but he was least successful in just these respects. He felt that political programs were less important than "spiritual bearing." Italian Fascism served him as an example of a movement which had started only with a will to national greatness.[47] As an activist who employed ideology more as a tactic than as a program he was slow in recognizing spirits fundamentally antagonistic to his. As late as 1929 he expressed his disappointment with the Nazis for not having given up their southern (that is, Italian and Bavarian) roots. He warned them that only from northeast Germany, from Prussia, could the ethos of national resistance to the foreign enemy come.[48] By early 1932 he had come out strongly against Hitler, but still for social conservative reasons. In his eyes, Hitler was too southern, too Catholic. "Wherever National Socialism enters," he wrote, "Prussia and Protestantism lose."[49] Slowly in that year Niekisch's ideology of resistance changed. He began to focus on resistance to Hitler and Nazism. He began, also, to attack Hitler for socialist reasons; the National Bolshevism of the years 1926-1931 slipped into the background. Now he charged Hitler with being "the last hope of the bourgeois world in Germany."[50] He continued to attack the Nazis in the pages

of these farmers to Nazism, *Landbevölkerung und Nationalsozialismus,* esp. pp. 130-33, and the account of the Schleswig-Holstein peasant movement in fictionalized form in Ernst von Salomon's *Die Stadt* (Berlin, 1932).

[47] *Gedanken,* pp. 355-56. Nevertheless, the *Widerstand* movement did profess an elaborate program, published in the early 1930s in a pamphlet entitled *Politik des deutschen Widerstandes,* pp. 25-28. Here stated in the form of a manifesto was the demand for a national policy oriented toward the "primitive East," withdrawal from the world economy, movement of the urban population into the underpopulated and undervalued countryside, authoritarianism and militarism, rejection of capitalism and the concept of private property, and the pursuit of social and economic policies that would lead to the restoration of the primacy of the state.

[48] "Der deutsche Nationalsozialismus," *Widerstand,* IV (1929), 135.

[49] "Vom deutschen Protest zum Faschismus," *Widerstand,* VII (1932), 15, 23.

[50] "Der grossen Worte nackten Sinn," *Widerstand,* VII (1932), 43-

of *Widerstand* and his new periodical, *Entscheidung*, until the Nazis suppressed them both.[51]

When Kurt Sontheimer characterized Niekisch as a "romanticist of revolution" in his review of Schüddekopf's book in the *Frankfurter Allgemeine Zeitung*, Niekisch replied in a letter to the paper. He admitted having opposed the Weimar Republic but denied that such opposition had aided Hitler's accession to power. He blamed the rise of Hitler on the politics of the Republic.[52]

Niekisch's defense was probably valid; Hitler's way to power was paved for him by the failures of the Weimar Republic. The most extreme charge which may be levelled against Niekisch is that he tried opportunistically to capitalize on existing discontent. But his failure lay precisely in his inability to move men to action. It may be true that the social conservative ideas which he *used*, and perhaps half believed, undermined confidence in democratic values; still, Niekisch was little more than a drummer boy in the war on the Weimar Republic. It is also true that his intentions were much grander than his accomplishments. In his autobiography he claims that his ideology of resistance was primarily a tactic for drawing middle class nationalists to the left.[53] This statement is puzzling.

Newly radicalized middle class Germans who admired the toughness and resoluteness of Communists could join the Communist Party. Nationalists with a social conscience could find like-minded comrades in the ranks of the Nazis.

---

44. He also wrote a book attacking Hitler entitled *Hitler—Ein deutsches Verhängnis* (Berlin, 1932), with excellent drawings by A. Paul Weber.

[51] *Entscheidung* was started on 9 October 1932 and suppressed by order of the Police President of Berlin on 30 November 1933, never to reappear. Niekisch was arrested in 1937. He was released at the end of the war, frail and nearly blind. He lectured at Humboldt University in East Berlin for a time and then retired to his home in the western half of the city, where he lived until his death on 23 May 1967.

[52] Niekisch's letter appeared in the letters-to-the-editor column of the *Frankfurter Allgemeine Zeitung*, 26 May 1961, p. 9.

[53] *Gewagtes Leben*, pp. 137, 146.

Those to whom the idea of Potsdam appealed were probably those least willing to embrace any of the essential features of Communism. Niekisch, unlike the Nazis and the Communists, repudiated party politics. How, then, did he propose to build a movement having a significant social base? The last annual meeting of the *Widerstand* circle attracted two hundred participants—and these only to hear speeches. Socialism, Potsdam, and Moscow constituted a trinity of faith for which neither the German worker nor the member of the Mittelstand longed.

The major premise of Niekisch's National Bolshevism was the equation of a class with a nation. Niekisch drew two fundamental insights from the revolutionary first days of the Republic. He decided that the German worker alone would not, or could not, fight for the creation of a socialist Germany. Moreover, his experience with the suppression of the Bavarian Republic taught him that a secessionist, anti-national brand of socialism was bound to fail. Germany was surrounded by the victorious capitalist powers of the West and their vassals; winning and preserving socialism in Germany had to be a national effort, or the movement was doomed. Niekisch hit upon a formula which identified the domestic oppression of German workers with the capitalism of the Entente powers. In this new light all of the German people could be considered wage-slaves of those who kept them in chains through the Treaty of Versailles and reparations payments. Conversely, all Germans had the obligation to struggle for national liberation as a means of overcoming the internal oppressors. The needs of the state and those of the working class, Niekisch concluded, were identical.

In large measure a ploy, but like many ploys half believed by its user, the ideology of resistance failed to lure many nationalistic members of the Mittelstand to the left. Although nationalism was important in the value system of the Mittelstand, it was not, as Niekisch learned, the prime value.

OSWALD SPENGLER: A NATIONALIST HAILS SOCIALISM

The Bavarian Revolution also taught Oswald Spengler a lesson about the relationship of the working class to the nation: it brought home to him how alienated from conservative national traditions many Germans were. Like Niekisch, he decided to clarify the true meaning of socialism for the benefit of his middle class readers. He was in Munich when the Free Corps from the North marched in to crush the Bavarian Soviet Republic. Socialism had been defeated in Bavaria, he saw; but he knew that Socialist ministers in Berlin still determined the fate of Germany. Would they rule as Socialists or as Germans? What would become of the great traditions of the defeated German Empire?

Five years before, in 1915, the disenchanted Werner Sombart had castigated the German Social Democrats for their ideological treason. Although Spengler's *Preussentum und Sozialismus (Prussianism and Socialism)* [54] was strongly reminiscent of *Händler und Helden*, the tone, of necessity, was more conciliatory. True, in Spengler's book the reader found the same contrast between English and German values, the same identification of commerce with England and of militarism with Prussia, and the same emphasis on the tensions between English-style parliamentary liberalism and Prussian *Gemeinschaft*. But, whereas Sombart had read the Social Democrats out of the German tradition, Spengler sought to integrate them into it. The workers now had a stake in the nation, he reasoned. They now had to take their places in the ranks of its defenders. Spengler, at least, was prepared to welcome them, for he argued that "the old Prussian spirit and the Socialist persuasion, which today hate each other with the hatred of brothers, are one and the same." [55]

Spengler first gained wide recognition in Germany when his *Decline of the West* appeared in July 1918. [56] Its publi-

[54] *Preussentum und Sozialismus* (Munich, 1920) —hereafter cited as *PS*.

[55] *Ibid.*, p. 4.

[56] *Der Untergang des Abendlandes: Umrisse einer Morphologie der Weltgeschichte*, I: *Gestalt und Wirklichkeit* (Munich, 1920), II:

cation coincided with Germany's defeat at the hands of her sister nations to the west. The *Decline* was about the fall of a civilization of which both Germany and her conquerors were a part. Many Germans could find spiritual comfort in Spengler's prediction that Britain, France, and the United States were as surely doomed as Germany seemed then to be.[57] The *Decline* was one of the longest and most obscure books to find favor with the reading public in postwar Germany. The public controversy it aroused was unprecedented for a book of its kind.[58] In a time of defeat, revolution, and economic dislocation Spengler proffered resolute, even oracular, answers.

The *Decline* offered German readers a diagram of the anatomy of world history. The metaphor Spengler used to explain the great changes in the life history of a culture or civilization was drawn from biology. The ages of a society were, in his morphology of world history, the same as the ages of man. The last of the great historical civilizations, that of the West (which he termed Faustian Civilization), was now in its old age.[59] Spengler assured his readers that

---

Welthistorische Perspektiven (Munich, 1922). All references are to the English translation by Charles Francis Atkinson, *The Decline of the West*, I: *Form and Actuality* (New York, 1926), II: *Perspectives of World-History* (New York, 1928) —hereafter cited as *Decline*. I have compared citations in the English edition with the German original and have slightly modified the wording where the change seems to make for a more accurate and clearer rendering.

[57] H. Stuart Hughes, *Oswald Spengler: A Critical Estimate* (New York, 1952), p. 89.

[58] See Manfred Schröter, *Der Streit um Spengler: Kritik seiner Kritiker* (Munich, 1922), on the early controversy about the historical merit of the *Decline*. Schröter expanded his discussion after the war in his *Metaphysik des Untergangs: Eine kulturkritische Studie über Oswald Spengler* (Munich, 1949), in which he included the contents of the earlier work.

[59] I have refrained from any elaborate discussion of the organization and themes of the *Decline* since this material, for the most part, adds little to our understanding of Spengler's Prussian Socialism. For good treatments of the historical and philosophical ideas of the *Decline*, see Hughes, *Oswald Spengler*, Chs. IV and V, and the appropriate sections in Pitirim A. Sorokin, *Social Philosophies of an Age of Crisis* (Boston, 1950). The excellent study by Ernst Stutz, *Oswald Spengler als*

the decline would be long and eventful, and not without redeeming features.

Contemporary Germans, he wrote, lived at a time in the evolution of Faustian Civilization "when money [was] celebrating its last victories and the Caesarism that is to come approach[ed] with quiet firm steps. . . ."[60] The end of the rule of men whose only qualifications were that they had access to great wealth would also herald the demise of the old nineteenth-century ideologies which made of money a cause for political conflict. Both liberalism and Marxism, then, were dying out.[61] Aligning himself with the social conservatives who identified liberalism and Marxism, Spengler argued that "from Adam Smith to Marx it is nothing but self-analysis of the economic thinking of a single culture on a particular level of development." Both were theoretical, systematic, unhistorical; both made claims to universal validity; both left the *soul* of a generation, of an estate, or of a people out of their calculations. Their false distinctions neglected the truth that economics and politics were only different aspects of "one living, flowering current of being. . . ." Spengler hailed this vulgarization of Spann's Universalism as "a new, a German outlook on economics, an outlook far beyond capitalism and Socialism. . . ."[62]

The new view of society that Spengler propounded did not acknowledge the existence of a separate working class. Everyone, from the entrepreneur down to the meanest tailor's helper, was a worker. But not all did work of the same importance. The economic realm, like the rest of life, was stratified. "Every stream of being consists of a minority of leaders and a huge majority of the led . . . ; every sort of economy consists in leading-work and in doing-work." The most important workers were clearly the leaders of production, the generators of wealth, not those who merely car-

---

politischer Denker (Bern, 1958), sees a closer and more coherent link between Spengler's historical and political theories than I have been able to discern in his writings.

[60] *Decline*, II, 507.
[61] *Ibid.*, p. 454.
[62] *Ibid.*, pp. 469-71.

ried out the directives of the creative stratum nor those
who lived from wealth gained through money transac-
tions.[63] It followed that the most important member of the
economy in a machine age was the engineer, "the priest of
the machine." Spengler saw no reason for social conflict between the manual worker and his employer; they
were both workers. The real conflict was between the forces
of creative production and the power of money. It was "the
desperate struggle of technical thought to maintain its liberty against money thought." Socialism, he concluded, was
the will, the organization, and the discipline which kept the
community in trim for the great battle of blood and money,
the battle between politics and capitalism.[64]

He entered more deeply into the problems of a socialism
for Germany in his *Preussentum und Sozialismus*. Whereas Niekisch sought to reconcile the demands of the workers
with the needs of the state by arguing that their problems
were identical and soluble only in combination, Spengler
argued that to embrace the Prussian virtues of authoritarianism, subordination, self-sacrifice, and national solidarity
was to embrace socialism. Hence he could offer the pardoxi-
cal formulation that "Friedrich Wilhelm I and not Marx
. . . was the first conscious socialist."[65] For, to Spengler,
socialism was a matter of "rearing" (*Züchtung*), of national
character. Frenchmen were middle class by national tradition, whereas "every genuine German is a worker. That be-
longs to the style of his life."[66] August Bebel, the architect
of the Social Democratic Party, was as much admired by

[63] *Ibid.*, pp. 479-80, 492-93. Spengler returned again and again to
this distinction between those who planned work and those who
carried out directives. See, e.g., his *Neubau des deutschen Reiches* (*Reconstruction of the German Reich*) (Munich, 1924), pp. 90-92—
hereafter cited as *NR*. See also his *Man and Technics: A Contribution
to a Philosophy of Life*, tr. Charles Francis Atkinson (New York,
1932), pp. 60-62, from the German original, *Der Mensch und die
Technik: Beitrag zu einer Philosophie des Lebens* (Munich, 1931).
The translation will hereafter be cited as *MT*.

[64] *Decline*, II, 505-6.

[65] *PS*, p. 42.

[66] *PS*, pp. 10-11.

Spengler as by Niekisch. He had been a true socialist, "a man of action, military and authoritarian through and through."[67] His party had degenerated after it had lost his firm guidance. It had become merely a Marxist party. Like Sombart, Spengler derided Marx for having based his thought, not on political assumptions, but rather on theological ones. In Marxism the conflict of socialism and capitalism was the conflict of good and evil: the bourgeoisie was the devil, the workers angels, and the collapse of bourgeois society the Last Judgment.[68] Contemporary Marxists were motivated by the Marxist theology, by greed, and by non-German, or non-Prussian, ideas of English extraction. "Marxism"—to quote one of Spengler's striking, if vacuous, paradoxes—"is the capitalism of the workers."[69] Spengler appealed to German workers to give up all illusions. They had only the choice of Prussian Socialism or nothing, he warned.[70]

Actually, as Spengler used the words, "Prussianism" and "Socialism" meant the same thing: they referred to the heroic virtues that Sombart had ascribed to the German character in contrasting it with the English tradesman's outlook. Spengler fit the distinction into his own theory by setting the English division of society into classes of the rich and poor over against the German separation of those who command from those who obey. English democracy offered one all the possibilities of becoming rich, German democracy the possibility of reaching every existing rank.[71] Spengler's conception of England, much like Sombart's, stressed the impossibility of transplanting English democratic institutions in Germany. Further, he argued that democracy as practiced in England was a sham anyway; the people were manipulated by the party leaders and had little voice in determining their own fate.[72]

Spengler offered a *Prussian* solution to German social, economic, and political questions. He called for an alliance between the best of the German working class and the ad-

---

[67] *PS*, pp. 15-16; see also p. 76.
[68] *PS*, p. 73.   [69] *PS*, p. 75.   [70] *PS*, p. 98.
[71] *PS*, pp. 43-44.   [72] See, e.g., *PS*, p. 56.

herents of the old Prussian patriotism (*Staatsgefühl*) to create a state that was both socialist and democratic in the Prussian sense.[73] Domestically, this new state would carry on the struggle against the "inner" England. Prussian Socialism would guarantee the all-important domination of commercial life by the state.

In its highest form, Spengler averred, socialism was a unique feature of Faustian Civilization. A truly socialist Germany would consequently lead the other nations of the West. Socialism, in its international manifestation, was the Faustian will-to-power, "the will to absolute military economic and intellectual world dominance; world-war, world revolution, determination by means of technology and invention to weld the mass of humanity into a whole, and most important . . . modern imperialism: what we believe, all should believe; what we want, all should want." Socialism, then, was the collective will of Germans for world domination.[74]

When *Preussentum und Sozialismus* was first published in December 1919, an eager middle class reading public searched its pages for formulas by means of which the troubled political reality might be understood. Political instability and disorder were still the norm in public life. The Berlin uprising of January had unleashed a momentary panic in both middle class and moderate Socialist circles. The revolutionary government of the Bavarian Soviet Republic had just been bloodily suppressed. A constituent assembly was meeting in Weimar to draft a constitution for a democratic republic. Plans were being laid by Wolfgang Kapp and a number of generals for a monarchist coup, which they finally attempted in March 1920. Spengler's small tract was welcomed by the fearful and confused members of the German middle classes for at least two reasons.

First, it attacked the radical socialists who were disrupting orderly public life and threatening to import the excesses of the Russian Revolution into Germany. Spengler clearly demonstrated, for those who wished to be convinced,

[73] *PS*, pp. 98-99.
[74] *PS*, pp. 23-24.

that Marxian socialism was not suited to German politics, German needs, and the German national character. He also offered the reassuring oracle, much like that of the *Decline*, that, whether or not Marxist leaders admitted it, their doctrine was now meaningless and dead.

More important, Spengler built an ideological bridge to the new era for his conservative readers. Like the other social conservatives we have discussed, Spengler sought to bring his own thinking and that of his readers into accord with the new problems and conditions of twentieth-century life. In the pamphlet he piously extolled a "monarchist-socialist order" and declared a prince to be "the sole protection of a government in the face of commercial values." But, only a month after the Kaiser had abdicated, he had written his friend Hans Klöres of his hope that the German Revolution would recapitulate the course of the French Revolution. To be sure, the German people had behaved disgustingly by betraying their ruler, as in the past they had betrayed Frederick the Great and Bismarck. But Germany could gain from the disruption in the lands of her enemies caused by the spread of the revolutionary ethos. As in late eighteenth-century France, the revolutionary situation could be the occasion for territorial aggrandizement. And at home, in the end, all would welcome a dictatorship, "something Napoleonic," which would once again restore political authority.[75]

Spengler was still attracted by the idea of aristocratic preeminence. As late as 1924 he bemoaned the social and political decline of the nobility. Speaking before an audience of nobles in that year, he charged them with the task of regaining their lost supremacy. But at the same time he called upon them to renounce the provincialism of their outmoded ideals. He asked them to give up what remained of their special privileges in the countryside. He urged them to accept the "world horizon," as the powerful and success-

[75] *PS*, pp. 91-92; Spengler to Klöres, 18 Dec. 1918, *Oswald Spengler: Briefe, 1913-1936*, ed. Anton M. Koktanek (Munich, 1963), pp. 111-14.

ful gentry of England had done. Only then would the nobility be once again fit to lead the German people in world
affairs.[76]

But after 1919 Spengler dropped his advocacy of the
nineteenth-century idea of a social monarchy. Monarchism
seemed to have little appeal to the right after the first few
years of the Republic.[77] In its place Spengler championed
a new Caesarism. And the nobility apparently did not
measure up fully to what Spengler required of them, for
we find no further references to their right to lead in his
writings after 1924. As a surrogate for the nobility he recommended the creation of a more open social elite.[78] This
elite, he proposed, would lead the struggle against commercial values. The subordination of all economic questions to
political values was the major premise of Spengler's Prussian Socialism. Spengler reasoned that a proper organization of political life would solve all the economic and social problems from which Germany suffered. What Spengler
believed these problems were now requires elucidation.

Spengler's concern for social questions stemmed from the
characteristically conservative assumption of the primacy of
foreign policy. "When a great misfortune befalls a man, how
much strength and good there is in him is manifested. When
fate crushes a people it lays bare its inner greatness or limitations. Thus the most extreme danger no longer permits an
error about the historical rank [*Rang*] of a nation."[79] Only
the clowns, the cowards, and the criminals who ruled Germany had the temerity to avoid pursuing an active and aggressive foreign policy, foolishly claiming that they were

[76] "Aufgaben des Adels," address delivered on 16 May 1924 at the
Annual Meeting of the German Nobility in Breslau, in *Reden und
Aufsätze*, ed. Hildegard Kornhardt (Munich, 1938), pp. 89-90, 93-95.

[77] Lewis Hertzman, *DNVP: Right-Wing Opposition in the Weimar
Republic, 1918-1924* (Lincoln, Neb., 1963), pp. 86-88; see further
Kaufmann, *Monarchism in the Weimar Republic*.

[78] See the discussion of Spengler's elite theory in Walter Struve,
"Elite versus Democracy" (Ph.D. diss., Yale University, 1962), pp.
240-78.

[79] *NR*, p. 3.

thereby freeing Germany from the unhappy consequences of the play of international political forces.[80]

Spengler's conception of man rested on Nietzsche's vision of man as a beast of prey. Man had fashioned tools and weapons with which to conquer nature and his rivals. Those of his activities that were directed toward the acquisition of power Spengler labelled "politics"; those that were aimed at gaining "booty" he called "economics."[81] Man has conquered nature by means of the machine, Spengler wrote. But the creative geniuses who had led the struggle against nature were now in terrible straits. Drawing upon Sombart, he pictured the old entrepreneurial spirit as a force already in its death throes. It was to him "a sort of pacifism of the battle against nature."[82] The workers, only adjuncts of the machine, were in rebellion against their destiny.[83] Finally, leaderless and served only by dumb creatures, the machine was running out of control. It was transforming the valued ideals of Spengler's society. "All things organic are dying in the grip of organization. An artificial world is permeating and poisoning the natural world. Civilization itself has become a machine that does, or tries to do, everything in mechanical fashion. We think only in horse-power now; we cannot look at a waterfall without mentally turning it into electric power...."[84]

As the leaders of production faltered, Spengler went on, a sinister new power began to invade and dominate the economy. Financiers finally captured control of the economy by means of a long-range maneuver which they had been plotting since the middle of the last century. The owner-property relationship, Spengler averred, had now been supplanted by pieces of paper rapidly circulating among the money men. The financial world continued to spread its tentacles into all features of public life. "The fluid [bewegliche] wealth which stands behind the banks, concerns, and individual factories has brought under its influence, to a degree undreamed of by the public, governments,

80 *NR*, p. 7; see also pp. 94-95.
81 *MT*, Ch. I.   82 *MT*, p. 97.
83 *MT*, p. 98.   84 *MT*, p. 94.

the political order, parties, the press, and public opinion."[85]

The fundamental economic task Germany had to carry out now was that of freeing herself from the money powers and reasserting the prerogatives of productive capital. Spengler felt that ownership of real property was somehow a more genuine condition than ownership of mere money or bonds. He seemed to hold that money was a greater abstraction than a deed to a farm, for example. This view evidently stemmed, at least in part, from a unique version of the labor theory of value; only here labor of higher value was elevated above all other kinds. For the rest, Spengler was aligning himself with that romantic strain in social conservatism which glorified the work of the peasant or the artisan as in itself more meaningful than that of the machinist or the field laborer.[86] But even the work of the machinist, for all its inferiority, he characterized as superior in moral quality to that of the banker. The former at least was a part of the realm of creative capitalism; the latter was nothing more than a parasitical activity.[87]

[85] Spengler, "Politische Pflichten der deutschen Jugend," first given as an address before Würzburg University students on 26 Feb. 1924, reprinted in *Politische Schriften* (Munich: Volksausgabe, 1933), pp. 138-41; *Hour of Decision, Part One: Germany and World-Historical Evolution* (New York, 1934), p. 143—tr. Charles Francis Atkinson from the German *Jahre der Entscheidung: Deutschland und die weltgeschichtliche Entwicklung* (Munich, 1933). The translation will hereafter be cited as *HD*. Spengler originally entitled this work, which he never completed, *Deutschland in Gefahr* (*Germany in Danger*) but changed the title to "avoid misunderstanding" with the new National Socialist government.

[86] *HD*, pp. 99-100. He took exception to Ernst Jünger's *Der Arbeiter* just because he felt Jünger had given short shrift to state officials, entrepreneurs, officers, artisans, and peasants. He reminded Jünger that "in Germany the peasantry [was] still a political force to be reckoned with." Spengler to Jünger, 5 Sept. 1932, *Briefe*, pp. 667-68.

[87] In Nazi terminology this distinction was formulated as a conflict between "creative" (*schaffende*) and "exploitive" (*raffende*) capitalism. See the work of its outstanding exponent in the NSDAP, Gottfried Feder, *Der Deutsche Staat auf nationaler und sozialer Grundlage: Neue Wege in Staat, Finanz und Wirtschaft* [1923], the Nationalsozialistische Bibliothek, Heft 35 (16./17. Auflage, Munich, 1933), pp. 20-21, 37. See also his *Das Manifest zur Brechung der Zinsknechtschaft*

Spengler considered the institution of private property to be of the greatest economic, political, and cultural significance. Not only was the recognition of the sanctity of private property essential for a well-functioning economic order, but it was absolutely necessary for the economic security of a ruling elite. Spengler believed, like most conservatives of the nineteenth century, that the existence of a tradition of high culture was intimately tied to the existence of a stratum of men living in wealth and luxury.[88] More innocent of the world than Sombart, Salin, or Spann, Spengler argued that wealth, per se, resulted from the innate superiority of the possessor; it was a badge of the worth of an individual.[89] A liberal businessman of the nineteenth century could have applauded this piece of Social Darwinian reasoning. Spengler's nostalgia for the lost social hierarchy of the nineteenth century did not always mesh with his social conservative theories.

Yet, like Spann, he wished to limit the producer's exercise of his right of private property. He reiterated the popular dictum "property creates obligations" (*Eigentum verpflichtet*), even though he remained vague as to what these obligations might be. The national interest was clearly one

---

(Munich, 1919). Actually, the Marxist theoretician Rudolf Hilferding, in the *Finanzkapital* (Vienna, 1923), which appeared originally in 1910, was the first to give this mode of thought theoretical formulation. It was then picked up and used by that enigmatic liberal, Walter Rathenau, in *Vom Aktienwesen* (Berlin, 1918). During the Weimar period Marxists showed relatively little interest in this now outdated, and inaccurate, distinction. See Chapter I of this study and Franz Neumann's *Behemoth*, pp. 259-68, for the refutation of the assertion that "finance capital" controlled the German economy in the 1920s.

[88] Cf. the classic nineteenth-century statement of this position by Heinrich von Treitschke—"the millions must plow, hammer, and grind in order that a few thousands might study, paint, and govern"—in his attack on the founders of the Verein für Sozialpolitik in the essay "Der Sozialismus und seine Gönner," *Aufsätze, Reden und Briefe*, ed. K. M. Schiller (Meersburg, 1929), IV, 136ff. See also his *Politik*, ed. Max Cornicelius (5th edn., Leipzig, 1922), I, 50ff.

[89] *MT*, p. 77; *HD*, esp. pp. 97, 102.

criterion. "Employ your property as if it had been given you in trust by the Folk," he admonished. For those who did not do so, he demanded especially strong laws against speculation for profit.[90] In sum, Spengler's views on private property were closer to the *Herr im Hause* mentality of nineteenth-century businessmen than to the normative view more typical of social conservative theorists.

So intensely did Spengler feel the necessity for defending the prerogatives of the creative stratum that in explaining the great depression he aimed his accusations in the most improbable directions. He traced the unemployment in the West, in the "white countries," to the emergence of productive capacity in the "colonial races." He alleged, further, that the whole depression was purely a consequence of the decline of the power of the state. Fundamentally, however, "the whole economic crisis . . . is not as the whole world supposes, the temporary consequence of war, revolution, inflation, and payments of debts. It has been willed. In all essentials it is the product of the deliberate work of the leaders of the proletariat." The concomitant unemployment, he charged, was attributable to the unduly high political wages the workers had exacted.[91]

Spengler tended to label any economic policy he deemed harmful as bolshevism. He denounced the industrial wage system, which the unions had forced upon management, because it punished superior performance and destroyed the German-Prussian ideal of work as duty. Its logical consequence, wage-bolshevism, was leeching the lifeblood out of

[90] *NR*, p. 93.

[91] *MT*, p. 102; *HD*, pp. 43, 147, 173. Soon after the appearance of *Hour of Decision*, which contained the samples of economic reasoning cited in the text, Spengler received a warm letter of appreciation from Edgar Salin. Salin wrote that there were details with which he disagreed; nevertheless, he praised Spengler, remarking that "the whole fate of Germany takes on another aspect when someone is there who see things so correctly and has the courage to say what he sees." Salin to Spengler, 28 Aug. 1933, *Briefe*, pp. 700-701. See further the even more enthusiastic comments of another Georgian, Karl Wolfskehl, on pp. 688-89, 701-3.

the national economy.[92] But even more pernicious than wage levels set uneconomically high through political means was a taxation policy he excoriated as tax-bolshevism. Just as the policies of high death duties and the income tax, initiated by David Lloyd George before World War I, were destroying the economic footing of Britain's traditional governing class, so in Germany democrats and leftists were carrying out "a hidden expropriation by means of the tax form." The social revolution, which in Russia could not be carried off without great bloodletting, was creeping forward almost unheralded in Germany, he warned. It was taxing away the high standard of living so essential to the culture-bearing stratum of society. The payment of niggardly pensions to the retired members of the Mittelstand and the inflation, which the state could not curb, were but two further instances of tax-bolshevism. Rent controls (*Wohnungsbolshevismus*) taxed the whole nation by pauperizing house owners. Such controls hurt the construction industry and produced unemployment among its largely artisan labor force. Spengler likened the devastation wrought in Germany by tax-bolshevism to the destruction left by a war or a revolution.[93]

We would be expecting too much of Spengler's thin knowledge of economics if we tried to find in his theories a clear formulation of specific policies that would lead to the overthrow of the power of the bourse and of the labor agitator. In his published writing he called for the convocation of an international congress of economics experts (not politicians, lawyers, or finance officials) to undertake a study to determine how taxes could best be collected with the least amount of damage to the economy. As an interim

[92] *NR*, p. 92; *HD*, p. 156. He suggested the factory work brigades of the Russian First Five Year Plan as a model more worthy of German emulation.

[93] *NR*, pp. 83-85. See also the address "Das Verhältnis von Wirtschaft und Steuerpolitik seit 1750" given before the conservative businessmen of the Verein zur Wahrung der wirtschaftlichen Interessen von Rheinland und Westfalen (Society for the Protection of the Economic Interests of the Rhineland and Westphalia) on 19 Sept. 1924, reprinted in *Politische Schriften*, pp. 309ff.

measure he put forward a tax reform program which he believed would benefit the beleaguered middle and upper classes.[94] Privately he proposed to Paul Reusch, general director of the great mining firm of Gutehoffnungshütte, that the leaders of German industry, agriculture, and commerce form a committee, formulate a tax policy, and present the government with their own draft of a new tax law.[95]

Spengler held that inflation could best be avoided by having the state assume absolute control of the currency. The solution of the 1923 inflation by the use of the new Rentenmark, in his estimation, had mortgaged German property, but the Germans had received nothing in return for taking on this debt. Spengler would accept only a currency that was not at the mercy of foreign powers. This reservation ruled out any currency based on the gold standard, for not only was the gold standard an invention of the materialistic liberal camp, but it was also an international medium of exchange. Spengler, like so many educated Germans who, in their smattering of economics, had been taught the state theory of money of G. F. Knapp, believed that the backing of the value of currency should be public confidence in the leadership of the state.[96] A strong and capable political leadership would, Spengler argued, guarantee a stable currency and a robust economy.[97]

An elite would rule over a state organized on authoritarian lines. The state would be run by competent bureaucrats. The goal of national policy would be to make Germany a great nation in world politics. Such a state could not permit strikes, since strikes would constitute a disruptive reversion to the tactics of private pressure groups attempting to influence the collectivity. Spengler suggested, but did

[94] *Politische Schriften*, p. 310. See the jumbled assortment of taxation measures proposed in *NR*, pp. 85-88.

[95] Spengler to Reusch, 30 Dec. 1924, *Briefe*, pp. 372-73.

[96] See the charitable, but critical, evaluation of Knapp's theory of money in Schumpeter, *History of Economic Analysis*, pp. 809-11 and esp. pp. 1090-91.

[97] *Politische Schriften*, pp. 257-63.

not develop, the familiar social conservative plan for the creation of some kind of economic council to adjudicate questions of pay. With Spann, he recommended the replacement of parliamentary bodies by corporate organizations hierarchically ordered. At the pinnacle would be a workers' council, comprising representatives of all aspects of labor —officers, bureaucrats, peasants, miners, and so forth. That is all he had to say about corporatism; he merely made brief allusions to it in his tract of revolutionary times, *Preussentum und Sozialismus*.[98]

It is likely that the idea of corporatism appealed less to Spengler than it had to Sombart and Spann because Spengler thought it too radical a form of economic organization. He was wary of limiting the prerogatives of the entrepreneur, the all-important "worker of higher quality."[99] On the eve of the Nazi accession to power in the depths of the depression Spengler took pains to clarify the meaning of his brand of socialism, lest any confusion remain in the minds of his readers. In the foreword to his *Politische Schriften*, dated October 1932, he wrote: "Those in nationalist circles who have picked up [the word] as a slogan have to this day not understood that 'socialism' is an ethos, not an economic policy. Even now idiots are still trying to preach a 'national communism.' Socialism, as I understand it, presupposes an economy based on private enterprise [*Privatwirtschaft*] with its old teutonic desire for power and for plunder."[100] Prussian Socialism, it seems, meant the institution of unrestrained capitalism in Germany as the economic basis for imperialist aggression.

How to reconcile the old and the new without abandoning the conservative heritage of the nineteenth century was Spengler's dilemma. His was far more acute than that of any other social conservative thinker treated in this study, even though it was no different in kind from the dilemmas Sombart, Salin, and Spann faced. Spengler was, of all these

98 *PS*, pp. 66, 77, 91.
99 Cf., e.g., *NR*, p. 92.
100 *Politische Schriften*, p. vii.

men, the one least able (or least willing) to break away
from the major values of prewar conservatism. Did his theories really offer so much that was new? Was not his talk
of an age of Caesarism as much an expression of nostalgia
for the lost monarchy as an affirmation of hope for a future
dictator? How different was his new elite to be from the
aristocracy of the nineteenth century? The prescriptions
and qualifications he set down described a new aristocracy
nearly as exclusive and socially independent as the old aristocracy of birth.[101]

Perhaps it was these basically nineteenth-century instincts
that kept Spengler out of the ranks of the Nazis. Although
they wooed him and considered him one of their own,[102]
he refused to make any firm commitment to National Socialism. Hitler did not seem to him the awaited Caesar on
the model of August Bebel, or Mussolini, or even Lenin;
nor did the SA men seem to measure up fully to his ideal
of the new elite. He disliked the parades, the drums, and
the noise. In good reactionary nineteenth-century fashion he
especially distrusted their enthusiasm. As he wrote in the
fall of 1932, in a remark apparently directed against Hitler:
"Enthusiasm is a dangerous burden on the road of politics. The pathfinder must be a hero, not a heroic tenor."[103]

The ideologies of Spengler and of Niekisch might best
be understood as, respectively, the right and the left limits
of social conservative thought and activity. In neither do
we find the doctrine in "pure" form; and yet, despite the
great differences between these men, both adopted varieties
of social nationalism and propagated them primarily to
readers of the educated middle classes. Both embraced social
conservative principles without fully giving up their earlier
ideological persuasions. This compromise forced them into
ambiguities of conceptualization and logical contradictions

---

101 Cf. Struve, "Elite versus Democracy," pp. 265ff.

102 See Hughes, *Oswald Spengler*, Ch. VIII.

103 *Politische Schriften*, p. x. Hughes explains Spengler's aloofness
from Nazism as "a combination of personal fastidiousness and political
illusion." *Oswald Spengler*, p. 156.

so blatant as to make them remarkable even within the context of social conservatism.

Spengler's zealous defense of the special prerogatives of the entrepreneur, for instance, seems rather curious in view of his assertion that conservatives had to make their peace with contemporary German democracy. Similarly, his attacks on bolshevism and social democracy clash sharply with his appeals to German workers (in *Preussentum und Sozialismus*, for example) to work for the good of the nation. He offered German workers only the certainty of a subordinate position in society, in exchange for which they were to acknowledge the leadership of a political and economic elite. Even the members of the white-collar middle classes who so eagerly read his books searched in vain for proposals, or even coherent formulas, for programs that would alleviate their social and economic plight. Spengler tended to be forthright only in his use of metaphors. The proposals for policies were usually either platitudinous, naive, or so abstract as to be without value.

Spengler might well be taken as a representative of the conservative emphasis of social conservatism; he virtually excluded the social dimension from his theories. Basically, Spengler knew little of economics. He knew only that economic problems had something to do with Germany's ills. The cure he prescribed amounted to the exclusion, to as great a degree as possible, of economic considerations from the important issues of domestic and international politics. To Spengler it somehow seemed that Socialists, Communists, and financiers were conspiring to weaken the state. If these treasonous elements could be cut down to mid-nineteenth-century size, important goals in the arena of world politics might be pursued unimpeded and in the fullness of national strength.

Niekisch, too, clung to a tradition which had its origins in the nineteenth century. His ideology of resistance rested on a heretical and rather singular use of Marxist principles, which he adorned with the trappings of social conservatism. He denigrated liberalism and cosmopolitanism as foreign to the German ethos. He praised the spirit of Potsdam, glorifying its heritage of authoritarianism and militarism. He urged the total subordination of the society and the economy to the requirements of national liberation. And he worked actively to convert uncommitted nationalists to his brand of socialism. Some members of the Bund Oberland seemed willing enough to listen to him when he spoke as a social conservative. As long as his Marxism was no more than a critique of existing society, he met with a degree of acceptance. But the rather elusive image which equated Moscow and Potsdam moved no one to action. A diplomatic policy oriented in the direction of Russia was one thing; emulation of Soviet society was quite another.

When Hitler forced Niekisch to choose between the "national" and the "bolshevik" in his ideology of resistance, he resolutely chose the latter. Had the social conservative aspects of his thought held him more firmly, he would have manifested greater indecision. The choice would have been made with greater anguish. Like Sombart and Spann, he might have embraced National Socialism on the basis of his hopes for its evolution in the desired direction; or, like Spengler, he might have coexisted with it, without giving it his approval. Instead, he fiercely attacked it until his publications were silenced.

For all their manifest differences, Spengler and Niekisch were playing essentially the same game. Both aimed their writings at a Mittelstand audience. Both employed the language of cultic heroism, of militarism, and of nationalism. Spengler's gambit aimed at eliminating the social revolutionary potential in the thinking of the dissatisfied Mittelstand; he intended his theories to function as a blotter for such tendencies. Niekisch, for his part, worked to further the radicalization of the Mittelstand, or at least those elements of it which he could reach in the military and the Bünde. He was enough of an ideological gambler to hope that members of the armed Mittelstand might be prepared for a Marxist solution to their problems, if this solution were well tinctured with heroic, nationalist, and military values. And both advocated a disciplined authoritarian society so organized as to enable Germans to free themselves from Western domination.[104]

The vague and ambiguous idea of Potsdam, with its connotations of a powerful, grand, and harmonious Germany, served to obscure nice ideological differences. The Prussian ideal permitted Spengler to attack the SPD and yet to turn aside charges that he was a reactionary by also allowing him to praise the *lost* heritage of the Prussian corporal's son, August Bebel. It permitted Niekisch to attend receptions at the Soviet Embassy, even in the Nazi era, and yet to drink with his friend Ernst Jünger and to maintain cordial relations with Count Reventlow. In the fall of 1932, when the DNVP and the NSDAP were still united in the Harzburg Front, Alfred Hugenberg offered to run *Widerstand* people on the DNVP lists. Although Niekisch firmly declined. Hugenberg's offer seemed not to have greatly surprised him.[105] Should it have come as a great surprise to a man who, for whatever reason, could write that "either a German state is founded upon the spirit of Potsdam, or it is no state," who employed the symbols of conservatism, who even awaited the coming of a Third Reich?[106]

[104] Niekisch considered Spengler a demagogue of the bourgeois masses (read Mittelstand); yet he found much that was of value in the *Decline of the West*. He also considered *Preussentum und Sozialismus* "noteworthy," even if it was a neat trick to identify capitalism and Prussianism. "Auf 'den politischen Lohn' gekommen," *Widerstand*, VIII (1933), 297-305, esp. 297, 299. In the autobiography he wrote after the war he has only harsh words for the German Socialisms of Moeller van den Bruck, Sombart, and, of course, Spengler. *Gewagtes Leben*, pp. 134-37.

[105] In his *Gewagtes Leben*, pp. 205-7, Niekisch asserts that the party's active defense of private property and its hostility to the East offended him. He told Hugenberg that the DNVP still had too much of the Imperial era about it.

[106] *Gedanken*, pp. 158-59. In the same passage he characterized the Weimar Coalition of the Democratic Party, the Catholic Center, and the SPD as "the triple alliance against the German spirit of the state. . . ." In 1930 Niekisch found the idea of a new Reich of North German orientation an attractive one. See his article "Das dritte Reich," *Widerstand*, V (1930), 134-39. Moeller van den Bruck's revival of the mystical ideal of a Third Reich found great resonance in new conservative circles. See his book of that title, *Das Dritte Reich*, ed. Hans

Ultimately, the idea of Potsdam appealed to members of the Mittelstand less as a vision of a happy society than as a mythology of shared danger. Much like the comradeship of the trenches, of which Ernst Jünger had written so powerfully,[107] the Prussian ideal bespoke a national comradeship in the face of internal social conflicts and of the continuing hostility of the Western powers. Some social conservative thinkers, Spengler for one, urged the domestic reordering of society so that internal conflict would not interfere with the implementation of nationalist foreign policy objectives. To some degree, this was Salin's position, too. Others, like Sombart and Niekisch, argued for a strong state and an active foreign policy so that domestic injustice and exploitation might be brought to an end.[108] That the Mittelstand needed a creditable myth of shared danger became supremely evident in 1929.

When the great world depression struck Germany in 1929, the adherents of the ideology of social conservatism were prepared both emotionally and intellectually to welcome the collapse. Sombart had spoken and written of the end of capitalism well before the beginning of the crisis. Economic theory and the lessons of Stefan George had taught Salin to accept the inevitability of the "healing crisis." Spann, Niekisch, and Spengler had been awaiting the

Schwarz (3rd edn., Hamburg, 1931), which first appeared in 1923. See also the critique by Fritz Stern, *The Politics of Cultural Despair*, pp. 253ff. In his *Antidemokratisches Denken in der Weimarer Republik*, pp. 300-303, Kurt Sontheimer presents an evaluation of the impact of the book and of the term on the National Socialists, as well as on the various circles of neoconservatives dedicated to the overthrow of the Weimar Republic.

[107] See, e.g., Jünger's *Stahlgewittern* (Berlin, 1942) and *Der Kampf als inneres Erlebnis* (Berlin, 1940).

[108] On Salin, see Chapter III of this study. Spengler, "Das heutige Verhältnis zwischen Weltwirtschaft und Weltpolitik," address given on 9 Nov. 1926 before the Industry Club of Düsseldorf, reprinted in *Politische Schriften*, pp. 316-17. On Sombart, see Chapter II of this study. Niekisch, "Sammlung zum Widerstand," *Widerstand*, III (1928), 156. And yet, when the spell of social conservatism on him was strong, Niekisch was capable of writing: "Never and nowhere will private property allow itself to be abolished." *Gedanken*, pp. 277-78.

eclipse of the liberal order since at least the end of the war. Social conservatives, like the Communists, greeted the economic collapse with a certain amount of *Schadenfreude*, of malicious glee. In company with the Marxists, who saw a positive side to the increasing misery of the unemployed members of the proletariat because their suffering guaranteed an earlier outbreak of the social revolution, social conservative thinkers observed the anguish of the middle classes with feelings both of commiseration and expectation. Ferdinand Fried, of the periodical *Die Tat*, spoke for all social conservatives when he wrote in 1932: "We are still in the midst of the process of dissolution, of collapse. . . . We cannot hold it back, and yet we need not just dumbly let it happen to us. We can master it the moment we realize its meaning and affirm it the moment we consciously organize the collapse."[109]

In the depression the writers of the *Tat*, especially Ferdinand Fried, the *Tat*'s specialist on economic questions, brought together the elements of social conservative ideology into a coherent and persuasive form. And it was during the depression that all elements of the middle classes were most prepared to listen to the revolutionaries of the right. Born of the discontent of the old middle classes, social conservative ideology was not yet fully oriented to the problems and interests of the new middle classes of white-collar workers. The writers of the *Tat* set themselves the task of reorienting the ideology to the needs of the intelligentsia of the new Mittelstand. The depression had momentarily united the old and the new middle classes by means of the common economic hardship to which both groups were exposed. The writers of the *Tat* sought to convert vague feelings of common hardship into firm commitments to a common ideology; they aimed at moving the middle classes to political action. The first task, of necessity, had to be the creation of a program for the revolution of the intelligentsia. The *Tat* circle made their magazine the organ of the vanguard of that revolution.

[109] Ferdinand Fried, "Gestaltung des Zusammenbruchs," *Die Tat*, XXIII (March 1932), 986.

VI. Ferdinand Fried

DIE TAT AND
THE THIRD FRONT

WERNER SOMBART aroused heated discussion at a meeting of the Verein für Sozialpolitik with his dire prognoses of the end of capitalism. By means of articles in scholarly journals such as the *Weltwirtschaftliches Archiv* and in conferences of the Friedrich List Society, Edgar Salin gained the attention of the academic world for his plans for the moral rejuvenation of Germany. Othmar Spann retailed his ideology to the leaders of neoconservative and nationalist movements, and perhaps occasionally tutored Hitler in economics.[1] But, without publicists like Oswald Spengler, Ernst Niekisch, and the writers in the circle around the periodical *Die Tat*, the politically unorganized members of the middle classes could not have learned so easily of the analyses and the programs of social conservatism. The importance of such "middle-brow" publicists in the diffusion of ideas must not be underestimated.[2]

[1] Gerhard Schulz, "Die Anfänge des totalitären Massnahmenstaates," Part II of Karl Dietrich Bracher, Wolfgang Sauer, and Gerhard Schulz, *Die nationalsozialistische Machtergreifung: Studien zur Errichtung des totalitären Herrschaftssystems in Deutschland, 1933-1934,* Vol. XIV of the Schriften des Instituts für Politische Wissenschaft, Berlin (2nd edn., Cologne, 1962), p. 400. Schulz has also discovered remarkable parallels of thought, and even of wording, between Hitler's *Mein Kampf* and the 1921 (1st) edition of Spann's *Der wahre Staat*; see p. 400, n. 98.

[2] For an analysis of the pattern of diffusion, see Paul Lazersfeld and Elihu Katz, *Personal Influence: The Part Played by People in the Flow of Mass Communications* (Glencoe, Ill., 1955), pp. 3-5, and the Foreword by Elmo Roper, esp. pp. xv-xvi. See also Franklin L. Baumer, "Intellectual History and its Problems," *Journal of Modern History,* XXI (1949), 193ff. For an approach to the writing of intellectual his-

In the depression-torn Germany of the early 1930s the Spenglers, the Niekischs and the other publicists of the right purveyed the social and economic ideas which could be molded into clichés at the beerhall *Stammtisch*, at the innumerable meetings of the societies and clubs to which so many members of the middle class belonged, at the political rallies, and in the pages of magazines of political commentary.

The political magazine was an institution of vital importance for the growth of social conservative thought in Germany. Whereas the Social Democrats and the Communists each had elaborate apparatus to guarantee dissemination of information and to maintain discipline, the Mittelstand, by virtue of its social composition, was not amenable to such thorough forms of organization. To be sure, the Nazis very quickly created an extensive bureaucracy and a system of regional organization, but only party officialdom had access to the communication machinery of the apparatus. And it must be remembered that the majority of social conservative theorists (and all of those under study here) remained outside the NSDAP until after the seizure of power, if they ever joined at all.

Every major neoconservative group had its own literary organ. Many magazines were founded with the specific intention of converting their readership into the nucleus of a movement.[3] Some of these periodicals were mere newsletters with editorials, but others were elaborate journals of opinion, with sufficient political impact to make it mandatory for the authorities to take their views into account.[4]

---

tory in terms of the diffusion of ideas downward from abstract thinkers to political activists, see Fritz Stern's *Politics of Cultural Despair*, esp. pp. 267-98.

[3] The example of Ernst Niekisch's *Widerstand* and *Entscheidung* has already been touched upon. An incomplete list of periodicals dedicated to "the conservative revolution" assembled by Armin Mohler includes eighty titles. *Die Konservative Revolution in Deutschland*, pp. 95-99.

[4] See, e.g., the statement of ex-Chancellor Heinrich Brüning that *Tat* had caused him "enormous difficulties," in a letter to Klemens von Klemperer, cited in von Klemperer's *Germany's New Conservatism*, p. 151.

Niekisch's periodical *Widerstand* had to carry frequent appeals to its readers for financial support; others—for example, *Tat*—had rich and powerful patrons.[5] A few such periodicals even proved self-supporting. Still, not many could depend on the generosity of rich patrons and the Reichswehr to purchase a party organ and on the devotion of the large number of followers who financed its operation, bought it, and distributed it. The National Socialist *Völkischer Beobachter* was unique in enjoying all of these advantages.[6]

The periodicals of the unaffiliated right fulfilled two important functions in twentieth-century German politics. First, they united readers from all levels of the Mittelstand, living all over Germany, into communities of the like-minded. The Frankfurt-am-Main bank clerk, the Bremen merchant, the petty government bureaucrat from Steglitz, the Bavarian Free Corpsman, the unemployed clerical worker, the university student—despite their different conceptions of the problems facing them—could all be united ideologically, and perhaps even be moved sufficiently to act together, through the pages of a periodical of social conservative orientation. A periodical such as *Tat* could dispense ideology and comfort by means of the mailbox or the magazine rack. Once politicized by social and economic conditions, members of the white-collar Mittelstand could then search for confirmation of their economic, social, and political ideals in the pages of such journals. They could assimilate neoconservative thought in monthly or weekly installments without leaving their armchairs. These periodi-

---

[5] Diedrichs had the *Tat* published at his Eugen Diedrichs Verlag in Jena. For a brief time General Kurt von Schleicher subsidized the Berlin newspaper *Tägliche Rundschau*, which Hans Zehrer, then editing *Tat*, took over in the summer of 1932. The newspaper also received subsidies from the commercial employees' association Deutschnationale Handlungsgehilfen-Verband. See Kurt Sontheimer, "Der Tatkreis," *Vierteljahrshefte für Zeitgeschichte*, VII (1959), 248, and n. 42 on the same page—hereafter cited as "Der Tatkreis."

[6] Georg Franz-Willing, *Die Hitlerbewegung: Der Ursprung, 1919-1922* (Berlin, 1962), pp. 177-98; see esp. pp. 180-85 on the purchase and financing of the *Völkische Beobachter*.

cals dusted off the boots of street politics and made them fit
to enter the *bürgerliche* household.

The neoconservative periodicals, secondly, permitted important revolutionaries of the right to devote all their energies to propagating their ideas. Here, too, comparison with
the orthodox political organizations is instructive. High officials of trade unions and of the SPD, whether of the party
bureaucracy or of the parliamentary faction, were guaranteed an adequate livelihood, even in the depths of the
depression. Communist leaders could also depend on their
party for support. All members of the Reichstag continued
to receive their salaries throughout the depression; in addition, they retained possession of their politically valuable
free railroad passes. Such institutionalized financial backing
enabled recipients to follow careers as full-time politicians
or political agitators.

Adherents of the nonaffiliated right, on the other hand,
not being able to depend on the regular support of a
party or of a pressure group organization, had to devote
more of their time to professional activities having little to
do with the political struggles of the day. Sombart, Salin,
and Spann enjoyed the relative security of their university
posts, but their professional obligations and the mores of
the academy restricted the extent of their direct participation in what would clearly have appeared to their colleagues
as "unorthodox" political activities. In addition to writing
books on politics, Spengler frequently lectured before organizations with largely bourgeois memberships. Niekisch
founded a *Widerstand* Press, which supplemented his
meager income and allowed him to concentrate his efforts
on building his movement. But the periodical *Die Tat* offered a group of neoconservative literati the wherewithal
to disseminate the ideals of the conservative revolution on
a full-time basis throughout the depression years.[7] It permitted the two most influential members of its editorial
staff, Hans Zehrer and Friedrich Zimmermann (better

[7] For a treatment of the political periodicals of the early years of
the Republic, see Helmut Hüttig, *Die politischen Zeitschriften der
Nachkriegszeit in Deutschland* (Magdeburg, 1928).

known under his pseudonym, Ferdinand Fried), to leave
their jobs on important Berlin daily papers and make of
Eugen Diedrichs's old periodical an "Independent Monthly
for the Creation of a New Reality."[8]

That was how the masthead read after Hans Zehrer assumed the editorship in October 1929. Although the magazine had been in existence since 1909 under that name and
had been in the hands of the publisher Eugen Diedrichs
since 1912, it had never occupied a significant place in German journalism.[9] When Zehrer assumed the editorship, it
was selling only approximately 800 of the 1,000 copies printed each month.[10] By 1932 Zehrer and the editorial staff he
assembled had so improved the quality and the political
relevance of the monthly that it could count a circulation of
30,000 copies,[11] with undoubtedly more than one reader
per copy.

Both Zehrer and Fried were gifted and experienced
journalists, who had worked together on the liberal, Ull-
stein-owned *Vossische Zeitung*.[12] Both had been compelled
to leave the university before they had completed their
studies.[13] Like many French intellectuals who could not

[8] Zehrer in a letter to Sontheimer admitted that one of the purposes
of the two newsletters that the *Tat* circle began after 1931 was to
help support some of the other contributors. *Tat* itself could maintain
only Zehrer and Fried. "Der Tatkreis," p. 230, n. 2.

[9] *Ibid.*, p. 230. On the history of the magazine in the days when it
was Diedrichs's organ for the propagation of the "New Romanticism,"
see Mosse, *The Crisis of German Ideology*, pp. 52ff.

[10] "Der Tatkreis," p. 232.

[11] *Ibid.* Struve ("Hans Zehrer . . . ," *American Historical Review*,
LXX, 1045, and n. 25 on the same page) estimates a circulation increase from something less than 3,000 in 1929 to more than 25,000 in
1933.

[12] Zehrer maintained his job at the foreign affairs desk of the "Voss"
even after he had begun to edit Diedrichs's journal. He left only when
Tat had come to occupy his full attention and gave promise of a
livelihood. Von Klemperer gives the date as October 1931. *Germany's
New Conservatism*, p. 130.

[13] At the University of Berlin, according to information given
Sontheimer by Zehrer, he had studied under Werner Sombart and
had discovered, to his edification, the *Preussentum und Sozialismus* of
Spengler. "Der Tatkreis," pp. 233-34, 243, n. 24.

achieve the security of a teaching post or a post requiring academic credentials,[14] Zehrer and Fried became alienated from their society, which they felt had no place for them —in this case, the capitalist and liberal society of Weimar Germany. Both became journalists. After Diedrichs had named him editor, Zehrer got in touch with his old friend from the "Voss," who was then writing for the business pages of the *Berliner Morgenpost* (another liberal paper), and asked him to write on economic issues for the periodical. From Heidelberg, the intellectually most productive university of the 1920s, Zehrer recruited the young social scientists Ernst Wilhelm Eschmann and Giselher Wirsing, the former to contribute articles on sociological topics, the latter to cover international politics and foreign trade. Fried supplied most of the economic ideas which appeared in *Tat*; Zehrer organized and homogenized the contributions of his co-workers; and together they led a small, close-knit, mutually complementary circle of intellectuals bent on revolution.[15]

Approximately a year after Zehrer and his friends had taken over *Tat*, the magazine presented what amounted to a position paper on the state of the ideological war against the Communists and the Socialists. The left, concluded the

[14] Cf. the section on "The Alienation of the Intellectuals," in Raymond Aron, *The Opium of the Intellectuals*, tr. Terence Kilmartin (New York: Norton Library paperback, 1962), pp. 203-94. Sontheimer, *ibid.*

[15] The organization of each issue, the forcefulness of the writing, and the impression the circle cultivated that they were independent and a little above the petty squabbles of daily politics all gave the reader a feeling of confidence in the writers and in the correctness of their views. Generally, a lead article, often unsigned, presented a clear and sharp critique or estimation of the contemporary political situation; detailed, well-researched articles on specific questions of the day followed; and brief paragraphs commenting on current events concluded the issue. The oracular effect was heightened by the frequent use of pseudonyms by members of the circle—giving the impression of a large circle of informed contributors in perfect agreement with one another on the vital issues of the day. Nor were the uncertainties of debate allowed to intrude. There was no regular book review page; the books the periodical recommended most often were the works in the series *Tat-Schriften*, which the *Tat* regularly advertised.

unsigned editorial, enjoyed "the tremendous advantage of
possessing a rigorously worked-out economic ideology, which
at the moment all the other nonbourgeois, noncapitalist
groups lack." The intellectuals of the *Tat* circle set themselves the task of closing the gap between an ideology at
least thirty years in the making and the realities of German
politics during the depression. Ferdinand Fried expressed
most succinctly the agenda of the new *Tat*: "He who wishes
to rebuild must first dismantle soberly and without passion
that which he wishes to rebuild. An analysis can never be
sufficiently acute or effective, it can never find its mark with
sufficient force, if there is not a passionate will behind it
to give form to the future."[16] The nature of this analysis
and of the kind of future projected by Ferdinand Fried
and his co-workers is the subject of this chapter.

In the worst year of the depression a writer for the trade
union organ *Gewerkschafts-Zeitung* noted with some surprise the appearance of a large number of new books and
articles heralding the demise of the capitalist order. What
the trade unionist found remarkable was that, although in
the past this kind of crisis literature had been common
enough in socialist circles, most of these new works were
by nonsocialists. The most popular book of the genre was
Ferdinand Fried's *Das Ende des Kapitalismus*.[17] Economic
autarky, Fried's alternative to capitalist international trade,
was an idea which, according to the contemporary observer,
had "an extraordinary power of attraction not only for
farmers and intellectuals, but also for many workers."[18]

The analysis of the causes of capitalist collapse that Fried
offered his readers was essentially an elaboration on the description of late capitalism that Werner Sombart had
worked out before the coming of the depression. Both men

[16] Unsigned article, "Die kalte Revolution," XXII (Oct. 1930), 500
(italics mine). All articles cited are from *Tat*, unless otherwise noted.
Foreword to Fried's *Das Ende des Kapitalismus, Tat-Schriften* (Jena,
1931). The contents of this book appeared first as articles in *Tat*.
It will hereafter be cited as *EK*.

[17] Franz Gross, "Das Ende des Kapitalismus: Bermerkungen zu
einigen Büchern," *Gewerkschafts-Zeitung*, XLII (1932), 313-14.

[18] *Ibid.*

put their main emphasis on the confluence of technological and psychological causes.

Like Sombart, Fried reasoned that the age of invention had drawn to a close. He expected no more new inventions of fundamental economic importance on the order of the steam engine or electricity. The technological phase of the industrial revolution had played itself out, and with it had expired the prime stimulus of growth in the capitalist economy.[19]

Of equal importance was the dotage both of the system and of the generation of once active entrepreneurs. As the generation of entrepreneurs who had owned their own firms passed away, the system of capitalism they had built passed away with them. The director of a corporation did not own the firm he headed; he was merely its first bureaucrat. He was not by nature competitive; rather, he planned. "The irrational impetus of speculation was being supplanted," Fried concluded, "by the rational factors of the card catalogue and the adding machine." His observations of industrial life disclosed only bureaucrats administering what their more adventuresome and imaginative fathers had bequeathed them. The spirit of capitalism was gone.[20]

The old rhythm of capitalist growth had been broken by the depression. Lacking new inventions, enterprising businessmen, and the stimulus of competition, it seemed to Fried unlikely ever to resume. Internationally, increasing customs barriers and the economic nationalism of many of the countries of Europe, Fried noted, had for all practical purposes destroyed the principle of free trade in a world economy. Fried predicted that the economic development of the future would tend toward stasis.[21] But it would not mean a return to the idyllic and the primitive. Fried as-

[19] *EK*, pp. 15, 22.

[20] *EK*, pp. 15, 21-22, 138, 141. Fried, "Das Kapital stirbt ab," XXI (Jan. 1930) , 722-35.

[21] *EK*, pp. 23, 147. See also the long citation from Werner Sombart's address at the Zurich Congress of the Verein für Sozialpolitik in the unsigned *Tat* article "Deutschlands Wege aus der Einkreisung," XXII (March, 1931) , 949ff.

sured his largely urban readers that the implications of his analysis were not "that driving automobiles [was] now at an end, and that tomorrow we will sit once again in the stagecoach [*Postkutsche*]."[22]

The range of choice Fried offered his readers, however, was typically narrow. It was felt by some that, if the economy could be reoriented to the play of forces in the marketplace, requiring the dissolution of cartels and the prohibition of monopoly pricing, capitalism might be rejuvenated. Like Salin, Fried argued that such a course was both psychologically and economically impossible. The capitalist spirit was dead; but, even if it were possible to revive it, chaos would follow in the wake of so drastic a reorganization of the economy.[23] The only other alternative Fried envisioned would necessitate "the complete rejection of capitalism and liberalism. It means the collapse of the economic system, and beyond that: repudiation of the idea of the world economy and the detachment [*Abkapselung*] of individual national economic areas; suspension . . . of reparations payments; erection of high customs barriers . . . ; and the further promotion of cartels and trade unions and their subordination to the state, which would thereby receive a firm economic foundation."[24]

The *Tat* circle offered their middle class readers a social conservative program that had something for both the old and the new middle classes. It advocated the nationalization of the large industrial and banking firms, which were so large and so important in the economy as to be considered basic industries; it proposed a policy of heavy taxation on large fortunes in private hands;[25] and, led by Fried, it espoused economic nationalism as a surrogate for international capitalism. The writers of *Tat* followed the social

[22] *EK*, p. 23.

[23] *EK*, p. 188.

[24] *EK*, p. 189. By June 1932 Fried was advocating that Germany declare herself bankrupt and stop reparations payments. "Ehrlicher Bankrott," XXIV (June 1932), 203-25.

[25] Zehrer, "Achtung, junge Front! Draussenbleiben!" XXI (April 1929), 38-39; "Die Situation der Innenpolitik," XXI (May 1929), 117-18.

conservative dictum of the primacy of foreign affairs. Applying the principle to economic relations, they concluded (as an unsigned editorial put it) that "a national Germany which aspires to independence and freedom can never rest on a capitalist base. Similarly, a capitalist Germany can never aspire to national autonomy."[26]

Since the beginnings of German industrialization free-trade advocates had waged a running battle with the advocates of protection. Protectionism had triumphed three times in modern German industrial history, each time more decisively. The occasion for the upsurge of protectionist policies in each case had been a moment of economic crisis. The historic tariff on iron and grain of 1879 followed in the wake of the crash of 1873, which was drawn out in the form of industrial and agricultural depression for several years thereafter. A second time, in 1902, tariff levels were raised during the Europe-wide depression of the turn of the century. The war required extraordinary autarkical measures; but, after the restoration of economic normalcy (by 1925), Germany moved once more in the direction of liberal trade policy. The great depression of 1929 provided the occasion for the third victory of the forces advocating import restrictions.[27]

The growth of policies restricting the free flow of international trade was by no means exclusively a German phenomenon. Despite the high-sounding declarations of the 1927 World Economic Conference in favor of the elimination of trade barriers in the cause of the revitalization of the world economy,[28] restrictive policies of high tariff walls, subsidies to industry and agriculture, currency controls, and dumping continued to be common weapons of the trade strategies of many countries. If Germany was a prime offender, France and the United States were not far behind.

[26] Unsigned article, "Deutschlands neue Einkreisung," XXII (Jan. 1931), 766.

[27] Wilhelm Röpke, German Commercial Policy (London, 1934), pp. 15-16.

[28] Cf. Heinrich Bechtel, Wirtschaftsgeschichte Deutschlands (3 vols.; Munich, 1956), III, 434.

Such policies were standard practice in Eastern Europe. Germany, however, had special problems that greatly complicated her trade position.

It will be recalled that the Treaty of Versailles had reduced Germany's control over her own trading policy, had burdened her with reparations debts, and had shorn from her a significant portion of her resources, arable land, and productive capacity. These disadvantages, along with Western unwillingness to buy German exports, complicated German commercial policy.

Causes of a more purely economic nature also played a role in German trade difficulties. The war and the accompanying economic dislocations had stimulated the expansion of the industrial and agricultural sectors of Germany's trading partners and competitors. The rapid growth of American agriculture and industry during the war and the years immediately preceding is a well-known fact of economic history. French and British industry also of necessity had to produce more during the war years. The increased capacities of these traditionally industrial lands and the beginnings of industrial production in the hitherto less developed regions of the world—Canada, Australia, South Africa, Japan, India, Latin America—together worked to put tremendous pressures on the German export industry and, consequently, on her domestic economy. Germany's Eastern and Southern European trading partners suffered from a shortage of foreign exchange; and Germany, now a capital-*importing* country, could not offer her potential markets the capital investments which in the past had accompanied their purchase of German goods.[29]

The consequence of the alterations in Germany's economic position as a result of the war and the structural alteration in the world economy was that, in the 1920s more than ever before, Germany was forced to export to stay alive, to keep her industry running, and to meet her foreign obligations. But, at the same time, her ability to export

[29] Franz Eulenberg, "Die deutsche Industrie auf dem Weltmarkte," *Strukturwandlungen*, I, 405ff., esp. 405-14.

had been seriously impaired. Germany on the eve of the depression ranked only fourth among the major exporting countries: Great Britain, the United States, and even France surpassed Germany in volume of exports.[30] She had to import approximately one-sixth of her food supply and the same proportion of her industrial needs.[31]

Because Germany led such a tenuous existence within the world economy, it was not surprising that strong forces re-emerged during the depression advocating a return to protection. The cry for "autarky" almost assumed the proportions of a popular slogan.[32]

Fried placed autarky at the top of the list of the economic demands of the *Tat* circle. He charged the West with having launched a credit offensive against Germany at the outbreak of the depression when Western creditors had begun to press their German debtors for immediate repayment. He interpreted the fierce competition for trade, which the depression had unleashed among the affected nations, as a declaration of economic war by the West. Not only did the Allies of World War I refuse to buy German goods, but they also competed aggressively with German exporters for markets. Recalling the last war, Fried forecast that the ultimate economic weapon of the West would be a return to the policy of blockade, which had proven so effective in bringing Germany to her knees in 1918. If Germany wished to survive, he warned, she would have to be prepared to weather such economic pressures. Fried proposed autarky as Germany's only hope in a hostile world.[33]

The *Tat* circle made itself the spokesman for all those who, out of motives of self-interest or hazy visions of economic recovery, demanded that Germany seal herself off

[30] *Ibid.*, pp. 400-401.

[31] *Ibid.*, p. 392.

[32] See Friedrich Hoffman, "Der Ruf nach Autarkie in der deutschen politischen Gegenwartsideologie," *Weltwirtschaftliches Archiv*, XXXVI (1932), 496-511, for a good survey of the many brands of full and partial autarky and of the various political groups advocating them during the depression.

[33] Fried, *Autarkie, Tat-Schriften* (Jena, 1932), pp. 31-32, 50ff.

from external economic and, hence, political pressures. The
policy seemed even to speak to the condition of bewildered
youth. It represented what one economic historian of the
day termed "the new spirituality of the younger generation," a generation struggling to oust foreign cultural values and to implant its own.[34] Large-scale agriculture was
incapable of surviving any degree of free international
trading in grains. Once prosperous family dairy-and-truck
farms, especially in Schleswig-Holstein, proved increasingly
unable to meet heavy mortgages and taxes, and many went
under the hammer. *Tat* encouraged the burdened small
farmers and, to a lesser extent, the Junkers by promising
that a better balance between agriculture and industry
within the German economy would follow from autarkical
policies.[35] German industry was even less fit to endure foreign competition. In July 1933, for example, bar-iron sold
on the international market for around 60 Reichmarks.
Well protected behind the high tariff walls (which had

[34] Franz Eulenberg, "Aussenhandel und Aussenpolitik," *Grundriss
der Sozialökonomik*, VIII, 224. Speaking before the executive committee of the Reichsverband der Deutschen Industrie in 1932, Clemens
Lammers defended the old liberal marketing policies by reference to
the age of the youth then entering industry and commerce. This
generation was still in its teens at the outbreak of the war, he argued,
and had never known "normal" economic conditions or a well-functioning world economy. Consequently, it did not understand why the
older generation prized economic liberalism so highly. Reprinted as
Clemens Lammers, *Autarkie, Planwirtschaft und berufsständischer
Staat* (Berlin, 1932), p. 5.

[35] E. W. Eschmann, "Nationale Planwirtschaft," XXIII (Jan. 1932),
827. The attitude of the *Tat* circle to the Junkers was equivocal. It
advocated national self-sufficiency, state guarantee of grain and cattle
prices, and the remission of burdensome mortgages—all of which would
have benefited the Junkers as much, if not more, than the peasant
cultivators. It also urged the parcelling out of large estates to the unemployed and the landless—"where it pays." Aside from the political
grounds for the land resettlement in the East in the years before and
during the Republic, a prime motivation had been to make cheap
German labor available to the large growers. Perhaps *Tat*'s ambiguity
mirrored that of its patron, the "social general" Kurt von Schleicher.
Cf. Fried, "Wo stehen wir?" XXIII (Aug. 1931), 383, and the unsigned article "Wohin treiben wir?" XXIII (Aug. 1931), 352.

permitted complete trustification of the steel industry), domestic bar-iron prices stood at 112 Reichmarks.[36] Workers too often saw no alternative under the conditions but to warmly second their employers.

The writers of Tat represented the policy of autarky as being forced upon the German people and as therefore essentially defensive.[37] Both the world and the domestic situation demanded that Germany seek self-sufficiency, argued the magazine; and Fried devised proof that Germany could achieve it. By improvements in efficiency, increased acreage, special protective tariffs, and abstinence Germany could produce enough grain, meat, potatoes, milk and dairy products, eggs, sugar, vegetables, fruit, herring, and wine to feed herself.[38] To be sure, Germans would have to forego coffee, tea, cocoa, and most spices and would have to cut down on their use of tobacco;[39] but only a modest patriotism would suffice for this purpose.

The *economic* folly of an industrialized country like Germany, with limited agricultural resources at her disposal, growing her own food is apparent. It would clearly have been more advantageous for her to have exported finished industrial goods, in which she had a relative trade advantage, and to have purchased what she could not efficiently grow. A reasonable international division of labor wherein each of the trading partners produces those goods for which it has a relative abundance of the requisite factors of production tends to yield the greatest economies and, therefore, the lowest consumer prices.[40] But it was just the

[36] *Die Wirtschaftskurve der Frankfurter Zeitung*, July 1933, p. 172; cited in Röpke, *German Commercial Policy*, p. 31.

[37] Giselher Wirsing, "Zwangsautarkie," XXIII (Sept. 1931), 428-38; Fried, *Autarkie*, p. 136.

[38] Fried, *Autarkie*, pp. 61-89, 92-94.

[39] *Ibid.*, pp. 89-92.

[40] On this point the reader may wish to consult the works of specialists, such as Bertil Ohlin, *Interregional and International Trade* (Cambridge, Mass., 1933), or Gottfried Haberler, *Theory of International Trade* (New York, 1937); but a reading of the relevant sections of a basic textbook of economics, such as Paul A. Samuelson's *Economics* (1st edn., New York, 1948), pp. 538-69, or the appropriate sections of any subsequent edition, should suffice.

resultant interdependence which Fried rejected. The political dangers of such a course outweighed the savings of a
few pfennigs the German consumer might enjoy. Was
not *Tat* struggling against the domination of the "How
Much?"[41]

Fried's argument that Germany could be self-sufficient in
the raw material requirements for her industry rested on an
even weaker basis. Here the argument was studded with
qualifying words like "perhaps" and with considerations of
possibilities. Fried had to admit that such vital resources
as iron ore would have to continue to be imported. His
conclusion that, "if necessary, we could manage without any
[raw material] imports" was not convincingly supported.[42]

Fried warded off being classified with the lunatic fringe
by more orthodox economists by denying that either he or
Tat were urging a total cessation of German foreign trade.
Naturally, Germany had to continue trading. His doctrine
of autarky did not oppose trade per se; rather, it aimed at
protecting Germany from the fearful consequences of the
collapse of the world economy.[43] An autarkical trade policy would restore what Fried felt was the proper relationship between the domestic economy and the world beyond
Germany's borders: Germany would import enough to cover
her needs in raw materials, and she would export enough
to pay for these primary goods.[44] Once emancipated from
foreign—that is, Western—economic pressures, Germany
might be better able to resist on the political level.[45]

Since autarky did not imply a complete end of trading,

[41] *EK*, pp. 30, 46. A further weakness of Fried's argument was that
it rested on the consumption figures of the depression years. Only
rigorous rationing measures could have restrained the eventual upsurge in demand. This relatively optimistic picture of how self-
sufficiency in food was to be achieved took no account of the possibility
of crop failures or of rationing.

[42] Fried, *Autarkie*, pp. 96-111.

[43] *Ibid.*, pp. 54ff., 126, 138. Fried, *Die Zukunft des Aussenhandels:
Durch innere Marktordnung zur Aussenhandelsfreiheit* (Jena, 1934),
p. 39—hereafter cited as *ZA*.

[44] *ZA*, p. 29.

[45] *ZA*, p. 39.

Fried saw the opposition to it as not originating merely from those interested in foreign commercial relations. He admitted that his critics correctly foresaw the implications of autarkical trading policies for internal organization. For, in Fried's words, "the implementation of autarky required, of necessity, regulation and guidance of the market, . . . an end to free and unrestrained economic activity [*Beweglichkeit*], and, as a consequence, an end to the chance for unlimited profits."[46]

Fried and his colleagues also realized fully the implications of what they advocated. Their recommendations for German commercial policy clearly required a state monopoly of foreign trade. This in turn required state control of international trade and payments and of domestic money and credit. Controls on production and distribution would necessarily follow. Autarky, then, presupposed a planned economy—in short, the complete domination of economic affairs by a powerful state.[47] An aura of morality clung to the idea of national planning in Eschmann's description of it as "*genuine* rationalization, avoidance of *wrong* investments, the formation of *genuine* economic capital."[48]

Fried and the members of the *Tat* circle admitted that a policy of autarky and a planned economy could be only the first steps in creating a buffered economy. Industrialists needed a certain supply of raw materials and markets for export of finished goods. Farmers had to sell surplus grain. The United States had Latin America as its economic appendage. The French had colonies, the British their Commonwealth. The Japanese had begun the creation of their Asian Co-Prosperity Sphere in 1931 with the invasion of China. For Germany *Tat* charted the "Course East-South-

[46] *ZA*, p. 42.

[47] Fried, "Wo stehen wir?" XXIII, 384-85; *EK*, p. 249. For an excellent analysis and refutation of the *economic* arguments for autarky and the planned economy of Fried, Salin, Sombart, and Spann, see Kurt Baumann, "Autarkie und Planwirtschaft," *Zeitschrift für Sozialforschung*, II (1933), 79-103.

[48] E. W. Eschmann, "Nationale Planwirtschaft," XXIV (June 1932), 229 (italics mine).

east!" Only in this direction could Germany break out dip-
lomatically and economically. *"For an anti-capitalist Germany can find its complement,"* wrote Wirsing, *"only in the
anti-capitalist peasant lands of the East."*[49] Germany's impossible indebtedness had forced her into the ranks of the
similarly burdened agrarian lands of Central Europe. She
was obligated, as the greatest sufferer of Western imposi-
tions, to lead Central and Eastern Europe in "the coming
world confrontation." She had to form a Central European
political confederation, which *"economically [would be]
tightly and centrally organized...."*[50]

The *Tat* circle expected close contact between the Ger-
man-led confederation and the Soviet Union. Diplomatical-
ly, keeping the line open to Moscow was essential for an
effective German foreign policy, as it was useful, too, for
Russia. And, like the peasant lands included in the proposed confederation, Russia would also serve as an important source for German raw materials and as a market for
her industrial products.[51] The USSR was a great anti-
capitalist power and the potential complement to Germany's political and economic needs.

Although *Tat* insisted that its plans for Germany's Eastern neighbors could not be implemented by force, it offered
its readers political forecasts which could have been realized
only by coercion or war. For the "closed national space"
(geschlossenen nationalen Raum) it projected included
more living space than contemporary Germany had at its
disposal. How could the Germans convince the future members of the confederation that economic direction from Berlin was what suited their own best interests? *Tat* answered
this question in part when it pointed out that "the contemporary young generation of Germans is growing up with
a thoroughly *grossdeutsch* outlook . . . ; the Central Euro-

[49] Fried, *Autarkie*, pp. 138, 143-44ff. Giselher Wirsing, "Richtung
Ost-Südost," XXII (Nov. 1930), 629-34 (italics in original).
[50] Fried, "Wo stehen wir?" XXIII, 384 (italics mine). *EK*, p. 264.
[51] Fried, "Wo stehen wir?" XXIII, 385; unsigned article "Deutschlands Weg aus der Einkreisung," XXII (March 1931), 952-55.

pean space, i.e., primarily the Balkans and the South East, dominates its imagination."[52] The next step, the writers of *Tat* concluded, was the political unification of the social groups in whose behalf *Tat* had devised this program.

Fried traced the long-range causes of the contemporary social crisis back to the triumph of the machine in the capitalist economy. The more industrialized Germany had become, the more impersonal had the process of production and the relationships between men become. Industrial capitalism had left "a field of rubble within men"; it had created the great chasm between capitalists and the masses that divided German society. As Wirsing wrote, "when today we look back at the agrarian-industrial debate of the turn of the century, we see how all the arguments of Adolf Wagner against the optimistic proponents of industrialism and exportation have turned out to be true. . . ."[53]

By the time of the great depression, Fried argued, the polarization of German society had gone so far that *not even* the traditional top "Four Hundred Families" controlled economic life anymore. Rather, he calculated that only one hundred and ten individuals or families owned a great proportion of the national wealth of Germany.[54] Fried did not use his findings to launch an attack on the wealthy; indeed, he chided the Social Democrats for the naïveté of their diatribes against the "money bags." He pointed, instead, to the destruction of the inherited social order as the true cause of this great conglomeration of economic power. Seemingly more "Marxist" than the Marxists

[52] "Deutschlands Weg aus der Einkreisung," XXII, 949, 952. See also Wirsing's book *Zwischeneuropa und die deutsche Zukunft, Tat-Schriften* (Jena, 1932), which von Klemperer has described as an "uninhibitedly offensive version of Naumann's Central Europe concept." *Germany's New Conservatism*, p. 130.

[53] *EK*, pp. 28, 46. Cf. also Fried's "Das Geld in der Krise," XXII (Oct. 1930), 523ff. Wirsing, *ibid.*, p. 249.

[54] They controlled, according to Fried, 3.4 billion marks of the national wealth. The next 2,300 men of wealth were worth only 2.3 billion. "Die oberen Vierhundert," XXI (Dec. 1929), 662-78.

themselves, Fried refused to denounce the men of wealth. The fault lay with the contemporary social order: it was "unmodern."[55]

Tat's analysis of the result of the Reichstag elections of September 1930 came to the novel conclusion that "56.6 per cent of the [newly elected] Reichstag was anti-capitalist." That is, over half of the representatives of the German people, comprising the Communists, the Social Democrats, and the NSDAP, opposed the existing economic order.[56] The depression had produced this revulsion against capitalist society. The emergency policies of Chancellor Brüning had only aggravated the disaffection; Fried observed that the crisis of capitalism had progressed so far during the Brüning era that state control and direction of the economy was necessary merely to insure that men's most basic needs of food and shelter were satisfied.[57] It was clear to Fried and his co-workers that the "system" of Weimar had lost whatever social basis it had ever had. The workers and peasants were beginning to move.[58] At their head, the *Tat* circle urged, should march the intelligentsia of the academic youth, the members of the white-collar middle classes, and those entrepreneurs they termed the "artisans of our time."[59]

These elements of the Mittelstand would provide the social basis of *Tat*'s economic and political program; indeed, the program was but an articulation of their demands. These strata were being pauperized, yet they refused to be "proletarianized." They were ready to join forces. "The Mittelstand is being pulverized between capital and the masses at an ever increasing rate. However, from it has emerged a new spiritual-political stratum, a stratum which

[55] *Ibid.*

[56] Unsigned article "Die kalte Revolution," XXII, 493.

[57] Fried, "Gestaltung des Zusammenbruchs," XXIII (March 1932), 978. See also his "Der Umbau der Welt," XXIII (May 1931), 81ff.

[58] *EK*, pp. 184-85.

[59] Zehrer, "Achtung! junge Front! Draussenbleiben!" XXI, 25-39. Heinrich Geiger, "Die Stosskraft der Angestellten," XXI (Jan. 1930), 758-65. Fried, "Der mittlere Unternehmer," XXI (Feb. 1930), 812. *EK*, pp. 95-96.

believes neither in the economic solutions of capital nor in those of the masses. For it has learned from its own misery that, contrary to Karl Marx, the spirit does triumph over matter."[60]

Tat published numerous investigations of the condition of the new middle classes. All these studies pointed to the same conclusion: these classes had to, and could, unite with the best elements from all the parties for political action. Fried described an estimated 0.84 million politically disaffected members of the white-collar Mittelstand as "puffballs"; broken, they would become liberating spores among the remaining 4.7 million.[61] Heinrich Geiger examined the problems of the unemployed and the lowness of the incomes of those who could work.[62] Despite their small numbers and low incomes, *Tat* assured them that they were in a position to exercise a great deal of political leverage.[63] Eschmann warned them to avoid the mistakes of the Italian middle strata, who had not understood the dynamism of Fascism and, as a consequence, had been left behind by it.[64]

Fried included the entrepreneurs of medium-sized enterprises which had not changed over to methods of mass production. It did not matter to him how large the factory of the producer of quality goods was; only the entrepreneur's attitude toward production was decisive.[65] He held up the industrialists Robert Bosch, Heinrich Freese, and Ernst Abbe as men who were ideal examples of this kind

[60] Fritz Leinweber, "Enteignung und Revolution des Mittelstands," XXII (Feb. 1931), 899. As an advertising prospectus put it, "*Tat* stands above the parties and rallies the forces of the middle."

[61] "Die Spaltpilze," XXI (Oct. 1929), 520-28.

[62] Heinrich Geiger, "Was verdient heute der Angestellte?" XXI (Feb. 1930), 836-41. See also Hans Thomas [Zehrer], "Akademisches Proletariat," XXII (Jan. 1931), 818.

[63] Geiger, "Die Stosskraft der Angestellten," XXI, 758-65, and Horst Grüneberg, "Mittelstandspolitik—Staatspolitik," XXIII (June 1931), 191-212.

[64] E. W. Eschmann, "Der Faschismus und die Mittelschichten," XXI (Feb. 1930), 851.

[65] Fried, "Der mittlere Unternehmer," XXI, 814.

of socially minded entrepreneur.[66] Fried praised the quality production of such manufacturers as "a higher form of
artisan industry" (*gesteigertes Handwerk*).[67] Like the rest
of the Mittelstand, they were caught "in between":[68] the
state would not recognize their special needs; the trade unions and Socialist policies were threatening the existence of
their factories; and the large capitalists who bought from
them or sold to them were exploiting their vulnerable position. Although they often sided with the large capitalists,
they were really a part of a Third Force. Fried expected them to come soon to a proper evaluation of their
position.[69]

Tat counselled German academic youth not to serve as
a prop for the decadent old order. Nor, it added, should
they hastily enter the ranks of the organized enemies of the
old order, whether they be of the right or of the left. The
"Young Front" must remain outside the old political align-
ments. *Tat* promised to include them in a new Third
Front.[70]

Tat welcomed recruits to the ranks of the Third Front
from all the parties, but not the parties themselves. The
chancellorship of Heinrich Brüning had exposed the bank-
ruptcy of the existing parties. Fried excluded the Social
Democrats from the Third Front, although *Tat* had counted their votes in its estimation of the size of the anti-capitalist alliance in the Reichstag. The heirs of Friedrich Engels,
the actual founder of the movement, had abandoned his
teachings in the era of late capitalism and had so closely
allied the movement with the one-time foe that Fried accused them of acting as the last crutch of the declining system of capitalism.[71] The Communists were clearly out of the

[66] *EK*, pp. 93-94.
[67] *EK*, pp. 83-84.
[68] *EK*, pp. 95-96.
[69] *Ibid.*; "Der mittlere Unternehmer," XXI, 823.
[70] Zehrer, "Achtung! junge Front! Draussenbleiben!" XXI, 25-29.
[71] *EK*, pp. 110, 113, 116, 124. Like Sombart and Spengler, Fried
denigrated Marxism—in contradistinction to socialism—as a secular
religion. In accordance with the familiar social conservative line of
criticism, he attacked the homeless Jew, Karl Marx, for having intro-

question. The Young Conservatives seemed to the *Tat* circle to be acting more like followers of Metternich than like the revolutionaries they claimed to be. And Hitler, who had focused his energies solely on the seizure of power, had exhausted himself in shadowboxing with the Brüning government. Zehrer dismissed the Nazis as vulgarians who offered no serious solutions to the fundamental questions of the day.[72] Who, then, would create the Third Front?

When President von Hindenburg asked Brüning to resign at the end of May 1932, Hans Zehrer urged the immediate formation of the Third Front. If the "true will" of the people could be engaged in a front which joined the authority of the President of the Reich with the power of the Reichswehr, the new state might be created, he wrote in *Tat*.[73] After Hindenburg had named Franz von Papen to replace Brüning, *Tat* published an appeal for an "interim cabinet" to be led by von Papen's minister of war, General Kurt von Schleicher.[74] The *Tat* circle expected this man, whom many Germans called the "social general," to translate their ideal into political reality. Schleicher stood above the parties. He enjoyed the confidence of the President. Moreover, he spoke in behalf of the army on political questions.

After the fall of Brüning, which in large measure Schleicher had caused, it was he who had prevailed upon Hindenburg to appoint Franz von Papen. Von Papen, in an interview with the President on 1 December 1932, proposed to go beyond the near dictatorial powers which Hindenburg had permitted him (and his predecessor) under Article 48 of the Weimar Constitution. He wished to continue to rule without concurrence of the Reichstag, to

---

duced into German socialism the foreign ideals of internationalism and the abolition of private property. "Kapital und Masse," XXII (Jan. 1931), 776-77, or *EK*, p. 114.

[72] Zehrer, "Die dritte Front," XXIV (May 1932), 117-18; unsigned article "Metternich Ära," XXII (July 1930), 299.

[73] "Die dritte Front," XXIV, 118.

[74] Zehrer, "Der Entscheidung entgegen," XXIV (June 1932), 198-200.

suppress the political parties and the paramilitary organizations by means of the police and the army, and to reform
the Constitution in an authoritarian direction.[75] As far
back as August *Tat* had attacked the Papen regime for
being reactionary, for pursuing a "monarchist-legitimist policy of restoration."[76] After von Papen had laid his plan before the President, Schleicher effected his dismissal. Von
Papen's reactionary coup d'etat, he believed would stop
neither the NSDAP nor the Communists. It could not build
the basis for stable government, and it might well lead to
the outbreak of civil war.[77] After the dismissal of Brüning
and von Papen it became impossible for Schleicher to continue his political maneuvers offstage. On 3 December he
reluctantly assumed the chancellorship, retaining the port-
folio of the Reichswehr Ministry.

It is extremely difficult to unravel the complex politics of
General Schleicher. He had Brüning dismissed because he
was unable to form an effective, durable political coalition.
Von Papen and his "cabinet of barons" had to go because
they were reactionary. Schleicher's actions and statements
while in office offer only meager evidence for a judgment
of his own ideological orientation. A few days after he had
taken office he began to repeal the reactionary economic program which von Papen had instituted. He earmarked funds
for vast public works projects. He reestablished state supervision over wage levels set in negotiated labor contracts. He
pushed through a special program of winter relief. All
these measures alarmed the business community but did not
win him more than an attitude of watchful toleration

75 Bracher, *Die Auflösung der Weimarer Republik*, p. 672.

76 Zehrer, "Revolution oder Restauration," XXIV (Aug. 1932), 365;
see also 353-91.

77 Bracher, *Die Auflösung der Weimarer Republik*, pp. 673-77. On
the political maneuvers of Schleicher, see the study by Thilo Vogelsang,
*Reichswehr, Staat und NSDAP: Beiträge zur deutschen Geschichte,
1930-1932* (Stuttgart, 1962). For the phase up to his accession to the
chancellorship, see pp. 65-334, esp. pp. 318-34. See also the section
by Bracher in *Die Nationalsozialistische Machtergreifung*, "Die Stufen
der Machtergreifung," pp. 38-44.

among the parties of the center and the left.[78] When he addressed the German people on the radio on 15 December, he, like the *Tat* circle, promised something for everyone. The workers were to get public works projects to relieve unemployment. Agriculture would receive increased duties on agricultural goods and an intensification of the program of rural resettlement. For the rest, he asked for the cooperation of all Germans, promising them (but not elaborating) a program beyond both capitalism and socialism. In the accurate phrase of Karl Dietrich Bracher, "the General courted everyone and aroused the mistrust of everyone."[79]

His tactical maneuvers appeared equally ambiguous. Since the Brüning era he had been conducting intermittent negotiations with representatives of the major parties of the Reichstag, with the exception of the Communists. He conferred frequently with Alfred Hugenberg of the DNVP and with representatives of the major businessmen's organizations. He spoke with leaders of the Socialist and the Catholic trade unions, as well as with Adolf Hitler.[80] His seemed to be the goal of the *Tat* circle: the creation of the Third Front.

The success or failure of his plan for creating parliamentary backing and perhaps a social base for a government which would ease the political crisis without civil war and without injury to the political independence of the army depended upon the cooperation of the largest party of the Reichstag, the NSDAP. At first Schleicher believed it possible to "domesticate" the Nazis by offering to include them in the cabinet. But Hitler refused anything short of the chancellorship. Schleicher, deciding now to split the party, initiated negotiations with Gregor Strasser, head of the party apparatus and leader of the left, or Northern, wing.[81]

[78] Bracher, *Die Auflösung der Weimarer Republik*, p. 680.

[79] *Ibid.*, pp. 680-81, 687.

[80] *Ibid.*, pp. 670, 687. Thilo Vogelsang, "Zur Politik Schleichers gegenüber der NSDAP, 1932," *Vierteljahrshefte für Zeitgeschichte*, VI (1958), 86-118.

[81] Vogelsang, *Vierteljahrshefte für Zeitgeschichte*, VI, 115-18.

At the same time, his talks with Adam Stegerwald, the leader of the Catholic trade unions, and Theodor Leipart, head of the Socialist unions, seemed to promise the possibility of a political alliance in that direction.[82]

In the two brief months of Schleicher's chancellorship these plans came to a head—and collapsed. Strasser controlled the party bureaucracy. He, Ernst Röhm, the leader of the SA, and Gottfried Feder,. the guardian of the Nazi economic program, all urged ending what seemed to them a fruitless opposition and accepting Schleicher's offer of ministerial posts. Leipart, in the tradition of the trade unions, seemed willing to gamble with an opportunistic policy which might stop Hitler. On 8 December Strasser dramatically resigned all his party posts and put his seat in the Reichstag at the disposal of the party. It appeared that he had acted to force Hitler's hand. But, instead of aligning his forces, Strasser left almost immediately with his family for a vacation in Italy. Feder, too, began a holiday. Within forty-eight hours Hitler, by threatening suicide, employing intimidation, and exploiting personal and factional rivalries, had brought the party once more firmly behind him.[83] On 6 January Rudolf Breitscheid of the SPD asked Leipart in the name of the party to break off negotiations with Schleicher.[84] Alfred Hugenberg, who had seemed willing to take his party into the Schleicher coalition, also broke away and undertook a series of negotiations with Oskar von Hindenburg, the son of the President, the vengeful Franz von Papen, and Hitler, which on 30 January 1933 brought a right-wing coalition government into power with Hitler as chancellor.[85]

Initially the members of the *Tat* circle did not seem to realize that the German Revolution had taken place without the mediation of their Third Front. As late as March

[82] For these negotiations, see Gerard Braunthal, "The German Free Trade Unions during the Rise of Nazism," *Journal of Central European Affairs*, XV (1955/56), 343-47.

[83] Bracher, *Die Auflösung der Weimarer Republik*, pp. 681-83.

[84] *Ibid.*, pp. 699-700.

[85] *Ibid.*, pp. 691-732.

1933 they still guided their readers' hopes in the direction of an alliance between the "social general" and the "socialist exponent of the NSDAP."[86] The alliance was never concluded. On 30 June 1934 Strasser and Schleicher paid the price for trying to flank Adolf Hitler: both were killed, along with many others who had advocated a second, a social revolution, presumably on the orders of Hitler, the leader of the national revolution.[87]

Tat continued to appear after 1933. Before the end of 1933 Hans Zehrer left political journalism. He had a Jewish wife, and, besides, he had been too closely linked with Schleicher not to have earned some enmity in the Nazi camp. It might have been, too, that he continued to hold his stated low opinion of Hitler and the slogans of National Socialism.[88]

Ferdinand Fried found a place in the Third Reich. With the failure of the Third Front he put himself and his magazine at the disposal of the government which he now hoped would carry out the program of social conservatism. He praised the early economic measures of National Socialism as steps in the right direction. He noted with gratification Germany's rapidly increasing economic self-sufficiency. His admiration for the producers of quality goods, such as I. G. Farben, grew even greater; he extolled them for their facility in producing synthetic materials to substitute for the missing imports.[89] He expressed his satisfaction with what economic reorganization the government had been able to accomplish by 1935.[90] He proved sufficiently attuned to the new order to merit an introduction to his book of 1934,

[86] Unsigned article "Schleicher und Strasser," XXIV (March 1933), 1068.

[87] Hermann Mau, "Die 'Zweite Revolution'—Der 30. Juni 1934," *Vierteljahrshefte für Zeitgeschichte*, I (1953), 119-37.

[88] During the war Zehrer recalled to the novelist Ernst von Salomon how superior as a man and as a politician Schleicher had been. He told von Salomon that the General's failure to stop Hitler had been nothing less than a tragedy. Reported by von Salomon in his *Der Fragebogen*, pp. 182-88.

[89] Fried, "Die Nationalwirtschaft," XXVI (Nov. 1934), 578-95.

[90] Fried, "Der Weg der Wirtschaft," XXVI (Feb. 1935), 814-33.

Die Zukunft des Aussenhandels (*The Future of Foreign Trade*), by Walther Darré, the Nazi authority on agriculture, Leader of the Peasantry, and minister of agriculture.

Gradually, like the Nazis, Fried abandoned the ideology of social conservatism. He ceased attacking the spread of technology and gave up his offensive against capitalism. Now that the Nazis could effectively manipulate German trade policy, he dropped his hostility to international trade.[91]

In 1942 he looked back to the days of the Weimar Republic when he and his co-workers on *Tat* had fought the domination of the state by big business. It had to be so, he now wrote, "for there existed no other force, no other authority." As in the days of Weimar, he looked ahead to "a future constitution of the economy" which would retain many features of older economic forms.[92] The reality of the Nazi era seemed to have caused him to leave behind the ideals of social conservatism. All that remained was his faith in the creative entrepreneur. The Nazi era disappointed him in all other respects. When the war ended, Fried was ready with a new interpretation of economic reality. The book he wrote in 1956 bore the title *Krupp: Tradition und Aufgabe* (*Krupp: Tradition and Mission*).[93]

[91] *Wende der Weltwirtschaft* (Leipzig, 1939), pp. 11, 46, 48-49, 82, 350. "Stunde des Aussenhandels," XXVI (May 1934), 142-44.

[92] *Die soziale Revolution* (Leipzig, 1942), p. 65: ". . . und sie musste es tun, weil sonst keine Gewalt, keine Autorität vorhanden war."

[93] (Bad Godesberg, 1956).

Conclusion
Organize and Perish

*The environment of my youth was
the circles of the petite bourgeoisie, a world which had very
little contact with that of the manual worker. Curious as it
may seem at first glance, the cleft between this by no means
economically well-situated stratum and the muscle worker
is often deeper than people realize. The reason for this,
we might almost call it animosity, is the fear of a social
group, which has only recently pulled itself up from the
level of the manual laborer, of falling back into the old,
little esteemed, estate—or at least of being reckoned in as
part of it. In addition, many remember with disgust the
cultural poverty of the lower classes, the coarseness of their
daily social intercourse. Their own position in society,
however modest it may be, makes any further contact with
this cultural and existential niveau, which they have left
behind, unbearable.*

—ADOLF HITLER in *Mein Kampf*[1]

Hitler's understanding of the needs of the middle classes
was primarily intuitive; but he understood them better than
the theorists of social conservatism. The tiny nationalist
organization which he joined in 1919 called itself the
German Workers Party. Like all German parties, it needed
a statement of its principles and program. Accordingly,
members Anton Drexler, a machinist by trade, and Gottfried Feder, an engineer, with a little help from Hitler,
composed a document setting forth twenty-five principles
and demands. The party soon changed its name to National
Socialist German Workers Party, and the Twenty-Five

[1] (Munich, 1933), p. 22.

Points, which were first publicly proclaimed before an audience at the Munich Hofbräuhaus on 24 February 1920, remained its official program for the next two and a half decades.

The first nine points demanded the union of all Germans into a Great Germany, abolition of the Treaties of Versailles and St. Germain, colonies for Germany's surplus population, exclusion of Jews from citizenship, appointment of only competent citizens to official posts without regard to party affiliation, state promotion of the welfare and economic activities of its citizens, an end to non-German immigration, and equality of rights and duties for all citizens. The program further called for improvement in the level of national health through obligatory physical activities, formation of a national army, legal measures against conscious political lies and their publication, a German press, and elevation of the common interest above self-interest.

The economic points demanded abolition of the "thralldom of interest," confiscation of war profits, nationalization of syndicates and trusts, introduction of profit-sharing in industry, and improved old-age insurance. Point Sixteen called for "the creation and maintenance of a healthy middle class" of artisans and merchants. Point Seventeen advocated land reform by means of "confiscation without compensation," the abolition of interest on mortgages, and prohibition of land speculation. The final plank urged the "creation of a strong central power of the Reich" and the "formation of diets and vocational chambers for the purpose of executing the general laws promulgated by the Reich and the various states of the federation."[2]

These demands clearly embodied the *Weltanschauung* of the many elements of the old middle classes in the depression year of 1920.[3] Equally clearly, they were framed with-

---

[2] An English text of the program with commentary by Gottfried Feder may be found in Feder's *Hitler's Official Programme, and its Fundamental Ideas* (London, 1934), pp. 38-43—tr. from *Das Programm der N.S.D.A.P. und seine weltanschaulichen Grundgedanken* (23. Auflage, Munich, 1930).

[3] Of the ample evidence on this point, see, e.g., Talcott Parsons, "Some Sociological Elements of the Fascist Movements," in his *Essays*

in the tradition of social conservatism. Here, in greatly vulgarized form, were Sombart's and Spengler's repudiation of the "inner England" and Salin's search for morality in public life. Here was the corporatism of Othmar Spann, with its contradictions between central authority and corporate decentralization. Here was the nationalism of all social conservatives and their outcry against foreign oppression. Here, finally, was the recognition of the special needs of artisans, small businessmen, and the peasantry. And yet it would be inaccurate simply to equate social conservatism with Nazism.

Like the middle classes, from which most of them stemmed,[4] the party members could not agree on any one economic ethic. Within the ranks of the NSDAP four different and distinct economic ideologies coexisted in the years before 1933.

At the center stood Gottfried Feder. Although fully committed to the program, he was willing to accept a few compromises if the party's struggle for political power required them. He led the struggle against the thralldom of interest,[5] but he denied that he or the movement opposed the institution of private property per se.[6] Anti-Semitism

---

in Sociological Theory (Glencoe, Ill., 1954), pp. 133ff.; Charles P. Loomis and J. Allen Beegle, "The Spread of German Nazism in Rural Areas," *American Sociological Review*, XI (1946), 729ff.; Carl J. Friedrich, "The Peasant as Evil Genius of Dictatorship," *Yale Review*, XXVI (1937), 724ff.; and Eduard Heimann, *Communism, Fascism, or Democracy* (New York, 1938). Bracher summarizes the electoral data in *Die Auflösung der Weimarer Republik*, pp. 645ff.

[4] Hans Gerth, "The Nazi Party: Its Leadership and Composition," in Robert K. Merton et al., eds., *Reader in Bureaucracy* (Glencoe, Ill., 1952); Daniel Lerner, *The Nazi Elite*, in Series B of the Hoover Institute Studies (Stanford, 1951). See in addition the works cited in n. 3.

[5] See his *Kampf gegen die Hochfinanz* (Munich, 1933), esp. the essay "Grundsätzliches über nationalsozialistische Wirtschaftspolitik," pp. 304-5; *Der deutsche Staat auf nationaler und sozialer Grundlage*, pp. 37ff.; *Hitler's Official Programme*, pp. 55-59, 93-98.

[6] Feder, "National Sozialismus und Eigentum," *Kampf gegen die Hochfinanz*, pp. 310-20, esp. p. 318; *Hitler's Official Programme*, pp. 88-89.

and the economic program of the party were of equal importance to him.[7] Feder was the "great projector" of the NSDAP. He advanced schemes for projects as diverse as termination of the credit shortage, nationalization of the banks, work creation during the depression, commercial autarky, and settlement of unemployed urban workers in the countryside.[8] He remained loyal to the party when the radicals were purged or executed.

The left was led by the Strasser brothers and their friends. Strongest in the Rhineland and in the industrial North, the Strasser wing took the socialist ideals of the party quite seriously. "We are socialists, economic socialists," proclaimed Gregor Strasser. "We speak for the 85 percent of the German people who own nothing and work for salaries and wages."[9] Otto Strasser left the party in 1930 to found the Kampfgemeinschaft revolutionärer Nationalsozialisten (Fighting Brotherhood of Revolutionary National Socialists) when Hitler refused to permit the party press in Saxony to support the trade unions during the great strike of that year.[10]

[7] See, e.g., *Hitler's Official Programme*, p. 71.

[8] *Ibid.*, pp. 96-98; Schweitzer, *Big Business in the Third Reich*, pp. 83-84. Hans Buchner, *Grundriss einer nationalsozialistischen Volkswirtschaftstheorie*, Nationalsozialistische Bibliothek, Heft 16 (Munich, 1930), is essentially a gloss on Feder with liberal supplementation from Spann and Walter Heinrich. For a critique of Feder's ideas up to 1926, see Franz Haber, *Untersuchungen über Irrtümer moderner Geldverbesserer* (Jena, 1926).

[9] Gregor Strasser, "National Sozialismus," in his *Kampf um Deutschland: Reden und Aufsätze eines Nationalsozialisten* (Munich, 1933), pp. 72-77, and in the same volume, "Gegen Marxismus und Reaktion," pp. 222-25.

[10] He soon renamed his organization the Black Front. It proved to be of no political importance in the remaining years of the Republic. His *Germany Tomorrow*, tr. Eden and Cedar Paul (London, 1940), has as Part III most of his earlier *Aufbau des deutschen Sozialismus* (1st edn., 1931). The 1940 English translation contains the gist of his program, which was little more than an elaboration of the original NSDAP program without the racism. It included all the modifications which had been made before his expulsion. It called for the abridgment of the right of private property, with the exception of landed "entail." It championed the *Arbeitsgemeinschaft* for big factories but left the

The right wing of the party was primarily a product of the depression years. It grew more powerful as the political fortunes of the party improved. Fritz Thyssen of the Vereinigte Stahlwerke and Albert Pietzsch, president of the Chamber of Industry in Munich, were the only important businessmen who joined the NSDAP before 1933. Several more joined after the accession to power.[11] But the majority of sympathetic business leaders chose to make their influence felt through official channels, personal contacts with important party figures, or unofficial circles of patrons, such as those around Wilhelm Keppler and Heinrich Himmler.[12] In 1931 Walther Funk left his post as editor of the *Berliner Börsen-Zeitung* to become an intermediary between the NSDAP and members of the commercial and industrial community. Many years later at the Nuremberg trials he testified that he had "tried to accomplish [his] mission by impressing on the Führer and the party as a whole that private initiative, the self-reliance of the businessman, and the creative powers of free enterprise should be recognized as the basic economic policy of the party."[13]

These first three theoretical tendencies within the

---

artisan fully in charge of his shop and its employees. It contained, finally, an elaborate model for a system of corporate estates. See pp. 126-89 of the translation, esp. pp. 142-44, 169-89.

[11] Such as Karl Krauch of I. G. Farben, who joined in 1937; Hermann Schmitz, treasurer and, in 1934, general director of the same firm, who became a NSDAP Reichstag deputy in November 1933; Albert Vögler, general director of the Vereinigte Stahlwerke, who also became a NSDAP Reichstag deputy in November 1933. Consult the biographical survey in Appendix C of Schweitzer's *Big Business in the Third Reich*.

[12] On the relationship of the Nazis to big business, see, in addition to the appropriate sections of *ibid.*, Schweitzer's article "Business Power in the Nazi Regime," *Zeitschrift für Nationalökonomie*, Dec. 1960, pp. 414-42; George W.F. Hallgarten, "Adolf Hitler and German Heavy Industry," *Journal of Economic History*, XII (1952), 222-46; and August Heinrichsbauer, *Schwerindustrie und Politik* (Essen, 1948). Louis Lochner's *Tycoons and Tyrants* (Chicago, 1954) should also be mentioned.

[13] Statement of Walther Funk before the International Military Tribunal, cited in Alan Bullock, *Hitler: A Study in Tyranny* (rev. edn., New York: Harper Torchbooks paperback, 1962), p. 172.

NSDAP corresponded to the three camps of social conservative ideology in the years before 1933. Sombart and Spann
were at the center.[14] Niekisch belonged clearly on the extreme left, and Spengler, deviations notwithstanding, belonged to the extreme right. Because of his wide range of
interests and his unique approaches to many problems,
Salin is more difficult to place in a category. Even if his
psychological set and his theory of economic analysis belied
economic liberalism, his commitment (as distinguished
from his sympathies) lay with the business community. In
the years of the depression, finally, the synthesis of the *Tat*
circle united all three camps. *Tat* advocated nationalization
of vital industries, with the left; it urged immediate improvement of the lot of the middle classes, with the center;
and it held up the creative entrepreneur as a model for all
classes of the society, with the right. None of the social
conservatives studied assigned racism a role of any significance in their theories.

The fourth complex of attitudes within the NSDAP was
not, properly speaking, a theory of economic values. It was,
rather, the position which subordinated the economic ideals
of the party to racism, to nationalism, and to the tactics of
winning power. This was above all the outlook of Hitler.

Hitler, like most members of the middle classes, knew
little about economics.[15] Problems in this realm he left to

[14] Feder's acknowledgment of his indebtedness to Spann (*Hitler's
Official Programme*, p. 54) is a rare instance in the National Socialist
economic literature of the acknowledgment of the *economic ideas* of any
of the twentieth-century social conservative studied here. But, as
we have seen throughout, most of these ideas were in circulation before 1914.

[15] Consider his statement made in the intimate circle of his secre-
taries in 1941: "All these things are simple and natural. The only
thing is, one mustn't let the Jew stick his nose in. The basis of Jewish
commercial policy is to make matters incomprehensible to a normal
brain. People go into ecstasies of confidence before the science of the
great economists. Any one who does not understand is taxed with
ignorance! At bottom, the only object of all these notions is to throw
everything into confusion." *Hitler's Secret Conversations, 1941-1944*, tr.
Norman Cameron and R. H. Stevens (New York: Signet Book paper-

the brothers Strasser, to Feder, and, after 1933, to Hjalmar
Schacht, onetime president of the Reichsbank. The only
two economic themes which cropped up with any regu-
larity in his writings, speeches, and conversations were his
hatred of bolshevism and of its ally, Jewish finance
capital.[16]

Soon after his release from prison in December 1924 Hitler had to quell a left-wing mutiny in the ranks of the reconstituted party. Gregor Strasser, speaking for the Northern wing, circulated the draft of a new party program,
which was essentially a radical gloss on the 1920 program.
The economic points called for, among other provisions,
entail of peasant farms, expropriation of large estates and
their redistribution as middling farms, nationalization of
major industries, introduction of compulsory gilds in enterprises employing fewer than twenty workers, and high
protective tariffs. The Strasser program further projected
the creation of five groups of regional and national corporate chambers covering agriculture, industry and commerce, labor, civil service and white-collar jobs, and the free
professions. It concluded by advocating the creation of a
Grossdeutsches Reich, a Central European customs union,
and a German-dominated United States of Europe. Domestically, an organically structured corporate system was
to replace parliamentary institutions. Economically, the
rights of the collectivity would be reconciled with the
deeply rooted human instinct of personal egoism.[17]

---

back, 1953), p. 89. This is a complete translation of the *Bormann-
Vermerke*, the notes Bormann had taken while Hitler rambled on at
the table after dinner.

[16] *Ibid.*, pp. 98, 357-58, 37, 456-57; see further the selection from
his statements on the Jews collected and edited by Norman H. Baynes,
The Speeches of Adolf Hitler, April 1922-August 1939 (2 vols.; London, 1942), I, 721-43; and, of course, *Mein Kampf*, e.g., pp. 420ff.,
444ff., and esp. the denunciations of the international Jewish financial
conspiracy, pp. 702ff.

[17] On this 1925/26 Strasser program, see one version and the commentary by Reinhard Kühnl, "Zur Programmatik der Nationalsozialistischen Linken: Das Strasser-Programm von 1925/26," *Vierteljahrshefte für Zeitgeschichte*, XIV (1966), 317-33, esp. 327-31, 333.

Hitler responded to this leftist version of social conservatism by forcing Strasser to withdraw the proposal and to
ask recipients to destroy their copies. Hitler followed up his
triumph in 1926 by declaring the program of 1920 unalter-
able. This move, at least temporarily, healed the ideological
and organizational rift. Now it was Hitler's turn to chart
the ideological course of the movement. But, unlike Gregor
Strasser, he acted quietly and privately.

At the request of Emil Kirdorf, Ruhr industrialist head
of Germany's top industrialists' organization, the Zentral-
verband deutscher Industrieller, Hitler offered his views on
Germany's current problems and proposals for their solution. His thoughts took the form of a secret pamphlet entitled *Der Weg zum Wiederaufstieg* (*The Road to Resurgence*). The covering letter, dated August 1927, was addressed to Emil Kirdorf himself, who, Hitler hoped, would
"help propagate these ideas in his circle."[18]

The National Socialist leader's statement began with the
premise that the contemporary belief that Germany had
finally attained economic stability was illusory. Rather, the
facts were that her international trade balance remained unfavorable, that international financiers were tightening
their grip on the German economy ("wiping out countless
middle and small enterprises [*Existenzen*]" in the process),
that the indebtedness of German industry and agriculture
was still growing, and that, "if this process continues un-
checked, in thirty years [?] the German people will have lost
the greater part of its once independent economy." Of
equal importance was the high rate of unemployment. The
increasing disposition of men out of work and men without

On Hitler's struggle to regain power after his release, see Konrad
Heiden, *Der Fuehrer: Hitler's Rise to Power*, tr. Ralph Manheim
(Boston, 1944), pp. 284-91.

[18] *Der Weg zum Wiederaufstieg* (Munich, 1927). I wish to express my
thanks to Professor Henry Turner, of Yale University, for supplying
me with a photocopy of the original text. All references, however,
will be to his publication of the pamphlet (with introduction and
translation), "Hitler's Secret Pamphlet for Industrialists, 1927," *Journal of Modern History*, XL (1968), pp. 348-74. The translations are
my own.

work to live off the community was also an alarming sign. These two factors alone—the spreading dominion of international finance capital in Germany and the domestic unemployment—proved to Hitler that no "consolidation," no "recovery," was taking place.[19]

No less crucial was the current level of business ethics. How could one speak of recovery in view of the extent of business fraud and speculation in Germany?[20]

For the future, Germany's greatest problem would be that of supporting herself economically. She could not do so solely from her own production. Germany had to export to survive. But the international competition was fierce. The advanced nations could not be expected to yield to Germany, and the underdeveloped lands were extending their own industrial capacities. Hitler reminded his industrialist readers that such international economic struggles were not won on the level of business activity but rather "by the power of the sword." That power was for Hitler the key variable. Thus, "in the highest sense, the task of politics is to make the life-struggle of a nation possible by the continued pursuit of a policy of adjusting [a people's] economic base [*Ernährungsgrundlage*] to the size of the population."[21]

In the remaining part of the statement Hitler laid out his political-ideological theories. These consisted primarily in a celebration of the importance of race, personality, and struggle in the fate of a nation.

Near the end of his message he reminded his readers that the National Socialist movement did not believe that the future of a people depended, in the first instance, on economic matters. Indeed, although the movement "views an independent national economy as a necessity," still, "the powerful nationalist state alone can give such an economy the protection and the freedom for survival and further development."[22]

[19] *Ibid.*, pp. 354-56.
[20] *Ibid.*, p. 356.
[21] *Ibid.*, pp. 356-58.
[22] *Ibid.*, p. 362. Actually, Hitler is playing on the ambiguity of the

We do not know the impact of Hitler's pamphlet on Emil Kirdorf's "circle." But we do know that in the following year, 1928, Hitler offered a reinterpretation of Point Seventeen of the party program in which he now specifically acknowledged the principle of private property in behalf of the NSDAP, proposing that the party expropriate only the land of Jewish speculators.[23]

In 1930, when Hitler forbade the party radicals to support the Saxon strikes, Otto Strasser in a final confrontation accused him of wanting "to strangle the social revolution for the sake of legality and your new collaboration with the bourgeois parties of the right." Hitler replied heatedly that he was still a socialist. Nationalization, he believed, was a possible recourse if business offended against the national interest, but its implementation was by no means obligatory. He told Strasser that, after the National Socialists had come to power, "things would remain as they were. Do you think I should be so mad as to destroy our economy?" He brushed aside Strasser's distinction between capitalism and socialism as "theoretical." "The only thing which the present system lacks," he assured Strasser, "is the ultimate responsibility of the nation. There can never be a system which is based on any other principle, . . . otherwise we should come to anarchist, bolshevik conditions. It is the result of the very nature of the process of production which remains always the same. . . ."[24]

Hitler had to expel Otto Strasser for several reasons. In the first place, Strasser threatened the policy of legality which

German word *Wirtschaft*. It can mean either "economy" (as I have translated it) or "business community." It can as well mean both, if one makes certain ideological assumptions—as Hitler seemed to be trying to convince Kirdorf and his friends he did.

[23] The text of Hitler's modification of the program may be found in Baynes, *Hitler's Speeches*, I, 105, or Feder, *Hitler's Official Programme*, p. 41.

[24] The only report of this conversation is that of Otto Strasser in his pamphlet *Ministersessel oder Revolution?* [n.pp., 1930], pp. 22-29. I have based my rendering of the cited passage on the excerpts in Baynes, I, 111-12.

Hitler had forced upon the party in 1930;[25] Hitler wished to become respectable. Moreover, the growing organization was in a constant state of financial crisis, and he feared that the radicals would jeopardize the party's increasingly cordial relations with rich and powerful patrons.[26] The party leftists believed National Socialism to be a *movement* bent on social revolution. Despite his frequent denunciations of the party system of the Republic, Hitler realized what neither the radicals nor the theorists of social conservatism realized, that the Third Reich could come into being only through the agency of a well-organized political *party* with an elaborate bureaucracy, a rich treasury, powerful friends, frequent compromises of principle for the sake of political advantage, and many voters. The course which Hitler charted for his followers brought him to power as German chancellor in a coalition government which included only three members of the NSDAP.

The events of the year 1933 forced social conservatives to take a stand on National Socialism. None of them, with the possible exception of Spann, had taken the Nazis seriously until the eve of their accession to power. Here was a possible solution to the theoretical and practical problem of how the transition to the new social conservative order would come about. All social conservatives had to ask themselves whether this was the beginning of the Third Reich that they had so long awaited. Each had to judge which economic tendency within National Socialism would become dominant now that the party had assumed the burdens and the responsibilities of government.

Confronted by the political reality of Nazism in power, the theorists of social conservatism, and with them the components of the ideology, splintered apart. Both the left and

[25] Ch. XVI—" 'Adolf Légalité!' "—of Heiden's *Der Fuehrer* tells the story.

[26] See, e.g., his important speech before the Düsseldorf Industry Club on 27 Jan. 1932, in which he flattered the industrialists and at the same time tried to win them over to his theories about foreign policy and race. Reprinted in its entirety in Baynes, *Hitler's Speeches*, I, 777ff.

the right unequivocally rejected the new order. Niekisch, the Marxist nationalist, and Salin, the seeker after a new morality, early and steadfastly opposed the regime of the NSDAP. Spengler, although considered a friend by the Nazis, refused to give them his imprimatur. The centrists, Sombart and Spann, welcomed the new order as a start in the proper direction; it was the Nazis who eventually rejected them. The *Tat* circle, the embodiment of all the tendencies within social conservatism, fell apart in 1933. Zehrer wrote bitterly that the masses had triumphed[27] and retired to his island in the North Sea. Fried alone, of all the social conservatives studied here, accepted a post with the National Socialist government. Working with Walther Darré in the Agricultural Estate soon brought him into the mainstream of Nazi racist thought.[28]

Once in power the Nazis continued to betray the ideals of social conservatism. What was left of the radical wing of the party was decimated in the purge of 1934. Gregor Strasser was murdered. Feder was safely shunted aside to an undersecretariat in the Ministry of Economics, where the spokesmen of business could keep an eye on him. The party's hold on the reins of government was too weak to risk alienating the wielders of massive economic power. In behalf of the business community, and of themselves, they outlawed the Socialist and Communist parties and dissolved the trade unions. But, in exchange for the benevolent toleration of business and of the army, they had to officiate over the liquidation of the remnants of their program of socialism for the middle classes.[29] Full employ-

[27] Hans Thomas [Zehrer], "Das Ende des Fortschritts," *Die Tat*, XXV (Aug. 1933), 358ff.

[28] He wrote a book in 1937 entitled *Der Aufstieg der Juden* (Goslar, 1937).

[29] Chs. III, IV, and V of Schweitzer's *Big Business in the Third Reich* are devoted to the defeat of the major economic ideals of the old middle classes. This otherwise excellent work makes too much of the working out in the Nazi era of intellectual tendencies and economic decisions, which, after all, had taken definite form before 1933. The cause of the middle classes was lost before Hitler came to power; after 1933, certainly after the purge of 1934, the struggle between big

ment stimulated by the creation of a war economy in peacetime,[30] some slight relief for the peasantry,[31] state-regulated trade policy, respect for the creative entrepreneur, and some pretty cottages[32] were all that remained of the positive ideals of social conservatism by 1936.

And yet the failure of social conservatism was not ultimately the work of willful generals and fearful big businessmen in connivance with the ruthless Nazis, for it bore within itself the seeds of its own defeat. As a response of the German middle classes to the growth of industrial economy and society social conservatism was in large measure an attempt to revitalize and to update a view of society deemed by many long dead. Its proponents tried to breathe new life into the old *dreams* of an agrarian idyll, of an aristocratic morality, of corporate harmony, of national grandeur, and of crisis-free existence. They blamed the evils of the twentieth century on liberalism and capitalism as the agencies of social change which had destroyed the good society of the past—a society which none of them had really known. In their eyes, socialism and communism were even

and small business was more a staged tragedy than a real duel. In this connection see the rather intriguing book by Harald Braeutigam, *Wirtschaftssystem des Nationalsozialismus* (3rd rev. and expanded edn., Berlin, 1936), which claimed to be interpreting Gottfried Feder but which cited (and followed) Ludwig von Mises, Friedrich von Hayek, Walter Eucken, Irving Fisher, and other extremely Manchestrian liberal economists.

[30] There is disagreement among economists on the mode of economic recovery. Burton H. Klein, *Germany's Economic Preparations for War* (Cambridge, Mass., 1959), pp. 77-82, argues that the German expenditures for rearmaments were modest and, therefore, not decisive in German recovery. René Erbé, *Die nationalsozialistische Wirtschaftspolitik, 1933-1939, im Lichte der modernen Theorie*, Publication of the Basle Centre for Economic and Financial Research, Series B, No. 2 (Zurich, 1958), p. 4, argues the contrary view. Schweitzer tends toward Erbé's view. *Big Business in the Third Reich*, pp. 297ff. Klein seems to have based his calculations on a very narrow interpretation of armaments expenditure; see his pp. 3-76.

[31] Schweitzer, *Big Business in the Third Reich*, pp. 197ff.

[32] See, e.g., the book of photographs put out by the German Library of Information in New York, *A Nation Builds*, ed. Dr. Mathias Schmitz (New York, 1940).

more culpable, for their adherents not only accepted the mode, the direction, and the pace of economic and social change but even wished to intensify these trends. Republican government had failed to protect the economic interests or salve the longings for status of the middle classes; it, too, had to be destroyed.

What the middle classes seemed to want—indeed, what the theorists of social conservatism offered them—would have been little more than palliatives had serious attempts been made to put their positive ideals into practice. More peasant farmers would not have helped those already in distress. A cutback in industry would perhaps have pleased the old middle classes but would have been a serious blow to the white-collar classes. True autarky would have so reduced consumption and so raised prices that the lot of the middle classes, rural or urban, would not have improved greatly. Imperialist expansion as a coordinate of autarky led only to a war which few would argue benefited any stratum of the middle classes in the long run. The planned economy and the corporately planned society might have satisfied the longings of the middle classes for status, but the price would have been oppression by an authoritarian, centralized, bureaucratic state. For other reasons, this was to be their fate in the Nazi era—without benefit of the corporate state.

Not only were the ideals of social conservatism inadequate to the situation, but they were self-contradictory as well. Sombart's proposals for the aid of the old middle classes would have injured the new middle classes. The late capitalism which he expected to decay could not have led to the peasant and artisan socialism he awaited. Salin accepted both the moral and aesthetic ideals of an aristocratic elite and the continuation of social forces which made such an ideal impossible to attain. Spann wished to adjust corporatism to the modern industrial state and drifted into totalitarianism. Niekisch wished to reconcile the worker to the nation and nationalists to Marxism, a hopeless task in Weimar Germany. Spengler proclaimed the decline of the West and yet spoke of a bright future for Germany. He longed for the translation of the Wilhelmian social structure into the society of the 1920s, but he understood the dynamics of neither society. Fried tried to combine the diverse interests of the old and the new middle classes. He argued for autarky in an industrial society. He proclaimed the end of capitalism and praised the entrepreneur. He took part in the support for a Third Front against Hitler and took office in the Third Reich.

In only one respect were the theorists of social conservatism correct in their proposals for solutions to the problems of the middle classes. This was in the primacy they assigned to politics over all questions of economics. What they wrote was poor economics, but it made political sense. There was little economic basis for the unification of the middle classes, yet there was a pressing need to bring all their problems into the political arena; only by gaining control of the state could the middle classes hope to improve their lot. Hitler realized this better than any of the theorists, and he worked steadfastly to bring his political union of the middle classes to power. The Mittelstand got from the Nazi era all that they could have reasonably expected—short of social revolution.

In a sense, National Socialism was only an episode in the history of German social conservatism. Those most unable and most unwilling to adjust to the improvement of technological and economic organization and to the growth of large-scale capital and big labor expressed their fears in the language of the social conservatism we have studied in the years between 1914 and 1933. The circumstances of German social, economic, and political organization caused them to look to National Socialism for help. The Nazis, like the leaders of both the Empire and of the Republic before them, would not and could not help them.

The sociologist Ralf Dahrendorf argues that the "odd combination of modernity in economic affairs and backwardness in social affairs" which dominated over seventy years of German history has now been resolved in postwar Germany. For the first time West Germany has a fully capitalist economy *and* society.[33] But surely the social conservative impulse is not dead in Germany nor in the rest of the West.[34] The specific problems differ, the programs differ, and the images of the "good old days" differ, but the impulse lives on. How well we deal with the problems of economic change and social organization, how soon we realize when an era has come to an end, will in large measure determine whether we will have to reckon with a few disadvantaged and dissatisfied people or with a social movement.

Today in Germany and, indeed, in the rest of the West the welfare state gives members of the Mittelstand the protection which the social conservative movements of the twenties, thirties, and forties were unable to confer on an earlier generation. Whether the welfare state proves to be a viable alternative to both the capitalism and the socialism of our own day is a question that must wait on events.

[33] "The New Germanies: Restoration, Revolution, Reconstruction," *Encounter* (April 1964), pp. 50-51ff.

[34] To be sure, the book by Friedrich Georg Jünger, the brother of Ernst, translated into English as *The Failure of Technology* (Los Angeles: Gateway Edition paperback, 1956), is more an anachronism than a portent. But consider the interpretation of Armin Mohler, *Die Fünfte Republik. Was steht hinter de Gaulle?* (Munich: Piper paperback, 1963), pp. 121-26, that in France today the technocrats are challenging the old social and economic order; and the analysis of Talcott Parsons, "Social Strains in America," in Daniel Bell, ed., *The Radical Right: The New American Right* (expanded ed., Garden City, 1963), pp. 175-93. Cf. also Senator William Proxmire's *Can Small Business Survive?* (Chicago, 1964).

Bibliographical Essay

THIS ESSAY is offered as a bibliographical outline for the study of German conservative social and economic thought in the late nineteenth and early twentieth centuries, including its institutional context. The notes to the various chapters should be consulted for specific titles. The student of this aspect of German history may also find useful the more detailed bibliography of my doctoral dissertation, "A Socialism for the German Middle Classes: The Social Conservative Response to Industrialism, 1900-1933" (Yale University, 1965), pp. 367-416, available from University Microfilms, Ann Arbor, Michigan. The books discussed here, together with the bibliographies which many of them contain, should serve as helpful introductions to the major topics treated in this study. The essay is divided into two major parts: (I) The Institutional Context, and (II) The Tradition of Social Conservatism.

I. THE INSTITUTIONAL CONTEXT

Perhaps the most underdeveloped aspect of contemporary German history is social and economic history. As the footnotes reveal, much of the best literature on the period 1914-1933 was written in the 1920s and 1930s.

Of the numerous histories of economic thought, analysis, and doctrine, the monumental work of Joseph A. Schumpeter, *History of Economic Analysis*, ed. from the manuscript by Elizabeth Boody Schumpeter (New York, 1954), towers above all others. Since Schumpeter set a high standard of theoretical excellence, few of the social conservative economists treated in this study received much treatment in his work. For economic thought in the nineteenth century, see W. Wygodzinski, "Die Entwicklung der deutschen Volkswirtschaftslehre im 19. Jahrhundert," in *Festgabe zu Gustav Schmollers 70. Geburtstag* (Leipzig, 1908); for the early decades of the twentieth, consult Adolf Weber, "Der Anteil Deutschlands an der nationalökonomischen Forschung seit dem Weltkrieg," in M. J. Bonn and M. Palyi, eds., *Festgabe für Lujo Brentano zum 80. Geburtstag* (2 vols.; Munich, 1925), Vol.

II. Also of great value in the same work and same volume is Karl Pribram's "Die Wandlungen des Begriffs der Sozialpolitik."

As for all modern industrial societies, the primary data on the German economy and society are rich and somewhat overwhelming. Of greatest importance are the publications of governmental agencies. Major sources of raw data are the publications of the Statistisches Reichsamt. Of special value are volumes carrying the results of the censuses of 1882, 1895, 1907, 1925, and 1933. The *Deutsche Wirtschaftskunde* contains summary data on the census of 1925, as well as useful historical data going back to the nineteenth century on population, occupational structure, and the various branches of the economy. The publications of the semi-official Institut für Konjunkturforschung, created on the model of the business cycle research institute at Harvard University, are also of prime value. Its bulletin, *Wirtschaft und Statistik*, is a mine of information on the Weimar era. In the middle of the Weimar period the Reichstag appointed a committee to investigate the state of all branches of the economy. The reports, which appeared in scores of volumes, were published under the general editorship of Bernhard Dernberg under the title *Erzeugungs- und Absatzbedingungen der deutschen Wirtschaft* (Berlin, 1927-1932). The final volume contains an index of all the works published in the series.

Of the many nonofficial serial publications, which are more interpretative than the government publications but of equal authority, the *Schriftenreihe* of the Verein für Sozialpolitik should be mentioned first. Despite the ideological and theoretical blindspots of its leading spirits, the work of the members of the Verein is still the best source of information on the economy and society of Germany in both the Imperial and Republican eras. The Appendix to Franz Boese's *Geschichte des Vereins für Sozialpolitik*, Vol. CLXXXVIII of the *Schriften* (Berlin, 1937), contains a complete listing of the publications of the Verein from its founding to its dissolution in 1937. The *Wirstschaftskurve* of the *Frankfurter Zeitung* is valuable. A repository of clear analysis and accurate statistics for the Weimar era is the weekly magazine edited by Gustav Stolper, *Der deutsche Volkswirt*. From 1925, the year of its founding, to 1933, when it was merged with *Der Arbeitgeber, Der deutsche Volkswirt* offered a valuable running commentary on all phases of the German economy. The articles by Stolper, especially those cited in the notes to Chapter I, are quite insightful. The *Weltwirtschaftliches Archiv*, published by the International Trade Institute at Kiel University, contains many useful interpretative articles and surveys.

There are no satisfactory economic or social histories of Germany for either the late Empire or the Weimar era. Some good essays, as well as notes, and a good bibliography may be found in Karl Erich Born, ed., *Moderne deutsche Wirtschaftsgeschichte*, Neue wissenschaftliche Bibliothek, No. 12 (Cologne, 1966), and Hans-Ulrich Wehler, ed., *Moderne deutsche Sozialgeschichte*, Neue wissenschaftliche Bibliothek, No. 10 (Cologne, 1966). The clarity and incisiveness of Gustav Stolper's *German Economy, 1870-1940* (New York, 1940) elevates it above other histories. Joseph Schumpeter's *Business Cycles: A Theoretical, Historical, and Statistical Analysis of the Capitalist Process* (2 vols.; New York, 1939) is too theoretical and schematic to serve as a basic history of the nineteenth and twentieth centuries, but the sections on Germany are brilliant. For the late nineteenth century, John H. Clapham's *Economic Development of France and Germany* (4th edn., Cambridge, Eng., 1961) is still of great value. We now have as well the provocative attempt by Hans Rosenberg to link the fluctuations of the business cycle during the great depression (1873-1896) with social and political events, in his *Grosse Depression und Bismarckzeit: Wirtschaftsablauf, Gesellschaft und Politik in Mitteleuropa* (Berlin, 1967). For the war years, Gerald Feldman's *Army, Industry, and Labor in Germany, 1914-1918* (Princeton, 1966) is a good starting point. For the Weimar period, there is the great collective effort by Gerhardt Albrecht et al., *Grundriss der Sozialökonomik* (Tübingen, 1926); Vol. IX brings together works of uniformly high quality to yield a picture of the German social structure in the 1920s and 1930s. We are also fortunate to have the collection of essays on the Weimar economy edited by Bernhard Harms, *Strukturwandlungen der deutschen Volkswirtschaft* (2 vols.; 2nd edn., Berlin, 1929); Harms's own essay in Vol. I, "Das neue Deutschland im neuen Europa," is a good short survey. The slim volume by M. J. Bonn, *Das Schicksal des deutschen Kapitalismus* (Berlin, 1931), is rich in insight.

On the various aspects of the German economy, see W. G. Hoffmann, J. H. Müller, et al., *Das deutsche Volkseinkommen, 1851-1957* (Tübingen, 1959). On wages, we have Gerhard Bry's *Wages in Germany, 1871-1945*, Vol. LXVIII of the General Series of the National Bureau of Economic Research (Princeton, 1960). On monetary policy, the excellent work by Rudolf Stucken,

Deutsche Geld- und Kreditpolitik (Hamburg, 1937), should be read. The pithy and incisive survey by Wilhelm Röpke, *German Commercial Policy* (London, 1934), is a good introduction. On agriculture, Alexander Gerschenkron's *Bread and Democracy in Germany* (Berkeley, 1943) is good but is marred by an undue fascination with the power of the Junkers. Most useful for the Weimar period is the collection of essays put out by the Friedrich List-Gesellschaft and edited by Edgar Salin et al., *Deutsche Agrarpolitik im Rahmen der inneren und äusseren Wirtschaftspolitik* (2 vols.; Berlin, 1933). On the organization of industry, see Alfred Kuhlo, *Die Organization der deutschen Industrie* (Berlin, 1928). On state social policy and social reform for the late nineteenth century, see Karl Erich Born, *Staat und Sozialpolitik seit Bismarcks Sturz: Ein Beitrag zur Geschichte der innenpolitischen Entwicklung des deutschen Reiches, 1890-1914* (Wiesbaden, 1957); for the twentieth, we are fortunate to have the brilliant work by Ludwig Preller, *Sozialpolitik in der Weimarer Republik* (Stuttgart, 1949).

Inevitably, histories of the upper classes are few and poor. Walter Görlitz's *Die Junker: Adel und Bauern im deutschen Osten: Geschichtliche Bilanz von 7 Jahrhunderten* (2nd expanded edn., Glücksburg, 1957), although unduly friendly, is the best work available. For the late Empire, Eckart Kehr's essays, appearing together as *Der Primat der Innenpolitik: Gesammelte Aufsätze zur preussischen Sozialgeschichte*, ed. Hans-Ulrich Wehler (Berlin, 1965), are full of insights. Gerschenkron's *Bread and Democracy* should also be consulted on the Junkers. The literature on the industrial and commercial bourgeoisie is thin. That serious studies are on the way is perhaps evidenced by the appearance of Lamar Cecil's *Albert Ballin: Business and Politics in Imperial Germany, 1888-1918* (Princeton, 1967). For the rest, the histories of industry and business cited in the course of the study will have to suffice.

On the lower classes, the *Grundriss der Sozialökonomik* is the best guide, especially Goetz Brief's "Das gewerbliche Proletariat" in Vol. IX, Part 1. Also of high quality is the general study by Theodor Geiger, *Die soziale Schichtung des deutschen Volkes* (Stuttgart, 1932).

On the middle classes, the basic work is still Emil Grünberg's *Der Mittelstand in der kapitalistischen Gesellschaft: Eine ökonomische und soziologische Untersuchung* (Leipzig, 1932), although it is marred by socialist illusions about the middle classes and their ultimate political destiny with the Social Democrats. Also valuable is George Neuhaus's "Die berufliche und soziale Gliederung der Bevölkerung im Zeitalter des Kapitalismus," in *Grundriss der Sozialökonomik*, Vol. IX, Part 1. See further the statistical study put out by the Bayerisches Statistisches Landesamt, *Sozial Auf- und Abstieg im deutschen Volk: Statistische Methoden und Ergebnisse* (Munich, 1930), Heft 117. Svend Riemer's Sozialer Aufstieg und Klassenschichtung," in *Archiv für Sozialwissenschaft*, LXVII (1932), and Friedrich Zahn's "Die Entwicklung der räumlichen, beruflichen und sozialen Gliederung des deutschen Volkes seit dem Aufkommen der industriellen-kapitalistischen Wirtschaftsweise," in Bernhard Harms, ed., *Volk und Reich der Deutschen* (Berlin, 1929), are both valuable supplements.

The middle classes should be divided into "old" and "new." The distinction rests on the group's relationship to industrial society. As a whole, the studies of the old middle classes are more informative and thorough than those on the new middle classes. Most social scientists, like most social conservatives, were—and still are—somewhat baffled by the complexities that analysis of this new social group involves. On the old middle classes in the nineteenth century, there is the masterful analysis of their early confrontations with industrial and commercial change by Theodore S. Hamerow, *Restoration, Revolution, and Reaction: Economics and Politics in Germany, 1815-1871* (Princeton, 1958); for the twentieth, the beginning chapters of Arthur Schweitzer's *Big Business in the Third Reich* (Bloomington, Ind., 1964) offer an excellent summary of the older literature with some valuable additions and corrections. David Schoenbaum, in *Hitler's Social Revolution: Class and Status in Nazi Germany, 1933-1939* (Garden City, N.Y., 1966), focuses on roughly the same topic as Schweitzer. Schoenbaum's work is heavily documented; but it is poor on the Mittelstand, and the theme—that Hitler's was a revolution of "nihilism"—seems to be contravened by the evidence presented.

On the new middle classes, the pioneer effort by Emil Lederer, *Die Privatangestellen in der modernen Wirtschaftsordnung* (Tübingen, 1912), raises most of the important questions; his work with Jakob Marschak, "Der neue Mittelstand," in *Grundriss der Sozialökonomik*, Vol. IX, Part 1, is still basic in the field. The novel by Hans Fallada (pseud. for Rudolf Ditzen), *Kleiner Mann, was nun?* (Berlin, 1932), is fictionalized sociology. It tells the story of a salesman in the era of the Republic. Fritz Croner's

Soziologie der Angestellten (Cologne, 1962) summarizes much of the literature of the past but is otherwise rather disappointing. For an excellent and succinct summary of the situation of the new middle classes in the years of the Weimar Republic, see the first part of Walter Struve's "Hans Zehrer as a Neoconservative Elite Theorist," *American Historical Review*, LXX (1965).

II. The Tradition of Social Conservatism

There exists no other study which attempts to relate the problems of the Mittelstand to the twentieth-century ideology of social conservatism. The short but excellent dissertation by Wolfgang Hock, *Deutscher Antikapitalismus: Der ideologische Kampf gegen die freie Wirtschaft im Zeichen der grossen Krise*, Vol. IX of the Wirtschaftswissenschaftliche Reihe of the Veröffentlichungen des Instituts für Bankwirtschaft und Bankrecht at the University of Cologne (Frankfurt-am-Main, 1960), presents an outline of the economic program of the "Conservative Revolution." But no analysis of the social or economic context is offered. Hock concentrates on the anti-capitalism of neoconservatives, paying little attention to their pro-capitalist and anti-Marxist tendencies. The focus, finally, is on the depression of the 1930s. Nevertheless, Hock's dissertation is a helpful, pithy introduction to the problems of studying social conservative modes of thought in the 1920s and 1930s. On the aspirations of the old Mittelstand (there is little on the new Mittelstand), Arthur Schweitzer's *Big Business in the Third Reich* is good. The work suffers, however, from oversystematization. It treats the conflict between small and big business in the Nazi era more seriously than even the evidence he presents warrants.

Of general studies of the "Conservative Revolution," the older study by Walter Gerhardt (pseud. for Waldemar Gurian), *Um des Reiches Zukunft: Nationale Wiedergeburt oder politische Reaktion* (Freiburg i. Br., 1932), has not been entirely supplanted by Klemens von Klemperer's *Germany's New Conservatism: Its History and Dilemma in the Twentieth Century* (Princeton, 1957). Less diffuse and more useful is Fritz Stern's *The Politics of Cultural Despair: A Study in the Rise of the Germanic Ideology* (Berkeley, 1961). Stern's approach via intellectual biographies of Paul de Lagarde, Julius Langbehn, and Arthur Moeller van den Bruck and the history of their intellectual connections has yielded an informative history of the origins of the high tradition of neoconservatism. Materials for many further studies may be found in the elaborate bibliography to Armin Mohler's *Die Konservative Revolution in Deutschland, 1918-1932: Grundriss ihrer Weltanschauung* (Stuttgart, 1950).

There exists no single comprehensive study of the roots of social conservative thought in the nineteenth century. Hans Freyer's *Die Bewertung der Wirtschaft im philosophischen Denken des 19. Jahrhunderts* (Leipzig, 1921) is a very insightful treatment by a man himself within the social conservative tradition. The classical statement of the origins of German uniqueness vis-à-vis the West is Ernst Troeltsch's "The Idea of Natural Law and Humanity in World Politics," an address delivered on the second anniversary of the Hochschule für Politik in October 1922, reprinted as an appendix to Otto Gierke, *Natural Law and the Theory of Society, 1500-1800*, tr. Ernest Barker (Boston: Beacon Press paperback, 1957). On Romantic political thought, Reinhold Aris's *History of Political Thought in Germany from 1789 to 1815* (London, 1936) is still good. On the late nineteenth century, there are Gerhard Masur's *Prophets of Yesterday: Studies in European Culture, 1890-1914* (New York, 1961), good for literary aspects, and the work by Fritz Stern.

What follows are works by, and about, the major figures treated in Chapters II-VI of this study.

I have found little of the secondary literature on Werner Sombart very helpful for my discussion. Most of the work deals either with his scholarly achievements as a student of capitalism or with his late years as a Nazi sympathizer. Not even Hock treats his intellectual development from the days when he was friendly to Social Democracy through his *Deutscher Sozialismus* of 1934. The best bibliographical compilation of Sombart's writings is at the end of Werner Krause's *Werner Sombarts Weg von Kathedersozialismus zum Faschismus* ([East] Berlin, 1962). Most useful on the theoretical implications of Sombart's theory of capitalism is the fine article by Talcott Parsons, " 'Capitalism' in Recent German Literature: Sombart and Weber," *Journal of Political Economy*, XXXVI (1928). On the same theme, but of poorer quality, is M. J. Plotnik's *Werner Sombart and his Type of Economics* (New York, 1937). Leo Rogin, in "Werner Sombart and the Uses of Transcendentalism," *American Economic Review*, XXXI (1941), treats the political implications of Sombart's method but does not do it well. Abraham L. Harris, "Sombart and German (National) Socialism," *Journal of Political Economy*, L (1942), is incorrect in simply labelling Sombart a Nazi. This is an inaccurate characterization both of the economics of the Socialist movement and of the economics of the man. Friedrich A. Hayek's *The Road to Serfdom* (Chicago: Phoenix Books paperback, 1944) contains a few misleading pages on the identity of Socialism, National Socialism, and Sombart's theories. Arthur Mitzman's "Anti-Progress: A Study in the Romantic Roots of German Sociology," *Social Research*, XXXIII (1966), is an essay in the school of Herbert Marcuse. A longer study, with a section on Sombart, is forthcoming.

Although there is no full-length biography of Sombart, the biographical information available is quite informative. The woman Socialist Lily Braun knew Sombart in his younger, "radical" years. Her *Memoiren einer Sozialistin* (2 vols.; Munich, 1909-1911) contains interesting insights on the young Sombart. Emil Ludwig recalls his former teacher in his memoirs, *Gifts of Life: A Retrospect*, ed. Ethel C. Mayne, tr. M. I. Robertson (Boston, 1931). Valuable information is presented in Leopold von Wiese's "Werner Sombart zum 70. Geburtstag," *Kölner Vierteljahrshefte für Soziologie*, XI (1932/33), and in the sketch by M. Epstein, Sombart's English translator, "Obituary, Werner Sombart (1863 - 13 May 1941)," *Economic Journal*, LI (1941). See further "Werner Sombart," in *Biographisches Jahrbuch und deutscher Nekrolog*, III (1898), and Waldemar Zimmermann's "Der proletarische Sozialismus ('Marxismus') von Werner Sombart," in *Schmollers Jahrbuch*, LVI (1932). Finally, there is the review of the first volume of *Der moderne Kapitalismus* (which received such severe criticism that Sombart essentially rewrote it) by Gustav Schmoller in his *Schmollers Jahrbuch*, XXVII (1903).

For the purposes of this study the following works were less useful:

Edgar Salin, "Sombart and the German Approach," in *Architects and Craftsmen in History: Festschrift für Abbott Payson Usher*, ed. Joseph T. Lambie (Tübingen, 1956). Salin is still interested in developing a new "conceptual" approach to economics.

Schmollers Jahrbuch, LIV (1930), is devoted to reviews and appreciations of Sombart's theoretical work *Die drei Nationalökonomien*.

Schmollers Jahrbuch, LVI (1932), contains a *Festschrift* dedicated to Sombart, but none of the articles discusses the aspects of Sombart's thought which would be of relevance here.

Leo Rogin, "Werner Sombart and the 'natural science method' in Economics," *Journal of Political Economy*, XLI (1933). Georg Weippert, *Werner Sombarts Gestaltidee des Wirtschaftssystems* (Göttingen, 1953)—a very abstruse discussion of Sombart's methodology.

Sombart's output was voluminous. The following works of his have contributed to my analysis of his social conservative ideas:

Beamtenschaft und Wirtschaft: Vortrag gehalten auf dem Mitteldeutschen Beamtentag am 11. September 1927 (Berlin, 1927).

Deutscher Sozialismus (Berlin-Charlottenburg, 1934), tr. Karl F. Geiser as *A New Social Philosophy* (Princeton, 1937)— a poor translation.

Die deutsche Volkswirtschaft im neunzehnten Jahrhundert und im Anfang des zwanzigsten Jahrhunderts (1st edn., Berlin, 1903; 7th edn., Berlin, 1927).

Die drei Nationalökonomien (Munich, 1930).

"Economic Theory and Economic History," *Economic History Review*, II (1929).

"Entfaltung des modernen Kapitalismus," in Bernhard Harms, ed., *Kapital und Kapitalismus* (2 vols.; Berlin, 1931), Vol. I.

Gewerbewesen, Sammlung Göschen (2 vols.; 1st edn., Leipzig, 1904; 2nd edn., Leipzig, 1929).

Händler und Helden (Munich, 1915).

"Die Idee des Klassenkampfes," address given at the meeting of the Verein für Sozialpolitik, Stuttgart, 1924, in Vol. CLXX of the *Schriften des Vereins für Sozialpolitik* (Munich, 1925).

The Jews and Modern Capitalism (London, 1913), tr. M. Epstein from the original, *Die Juden und das Wirtschaftsleben* (Leipzig, 1911).

Der moderne Kapitalismus (3 vols. in 4; 7th edn., Munich, 1924-1928).

Die Ordnung des Wirtschaftslebens (Berlin, 1925).

"Die prinzipielle Eigenart des modernen Kapitalismus," *Grundriss der Sozialökonomik* (Tübingen, 1925), Vol. IV.

Der proletarische Sozialismus ("Marxismus") (2 vols.; Jena, 1924).

Die Rationalisierung in der Wirtschaft (Düsseldorf, 1927).

Die Romanische Campagna, from the *Archiv für soziale Gesetzgebung und Statistik,* II (1889).

Socialism and the Social Movement in the Nineteenth Century, tr. from the German by Anson P. Atterbury (New York, 1898).

"Wandlungen des Kapitalismus," address given at the meeting of the Verein für Sozialpolitik, Zurich, 1928, in Vol. CLXXV of the *Schriften des Vereins für Sozialpolitik* (Munich, 1929).

Die Zukunft der Juden (Leipzig, 1912).

Die Zukunft des Kapitalismus (Berlin-Charlottenburg, 1932).

"Die Zukunft der Weltwirtschaft," *Ständisches Leben,* II (1932) —a reprint of part of *Die Zukunft des Kapitalismus.*

"Zur Kritik des ökonomischen Systems von Karl Marx," *Archiv für Gesetzgebung und Statistik,* VII (1894).

"Zur neueren Litteratur über das Handwerk," *Archiv für Gesetzgebung und Statistik,* IX (1896).

I have been able to discover little secondary literature on Edgar Salin. On his seventieth birthday a number of his friends put together the *Festschrift, Antidoron, Edgar Salin zum 70. Geburtstag,* ed. Erwin von Beckerath, Heinrich Popitz, Hans Georg Siebeck, and Harry W. Zimmermann (Tübingen, 1962). The *Festschrift* contains a complete bibliography of Salin's publications up to 1962. Most of the essays in the *Festschrift* are irrelevant to the issues of this study, with the possible exception of Raymond Aron's "Edgar Salin," which deals with Salin's postwar attitudes toward economic development. The respect which Salin has deservedly gained in the economic profession for his non-social conservative work is evidenced in the tribute paid to him by his greatest theoretical opponent, Wilhelm Röpke.

On the conference which Salin attended with Hans Luther of the Reichsbank, see the report of a liberal participant in Walter Eucken's *This Unsuccessful Age* (London, 1951) and a secondary account in Wilhelm Grotkopp's *Die Grosse Krise: Lehren aus der Überwindung der Wirtschaftskrise, 1929-1932* (Düsseldorf, 1954). The List Society has an adequate history for the first ten years of its existence: Hermann Brügelmann, *Politische Ökonomie in kritischen Jahren: Die Friedrich List-Gesellschaft e.V. von 1925-1935,* Veröffentlichungen der List Gesellschaft, Vol. I (Tübingen, 1956).

Of the works of Salin, the following have been most helpful in the preparation of this study:

"Am Wendepunkt der deutschen Wirtschaftspolitik," *Deutsche Agrarpolitik*, Veröffentlichungen der List Gesellschaft, Vol. VI (Berlin, 1932).

"Die Bedeutung des Transferschutzes," Salin, ed., *Das Reparationsproblem*, Vol. II: *Verhandlungen und Gutachten der Konferenz von Berlin* (Berlin, 1929).

"Bernard Harms in Memoriam," introduction to Hermann Brügelmann, *Politische Ökonomie in kritischen Jahren: Die Friedrich List-Gesellschaft e.V. von 1925-1935*, Veröffentlichungen der List Gesellschaft, Vol. I (Tübingen, 1956).

Civitas Dei (Tübingen, 1926).

Die deutschen Tribute: Zwölf Reden (Berlin, 1930).

"Die deutsche volkswirtschaftliche Theorie im 20. Jahrhundert," *Zeitschrift für schweizerische Statistik und Volkswirtschaft*, LVII (1921).

"Die Entthronung des Goldes. (Bemerkungen zu Keynes: 'A Tract on Monetary Reform')," *Schmollers Jahrbuch*, XLVIII (1924).

Geschichte der Volkswirtschaftslehre (1st edn., Berlin, 1923; 4th edn., Bern, 1951).

Goldwäscherei und Goldbergbau am Klondike und in Alaska (Tübingen, 1914).

"Stellung und Bedeutung des Unternehmers in der deutschen Wirtschaft der Gegenwart," *Berichte des Arbeitgeberverbandes Nord-West* (Düsseldorf, 1929).

"Theorie und Praxis staatlicher Kreditpolitik der Gegenwart (Antrittsvorlesung)," *Recht und Staat*, Vol. LVII (Tübingen, 1928).

Um Stefan George: Erinnerung und Zeugnis (2nd expanded edn., Munich, 1954).

"Von den Wandlungen der Weltwirtschaft in der Nachkriegszeit," *Weltwirtschaftliches Archiv*, XXXV (1932).

Wirtschaft und Staat: Drei Schriften zur deutschen Weltlage (Berlin, 1930).

I have also consulted the following works but have found them to be of less value for an understanding of the social conservatism of Salin:

Amerikanische Impressionen (2nd edn., Tübingen, 1953).

"Bachofen als Mythologe der Romantik. (Zur Neuherausgabe von Bachofens Werken)," *Schmollers Jahrbuch*, L (1926).

"Die drei Nationalökonomien in geschichtlicher Beleuchtung," *Schmollers Jahrbuch*, LIV (1930).

"Das Ende der Tribute," *Wirtschaftsdienst*, XVIII (1933).

"Friedrich List und die Gegenwart," *Deutsche Wirtschaftszeitung*, XXV (1928).

"Hochkapitalismus: Eine Studie über Werner Sombart, die deutsche Volkswirtschaftslehre und das Wirtschaftssystem der Gegenwart," *Weltwirtschaftliches Archiv*, XXV (1927).

"Das Kapital in der vorklassischen Wirtschaftslehre," in Bernhard Harms, ed., *Kapital und Kapitalismus*, Vol. I.

"Organische Geschichtsschreibung," *Archiv für Sozialwissenschaft und Sozialpolitik*, XLVI (1919/20).

Platon und die griechische Utopie (Munich, 1921).

"Sombart and the German Approach," *Architects and Craftsmen in History. Festschrift für A. P. Usher*, ed. Lambie (Tübingen, 1956).

"Der 'Sozialismus' in Hellas," *Bilder und Studien aus drei Jahrtausenden: Festschrift für Eberhard Gothein* (Munich, 1923).

"Standortsverschiebungen der deutschen Wirtschaft," *Strukturwandlungen der deutschen Volkswirtschaft* (Berlin, 1929).

"Die Tragödie der deutschen Gegenrevolution: Bemerkungen über den Quellenwert der bisherigen Widerstandsliteratur," *Zeitschrift für Religions- und Geistesgeschichte*, I (1948).

Stefan George was both a poet and a social critic. His critique of modern society, rather than the value of his writings as literature, was my prime interest. The best critique of George's position in the history of social ideas is Claude David's "Stefan George: Aesthetes or Terrorists?" in the UNESCO-sponsored volume, *The Third Reich*, ed. Maurice Baumont et al. (New York, 1955). A good interpretative essay on George and his poetry, with an excellent selection of illustrations, is Franz Schonauer's *Stefan George* (Reinbek-bei-Hamburg: Rowohlt Taschenbuch paperback, 1960). The exclusiveness and elitist aspects of his circle are treated by Dominik Jost in *Stefan George und seine Elite* (Zurich, 1949) and by Hansjürgen Linke in *Das Kultische in der Dichtung Stefan Georges und seiner Schule* (2 vols.; Munich, 1960). The aristocratic humanism of the George circle is the topic of Franz Josef Brecht's *Platon und der George-*

Kreis (Leipzig, 1929) and of the brief section in E. M. Butler's *The Tyranny of Greece over Germany* (Boston: Beacon Press paperback, 1958). E. K. Bennett's *Stefan George* (New Haven, 1954) is a poor introductory survey. The postwar literature (to 1954) on George is discussed by Karl Josef Hahn in "Stefan George—Mythos und Wahrheit," *Hochland*, XLVI (1954). Hahn, like many students of George's ideas, comments on the difficulty of getting accurate information from the works of his disciples.

It is safer to treat studies by Georgians as primary sources. I have benefited most from Robert Boehringer's *Mein Bild von Stefan George* (Munich, 1951), Salin's *Um Stefan George*, and Friedrich Wolters's *Stefan George und die Blätter für die Kunst* (Berlin, 1930).

I have cited from George's poetical output his *Hymnen, Pilgerfahrten, Algabal* (Berlin, 1905), *Der Krieg* (Berlin, 1917), and *Der Teppich des Lebens und die Lieder von Traum und Tod. Mit einem Vorspiel* (Berlin, 1932).

The secondary literature on Othmar Spann is of very uneven quality. The most complete bibliography of secondary works and works by Spann is Hans Riehl's "Schriften von und über Othmar Spann," in his *Das philosophische Gesamtwerk von Othmar Spann im Auszug* (Vienna, 1950). Andree Emery's "The Totalitarian Economics of Othmar Spann," *Journal of Social Philosophy*, I (1936), is a helpful introductory guide through the maze of Spann's Universalism. For anyone wanting more detail, there is Otto Hausmann's "Othmar Spann und seine Schule" (Ph.D. diss., University of Vienna, 1962). Justus Beyer's *Die Ständeideologien der Systemzeit und ihre Überwindung* (Darmstadt, 1941), if used with great caution, will yield good insights into Spann's system. Also informative is Franz Arnold's "Wiener Richtungen," in *Staatslexikon der Görres-Gesellschaft* (5th edn., 1932), Vol. V. The continued influence of Spannian ideas in Austrian academic life is revealed in the *Festschrift* edited by Walter Heinrich entitled *Die Ganzheit in Philosophie und Wissenschaft: Othmar Spann zum siebzigsten Geburtstag* (Vienna, 1950).

On Spann's role in Austrian politics, there are good treatments by Alfred Diamant in *Austrian Catholics and the First Republic* (Princeton, 1960); Charles A. Gulick in *Austria from Hapsburg to Hitler* (2 vols.; Berkeley, 1948), esp. Vol. II: *Fascism's Subversion of Democracy*; and Adam Wandruszka in

"Österreichs politische Struktur: Die Entwicklung der Parteien und politischen Bewegungen," in Heinrich Benedikt, ed., *Geschichte der Republik Österreichs* (Munich, 1954). The memoirs of Spann's special student, Ernst von Salomon—*Der Fragebogen* (Reinbek-bei-Hamburg: RoRoRo paperback, 1961) —are an important primary source on Spann's political activities. Taylor Cole's "Corporative Organization of the Third Reich," *Review of Politics*, II (1940), has been in part supplanted by Schweitzer's *Big Business in the Third Reich*, but the treatment of the impact and defeat of Spann's doctrines of corporatism in Cole's article is still the best available.

Perhaps the most important traditions of corporatism are the Catholic varieties. For Catholic social thought, the most useful study is *Church and Society: Catholic Social and Political Thought and Movements, 1789-1950*, ed. Joseph N. Moody (New York, 1953). In addition, the reader might find useful:

> Edgar Alexander, "Social and Political Movements and Ideas in German and Austrian Catholicism, 1789-1950," in Moody, ed., *Church and Society*.
>
> Heinz Herberg, "Eine wirtschaftssoziologische Ideengeschichte der neueren Katholischen Soziallehren in Deutschland" (Ph.D. diss., University of Bern, 1933).
>
> Paul Jostock, *Der deutsche Katholizismus und die Überwindung des Kapitalismus* (Regensburg, [1932?]).
>
> Karl Pawek, "Spanns Universalismus der Scholastik gegenübergestellt. Das Untersuchungsergebnis einer Innsbrucker Diss.," *Schönere Zukunft*, VIII (1932).

The following works on Spann, Austria, and corporatism, although useful, have been less valuable for my purposes:

> Arnold Bergsträsser, "Neuere Literatur zum Gedanken des berufständischen Staats," *Schmollers Jahrbuch*, XLVII (1923).
>
> Ralph Bowen, *German Theories of the Corporate State: With Special Reference to the Period 1870-1919* (New York, 1947).
>
> Francis W. Coker, *Organismic Theories of the State*, Vol. XXXVIII of the Columbia Studies in History, Economics, and Public Law (New York, 1910).
>
> F. Ermath, *The New Germany* (Washington, D.C., 1936).
>
> Emil Januschka, *The Social Stratification of the Austrian*

Population, United States WPA Foreign Social Science Monographs, No. 21 (New York: Columbia University, 1939).

August M. Knoll, "Die Frage nach der 'besten' Wirtschaftsform bei Othmar Spann," *Soziale Revue*, XXVIII (1926)—good on Spann's confounding of fact and value.

Barth Landherr, "Othmar Spann's Social Theories," *Journal of Political Economy*, XXXIX (1931)—poor article by a Dutch follower of Spann's sociology.

Frederick D. Rodeck, "Obituary of Othmar Spann, 1878-1950," *American Sociological Review*, XV (1950)—an apologia for Spann which claims the Nazis placed Spann in jail at one point. Rodeck is the first author to mention this event.

Wilhelm Rössle, *Ständesstaat und politischer Staat* (Tübingen, 1934)—a National Socialist critique of corporatism.

Max Weber, *Wirtschaft und Gesellschaft* (Tübingen, 1922)—incisive critique of use of the concept of "estate" in modern social science.

Guido Zernatto, *Die Wahrheit über Österreich* (New York, 1938).

Of Spann's prolific output, the following have aided my inquiry greatly:

Fundamente der Volkswirtschaftslehre (4th edn., Jena, 1929).
The History of Economics, tr. from the 19th German edn. by Eden and Cedar Paul (New York, 1930).
"Die politische-wirtschaftliche Schicksalstunde der deutschen Katholiken," *Schönere Zukunft*, VIII (1932).
Tote und lebendige Wissenschaft (2nd edn., Jena, 1925).
"Vom Interessenverband zum Berufstand," *Der Arbeitgeber*, XIV (1922).
Der wahre Staat: Vorlesungen über Abbruch und Neubau der Gesellschaft (1st edn., Jena, 1921; 2nd edn., Jena, 1923; 3rd edn., Jena, 1931; 4th edn., Jena, 1938).
"Die wissenschaftliche Überwindung des Marxismus," *Stahl und Eisen*, XLII (1922).

Spann's most important articles in his periodical *Ständisches Leben* for the years 1932-1936 have been noted in the text of Chapter IV.

The works of Spann that I found less important for the story of his social conservatism are:

Geschichtsphilosophie (Jena, 1932)—his theory of history.
Gesellschaftslehre (Leipzig, 1923)—his sociology.
Die Kategorienlehre (Jena, 1924)—his metaphysics.
Der Schöpfungsgang des Geistes: Die Wiederherstellung des Idealismus auf allen Gebieten der Philosophie (Jena, 1928)—more metaphysics.

Spann had a number of academic disciples. Useful on explicating what Spann and his school meant by Universalism are:

Walter Heinrich, "Universalismus," *Staatslexikon der Görres-Gesellschaft* (5th edn., 1932), Vol. V. This is an excellent summary of the ideology by the chief of Spann's disciples.
J. Roloff, "Der Begriff des Ständesstaates," *Ständisches Leben*, IV (1934).
———, "Misverständnisse über den Universalismus Othmar Spanns," *Ständisches Leben*, V (1935).

Although I have not made use of these works, the reader may find more on Universalism in the following books by disciples:

Jakob Baxa, *Gesellschaftslehre* (Leipzig, 1928).
Deutsche Beiträge zur Wirtschafts- und Gesellschaftslehre, ed. Spann and Georg von Bülow, is a series of works dedicated to the development of a Universalist theory of economics, money, banking, *Sozialpolitik*, industrial relations, etc.
Karl Faigl, *Ganzheit und Zahl* (Jena, 1928).
Walter Heinrich, *Grundlagen einer universalistischen Krisenlehre* (Jena, 1928).

There is no secondary literature which examines in depth the social conservative aspects of Ernst Niekisch's ideology of resistance. A chapter on Niekisch in Otto-Ernst Schüddekopf's *Linke Leute von Rechts: Die nationalrevolutionären Minderheiten und der Kommunismus in der Weimarer Republik* (Stuttgart, 1960) brings together a great deal of data but concentrates on Niekisch's National Bolshevism. The chapter, as well as the book, suffers from loose organization and lacks thematic unity. The article by Hans Buchheim, "Ernst Niekischs Ideologie des

Widerstands," *Vierteljahrshefte für Zeitgeschichte*, V (1957), is
less detailed and attempts a general evaluation of Niekisch's role
in the demise of the Weimar Republic. It may be that Buchheim
wrote the article as a brief on the court action Niekisch initiated,
upon his retirement from Humboldt University in East Berlin,
for restitution from West Germany for what he had suffered in
the Nazi era. Neither author has worked carefully through
Niekisch's periodicals, *Widerstand* and *Entscheidung*.

It is curious that the historically unimportant movement of
National Bolshevism, in whose ranks Niekisch is usually included,
has received so much attention from scholars. See, for example,
the work by Schüddekopf and the following studies:

> E. H. Carr, "Radek's 'Political Salon' in Berlin, 1919," *Soviet
> Studies*, III (1951/52).
> Klemens von Klemperer, *Germany's New Conservatism* (Prince-
> ton, 1957) with a chapter on conservatism and National
> Bolshevism but only a page on Niekisch.
> Erich Müller, *National Bolschewismus* (Hamburg, 1933), which
> should be viewed as a primary source.
> Arthur Spencer, "National Bolshevism," *Survey* (Oct. 1962)—
> a good survey, although wrong on the KPD.

All of Niekisch's books and pamphlets written before 1933 are
important for an understanding of his ideology of resistance
and for the extraction of the social conservative dimension of it:

> *Gedanken über deutsche Politik* (Dresden, 1929), composed of
> articles from *Widerstand*.
> *Gewagtes Leben: Begegnungen und Begebnisse* (Cologne,
> 1958)—his autobiography, which like so many works of this
> kind, gives rise to many questions by its explanations.
> *Grundfragen deutscher Aussenpolitik* (Berlin, 1924).
> *Hitler—Ein deutsches Verhängnis* (Berlin, 1932).
> *Politik des deutschen Widerstandes* (Berlin [1932?]). Although
> this pamphlet bears no author's name, it clearly represents
> the thinking of Niekisch. Schüddekopf ascribes the work to
> Niekisch with little hesitation. It is composed largely of
> sections from *Gedanken über deutsche Politik* and articles
> by Niekisch.
> *Politik und Idee* (Dresden, 1929).
> " 'Romantiker der Revolution,' " letter to the editor of the
> *Frankfurter Allgemeine Zeitung*, 26 May 1961.

Der Weg der deutschen Arbeiterschaft zum Staat (Berlin, 1924).

Perhaps the most important source on Niekisch is his periodical articles. The notes to Chapter V contain citations to the most important articles by Niekisch in *Widerstand* from 1927 to 1933. The short-lived *Entscheidung* (Oct. 1932 to March 1933) duplicates information available from his other writings.

These works written by Niekisch after 1933 throw little light on his thought and activities during the Weimar period:

Deutsche Daseinsverfehlung (Berlin, 1946).
Die dritte imperiale Figur (Berlin, 1935)—a tract against Hitler.
Ost-West: Unsystematische Betrachtungen (Berlin, 1947).
Zum Problem der Freiheit (Berlin, 1948).

Although there is a large body of secondary literature on Oswald Spengler, most of it concerns his theories of history. The best works are Ernst Stutz's *Oswald Spengler als politischer Denker* (Bern, 1958), which contains a short analysis of his ideas on economics, and the very readable general study by H. Stuart Hughes, *Oswald Spengler: A Critical Estimate* (New York, 1952).

For a survey of his historical system, see Pitirim Sorokin, *Social Philosophies of an Age of Crisis* (Boston, 1950). Theodor Adorno, in "Spengler nach dem Untergang: Zu Oswald Spenglers 70. Geburtstag," *Der Monat*, II (May 1950), reassesses Spengler's ideas.

See, in addition, the less important works:

Erwin von Beckerath, "Spengler als Staats- und Wirtschaftsphilosoph," *Schmollers Jahrbuch*, XLVII (1924).
J. von Leers, *Spenglers weltpolitisches System und der Nationalsozialismus* (Berlin, 1934)—a National Socialist evaluation.
Manfred Schroeter, *Metaphysik des Untergangs: Eine kulturkritische Studie über Oswald Spengler* (Munich, 1949)—a metaphysical appreciation by a latter-day Spenglerian, which includes Schroeter's earlier work *Der Streit um Spengler*.
S. D. Stark, *The Prussian Spirit: A Survey of German Literature and Politics, 1914-1940* (London, 1941) has a poor chapter on Spengler.

The following works by Spengler have been useful for this study:

Briefe, 1913-1936, ed. Anton M. Koktanek (Munich, 1963).

The Decline of the West, I: Form and Actuality, II: Perspectives of World-History (New York, 1926-1928), tr. Charles Francis Atkinson from *Der Untergang des Abendlandes: Umrisse einer Morphologie der Weltgeschichte, I: Gestalt und Wirklichkeit, II: Welthistorische Perspektiven* (Munich, 1920-1922). Vol. II is the more important as far as his social conservative ideas are concerned.

The Hour of Decision, Part One: Germany and World-Historical Evolution (New York, 1934), tr. Charles Francis Atkinson from *Jahre der Entscheidung: Deutschland und die weltgeschichtliche Entwicklung* (Munich, 1933).

Man and Technics: A Contribution to a Philosophy of Life (New York, 1932), tr. Charles Francis Atkinson from *Der Mensch und die Technik: Beitrag zu einer Philosophie des Lebens* (Munich, 1931).

Neubau des deutschen Reiches (Munich, 1924).

Politische Schriften (Munich, 1933).

Preussentum und Sozialismus (Munich, 1920).

Reden und Aufsätze, ed. Hildegard Kornhardt (Munich, 1938).

Although there are a number of valuable short studies of the *Tat* circle, none but that of Hock deals with the economic thought of the periodical to any significant extent. Hock limits himself to describing the contents and exposing the falsity of the *Tat* program of autarky and a planned economy. He does not evaluate the causes behind this program or identify those whom it was intended to benefit. The only important published study of the circle as a whole is Kurt Sontheimer's "Der Tatkreis," *Vierteljahrshefte für Zeitgeschichte*, VII (1959). In the unpublished dissertation by Walter Struve, "Elite versus Democracy: The Conflict of Elite Theories with the Ideals of Political Democracy, 1918-1933" (Yale University, 1962), a chapter on Hans Zehrer deals with the elitist aspects of the *Tat* program. Struve's article "Hans Zehrer as a Neoconservative Elite Theorist," *American Historical Review*, LXX (1965), which is based on this chapter, is also valuable. The older study by Edmond Vermeil, *Doctrinaire de la Révolution Allemande, 1918-1938*

(Paris, 1939), aligns *Tat* with the tradition of National Socialism. Klemens von Klemperer's *Germany's New Conservatism* contains a short discussion of the *Tat* circle.

On *Tat's* economic program, which consisted largely of the ideas of Fried, most of the contemporary literature should be treated as primary source material. The most important items are Kurt Baumann's "Autarkie und Planwirtschaft," *Zeitschrift für Sozialforschung*, II (1933), which deals with these ideas in the work of Salin, Sombart, and Spann as well, and Friedrich Hoffmann's "Der Ruf nach Autarkie in der deutschen politischen Gegenwartsideologie," *Weltwirtschaftliches Archiv*, XXXVI (1932). Less important are:

> Franz Grosse, "Das Ende des Kapitalismus: Bemerkungen zu einigen Büchern," *Gewerkschafts-Zeitung*, XLII (1932).
> Michael A. Heilperin, *Studies in Economic Nationalism* (Geneva, 1960), opposing economic nationalism.
> Clemens Lammers, *Autarkie, Planwirtschaft und berufsständischer Staat* (Berlin, 1932).

The following works by Fried have been used in my discussion:

> *Der Aufstieg der Juden* (Goslar, 1937).
> *Autarkie* (Jena, 1932).
> *Das Ende des Kapitalismus. Tat-Schriften* (Jena, 1931).
> *Krupp: Tradition und Aufgabe* (Bad Godesberg, 1956).
> *Die soziale Revolution* (Leipzig, 1942).
> *Wende der Weltwirtschaft* (Leipzig, 1939).
> *Die Zukunft des Aussenhandels: Durch innere Marktordnung zur Aussenhandelsfreiheit* (Jena, 1934).

See further the book by Giselher Wirsing, *Zwischeneuropa und die deutsche Zukunft. Tat-Schriften* (Jena, 1932). The articles in *Tat* for the years between 1928 and 1935 which bear on the theme of this study are cited in the notes to Chapter VI.

The secondary literature on National Socialism which I have used has been of fairly high quality. The most valuable single volume survey of National Socialism is the collection of essays sponsored by UNESCO and edited by Maurice Baumont et al., *The Third Reich* (New York, 1955). Unfortunately, this collection also contains several pointless and even poor articles. In addition to the essays by Claude David, Louis R. Franck, and Friedrich Lütge in this volume, I have profited from:

Karl Dietrich Bracher, Wolfgang Sauer, and Gerhard Schulz, *Die nationalsozialistische Machtergreifung: Studien zur Errichtung des totalitären Herrschaftssystems in Deutschland, 1933-1934*, Vol. XIV of the Schriften des Instituts für Politische Wissenschaft, Berlin (2nd edn., Cologne, 1962).

Alan Bullock, *Hitler, A Study in Tyranny* (rev. edn., New York, Harper Torchbook paperback, 1962).

Ernst M. Doblin and Claire Pohly, "Social Composition of the Nazi Leadership," *American Journal of Sociology*, LI (1945).

René Erbé, *Die nationalsozialistische Wirtschaftspolitik, 1933-1939, im Lichte der modernen Theorie*, Publication of the Basle Centre for Economic and Financial Research, Series B, No. 2 (Zurich, 1958).

Georg Franz-Willing, *Die Hitlerbewegung: Der Ursprung, 1919-1922* (Berlin, 1962)—a very good study.

Carl J. Friedrich, "The Peasant as Evil Genius of Dictatorship," *Yale Review*, XXVI (1937).

Hans Gerth, "The Nazi Party: Its Leadership and Composition," in Robert K. Merton et al., eds. *Reader in Bureaucracy* (Glencoe, Ill., 1952).

Franz Haber, *Untersuchungen über Irrtümer moderner Geldverbesserer* (Jena, 1926)—an early critique of Feder's monetary ideas.

Georg W.F. Hallgarten, *Hitler, Reichswehr und Industrie* (Frankfurt-am-Main, 1955).

Konrad Heiden, *Der Fuehrer: Hitler's Rise to Power*, tr. Ralph Manheim (Boston, 1944)—still valuable and not completely surpassed by Bullock.

Burton H. Klein, *Germany's Economic Preparations for War* (Cambridge, Mass., 1959)—not as good as Erbé or Schweitzer on the same topic.

Daniel Lerner, *The Nazi Elite*, in Series B in the Hoover Institute Studies (Stanford, 1951).

Charles P. Loomis and J. Allen Beegle, "The Spread of German Nazism in Rural Areas," *American Sociological Review*, XI (1946).

Hermann Mau, "Die 'Zweite Revolution'—Der 30. Juni 1934," *Vierteljahrshefte für Zeitgeschichte*, I (1953)—good on the purge of the social revolutionaries in the NSDAP.

Franz Neumann, *Behemoth: The Structure and Practice of National Socialism* (London, 1942)—a classic study.

Talcott Parsons, "Some Sociological Elements of the Fascist Movements," in his *Essays in Sociological Theory* (Glencoe, Ill., 1954).

Thilo Vogelsang, *Reichswehr, Staat und NSDAP: Beiträge zur deutschen Geschichte, 1930-1932* (Stuttgart, 1962).

————, "Zur Politik Schleichers gegenüber der NSDAP, 1932," *Vierteljahrshefte für Zeitgeschichte*, VI (1958)—good on Schleicher's policies and negotiations.

Alfred Werner, "Trotsky of the Nazi Party," *Journal of Central European Affairs*, XI (1951), deals with Otto Strasser.

As primary sources on the economic ideologies within the NSDAP, I have made use of the following works:

Harold Braeutigam, *Wirtschaftssystem des Nationalsozialismus* (3rd rev. and expanded edn., Berlin, 1936), on "liberal" Nazism.

Hans Buchner, *Grundriss einer nationalsozialistischen Volkswirtschaftstheorie*, Nationalsozialistische Bibliothek, Heft 16 (Munich, 1930), is friendly to Gregor Strasser.

Gottfried Feder, *Der deutsche Staat auf nationaler und sozialer Grundlage, Neue Wege in Staat, Finanz und Wirtschaft*, Nationalsozialistische Bibliothek, Heft 35 (16./17. Auflage, Munich, 1933).

————, *Kampf gegen die Hochfinanz* (Munich, 1933).

————, *Das Manifest zur Brechung der Zinsknechtschaft* (Munich, 1919).

————, *Das Programm der N. S. D. A. P. und seine weltanschaulichen Grundgedanken*, Nationalsozialistische Bibliothek Heft 1 (23. Auflage, Munich, 1930).

Adolf Hitler, *Hitler's Secret Conversations 1914-1944*, tr. Norman Cameron and R. H. Stevens (New York, Signet Book paperback, 1953)—the full text of *Bormann-Vermerke*.

————, *Mein Kampf* (Munich, 1933).

————, *Sozialismus wie ihn der Führer sieht: Worte des Führers zu sozialen Fragen*, collected by Fritz Meystre (Munich, 1935).

————, *The Speeches of Adolf Hitler, April 1922-August 1939*, ed. Norman H. Baynes (London, 1942)—the best collection of Hitler's speeches.

————, *Der Weg zum Wiederaufstieg* (Munich, 1927).

Hans Reupke, *Der Nationalsozialismus und die Wirtschaft* (Berlin, 1931).

———, *Das Wirtschaftssystem des Faschismus* (Berlin, 1930).

Alfred Rosenberg, *Der Mythos des 20. Jahrhunderts* (12th edn., Munich, 1933).

Richard Schapke, *Die Schwarze Front: Von den Zielen und Aufgaben und vom Kampfe der deutschen Revolution* (Leipzig, 1933).

Mathias Schmitz, ed., *A Nation Builds*, German Library of Information (New York, 1940)—pictures of the architectural wonders of the Third Reich.

Gregor Strasser, *Kampf um Deutschland: Reden und Aufsätze eines Nationalsozialisten* (Munich, 1932).

———, "Zur Programmatik der Nationalsozialistischen Linken: Das Strasser-Programm von 1925-26," in Reinhard Kühnl, ed., *Vierteljahrshefte für Zeitgeschichte*, XIV (1966).

Otto Strasser, *Aufbau des deutschen Sozialismus* (1st edn., Leipzig, 1932; 2nd edn., rev. and enlarged, Prague, 1936).

———, *Exil* (Munich, 1958).

———, *Germany Tomorrow*, tr. Eden and Cedar Paul (London, 1940).

———, *History in my Time* (London, 1941).

———, *Hitler and I*, tr. Gwenda David and Eric Mosbacher (Boston, 1940).

———, *Ministersessel oder Revolution?* [n.p.p, 1930].

Fritz Thyssen, *I Paid Hitler* (New York, 1941).

Index

Lightning Source UK Ltd.
Milton Keynes UK
UKHW021830121222
413815UK00006B/453